Chaucer, Langland and the Creative Imagination

David Aers

Chaucer, Langland and the Creative Imagination

Routledge & Kegan Paul
London, Boston and Henley

First published in 1980
by Routledge & Kegan Paul Ltd
39 Store Street, London WC1E 7DD,
Broadway House, Newtown Road,
Henley-on-Thames, Oxon RG9 1EN and
9 Park Street, Boston, Mass. 02108, USA

Set in Compugraphic English Times
and printed in Great Britain by
Ebenezer Baylis and Son Limited,
The Trinity Press, Worcester and London

British Library Cataloguing in Publication Data

Aers, David
Chaucer, Langland and the creative imagination
1 Chaucer, Geoffrey – Criticism and interpretation
2 Langland, William. Piers Plowman
I Title
821'.1 PR1924 79-41239
ISBN 0 7100 0351 X

To Elizabeth Salter and Derek Pearsall

Contents

Preface · ix

Acknowledgments · xi

1 **Imagination and Traditional Ideologies in** *Piers Plowman* · 1

2 **Langland and the Church: Affirmation and Negation** · 38

3 **Langland, Apocalypse and the** *Saeculum* · 62

4 **Chaucer: Reflexive Imagination, Knowledge and Authority** · 80

5 **Chaucer's Criseyde: Woman in Society, Woman in Love** · 117

6 **Chaucer: Love, Sex and Marriage** · 143

7 **Imagination, Order and Ideology:** *The Knight's Tale* · 174

Notes · 196

Index · 233

Preface

This study of two remarkable English poets who wrote in the later fourteenth century concentrates on some major and representative aspects of their work. It aims to show how due attention to the writers' contexts is necessary in the attempt to grasp the specific meaning and resonance of their poetry. I do not see my task as offering some general 'background' for the literature of the period – this easily leads either to a simple dualism between 'background' and text, or, to fixing what 'the medieval mind' thought, and so, *a priori*, what all the literature of the epoch must mean. In my own view, erecting a static dualism between text and contexts is bound to miss the vital interaction between individual work and the living milieu within which the writer gains the particular experiences, ideological forms and languages fundamental to his aesthetic activity. The implications of certain ideas and expressions are best grasped if we situate them, as far as we can, within the concerns and practices of the society in which the artist's consciousness developed. The explication of meaning must include reference to the relevant and specific forms of life, for language itself is an activity expressing the consciousness of social beings. Different forms of language articulate different forms of life and outlook, and in his language, whether conventional or striving towards fresh perspectives, the writer works with and on inherited ideological forms. These are themselves the shaping paradigms through which men perceive themselves, their world and the processes of historical change. The great achievements of Langland and Chaucer are dialectically related to traditional ideologies, contemporary practices and problems in ways I shall attempt to describe.

The two writers with whom I am concerned were genuinely exploratory in a period when many dominant ideologies, institutions and systems of authority were showing signs of strain and inadequacy. As always, in such periods of change and increasing complexity, one could respond, as many did, by merely reasserting traditional ideologies. Instead, in their very different ways, Chaucer and Langland created works which actively questioned received and still dominant ideologies, even those which they themselves revered and hoped to affirm. They made problematic topics for dramatic investigation what poets such as Gower and Lydgate continued to take as simply given. For Chaucer and Langland the imagination was indeed creative, involved in the active construction of meanings. The texts which they created are never the mirror of closed and given forms of thought and practice, never the passive reflection of the dominant attitudes in their ideological and social environment. On the contrary, they engage in a critical dialectic with traditional ideologies and social practices, one which involves both negation and constantly qualified affirmation in the creation of a poetry striving for what seemed more relevant and satisfactory perceptions of reality, both human and divine.

In following their poetry, I have aimed at a literary, critical response which moves from close reading of particular texts to the relevant contexts (social, theological, ecclesiastic) and back to the texts with what I hope is an enriched and sharpened understanding of the individual work and the writer's experience of his world, an increased understanding and enjoyment of the literature at the heart of this book.

Acknowledgments

There are many people whom I wish to thank. Professor Rodney Hilton, Ms Fiona MacDonald and Dr Roger Virgoe are historians who kindly read and commented on the draft of the first chapter. I found their advice extremely helpful, although they are not, of course, responsible for my judgments. Professor Gordon Leff kindly replied to my questions about the problems of future contingents in fourteenth-century philosophy. I am aware of considerable debts to scholars from various disciplines whom I have acknowledged at the appropriate places in texts and notes. My especial thanks are due to Bob Hodge and Gunther Kress, neither medieval scholars, but both concerned in the range of interests and problems that continue to preoccupy me and with whom, and from whom, I have enjoyed learning. Their own recent book, *Language as Ideology* (Routledge & Kegan Paul, 1979), should prove as important to literary critics as to linguists and historians of culture. I have also to thank Yvonne McGregor with whom I discussed the chapters on Chaucer. Finally, I wish to thank Elizabeth Salter and Derek Pearsall. They have discussed the whole project with me from its initiation, and read much of the book in draft, always offering me attentive and detailed criticism. For their intellectual generosity and sustaining interest in my work I am immensely grateful, and to them this book is dedicated.

My grateful acknowledgments are due to the British Academy for a grant towards the preparation of my manuscript; to the editors of *Literature and History* who published an earlier version of chapter 1; to the editors of *Chaucer Review* who published an earlier version of chapter 5. Acknowledgments are also due to the publishers who have given permission for quotation from copyright sources: Athlone Press for quotations from *Piers Plowman*.

The B Version, ed. E. T. Donaldson and G. Kane, 1975; Oxford University Press for quotations from *The Works of Geoffrey Chaucer*, ed. F. N. Robinson, 2nd edn., 1957; Cambridge University Press for quotations from *Medieval Women* by E. Power, 1975 and *Saeculum: History and Society in the Theology of St Augustine* by R. A. Markus, 1970; Penguin Books Ltd for quotations from *Western Society and the Church in the Middle Ages* by R. W. Southern, 1970; Manchester University Press for quotations from *Heresy in the Later Middle Ages* by G. Leff, 1967; Edward Arnold for quotations from *Medieval Heresy: Popular Movements from Bogomil to Hus* by M. Lambert, 1977; Presses Universitaires de France for quotations from *L'Église et la vie religieuse en occident à la fin du moyen âge* by F. Rapp, 1971; Rutgers University Press for quotations from *Piers Plowman as a Fourteenth Century Apocalypse* by Morton W. Bloomfield, 1962; University of Michigan Press for quotations from *Merchant Class of Medieval England* by S. L. Thrupp, 1962.

CHAPTER 1

Imagination and Traditional Ideologies in *Piers Plowman*

> And þoruȝ hir wordes I wook and waited aboute,
> And seiȝ the sonne euene South sitte þat tyme,
> Metelees and moneilees on Maluerne hulles.
> Musynge on þis metels a myle wey ich yede.
> Many times þis metels haþ maked me to studie
> Of þat I seiȝ slepynge, if it so be myȝte . . .
>
> *Piers Plowman* (B version), VII. 145–50

Traditional ideologies expressed the patterns through which self and world were perceived and understood. They depicted the features of legitimate authority and practice in different areas of the culture; they presented conventionally accepted beliefs, standards and values; they naturalized certain symbols and images which helped shape individual and collective experience. In short, they encouraged certain ways of seeing and thinking while discouraging others. No one has ever doubted the fundamental importance of traditional ideologies to Langland's perception and judgment. What has been less well recognized is the way writing poetry constantly released his imagination to embrace realities which pressed against received ideologies, his art putting these into solution despite the essential place they held in his conscious values and hopes. This is the relationship I wish to explore, between affirmation of established ideologies and their negation in the same poem, for this interplay turns out to be a central factor in the organization and magnificent achievement of *Piers Plowman*. I hope the study may also contribute to a more general discussion of the interactions between literature, social change and strains in received ideological structures. For Langland's great poem does invite attention to the ways in which traditional ideologies were themselves historical phenomena subject to diverse processes of change. With the gradual emergence of new social and economic situations, ideologies generated in earlier periods inevitably came under strain. Their authority was challenged and slowly undermined in the face of fresh problems, anomalies and confusions, leaving the community the long task of constructing ideologies and institutions appropriate to living in the changed circumstances.[1]

In the present chapter we shall be especially concerned with the major social ideology of Langland's world. This envisaged society as a static hierarchy of estates, fixed in occupations which were organically related, mutually beneficial, harmonious and divinely ordained. Society was often presented as a human body, with head and hands as king and nobility, feet as peasantry, and so on. As common was the tripartite division into those who pray, those who fight and those who labour to maintain fighters and praysters. Thomas Wimbledon states the view typically in 1388:

> in þe chirche beeþ nedeful þes þre offices: presthood, knyȝthod, and laboreris. To prestes it falliþ to kutte awey þe voide braunchis of synnis wiþ þe swerd of here tonges. To knyȝtis it falliþ to lette wrongis and þeftis to be do and to mayntene Goddis Lawe and hem þat ben techeris þerof, and also to kepe þe lond fro enemyes of oþer londes. And to laboreris it falleþ to trauayle bodily and wiþ here sore swet geten out of þe erþe bodily liflode for her and for oþer parties. And þese statis beþ also nedeful to þe chirche þat non may wel ben wiþouten oþer. For ȝif presthod lackede þe puple for defaute of knowyng of Goddis Lawe shulde wexe wilde on vices and deie gostly. And ȝif þe knythod lackid and men to reule þe puple by lawe and hardnesse, þeues and enemies shoden so encresse þat no man sholde lyuen in pes. And ȝif laboreris weren not, boþe prestis and knyȝtis mosten bicome acremen and heerdis, and ellis þey sholde for defaute of bodily sustenaunce deie.

He develops this picture of mutual dependence adding that 'euery staat shul loue oþer'.[2] Traditional divisions of labour, distribution of products and forms of life are presented as eternal, while the hierarchy of power and privilege is to remain absolutely static. Thomas Wimbledon, for example, adds, 'ȝif þou art a seruant oþer bondman, be soget and low in drede of displesynge to þy Lord', just as Gower, using the corporate image, asserts

> Quant pié se lieve contre teste,
> Trop est la guise deshonneste;
> [When the foot rebels against the head
> the behaviour is wholly illegitimate]

Similarly, another conventional preacher reminds 'kny3thes and oþur gentils' to concentrate on 'good gouernaunce' and military efficiency, priests on Christ's law, 'lower men' on labour, and concludes: 'iff euery parte of Cristes churche wold hold hem content with here own occupacions and not to entermet farþur þan reson and lawe rewels hem to, þan þe grace of almyghty God shuld floresh and þe more freshly contynue among.' So fixed are the boundaries that it seemed natural to perceive human identity almost completely in these classifications: 'There be in þis world þre maner of men, clerkes, kny3thes, and commynalte.'[3] When writers criticized deviations from this order in sermons or 'estates satire' their vision was firmly structured by the normative paradigm which never came into any kind of question: deviations were sinful and frequent, but corrigible. This attitude is evident in Lollard texts and Wyclif's work as well as in the orthodox writers referred to above.[4] The leading ideology thus made the inherited social world, with its distribution of power, work and wealth, so natural that any opposition to it seemed literally monstrous, as well as iniquitous.[5]

Of course, there was opposition and some signs of alternative social ideologies significantly at odds with the dominant one, as the Peasants' Uprising of 1381 indicated. For instance, their demands seem to have included freedom from serfdom and lordship, the termination of traditional manorial jurisdiction and services as well as of existing lawyers and law, and the abolition of the ecclesiastical hierarchy with the material wealth on which its power rested. Such ideas expressed interests, aspirations and experiences different to those legitimated and sanctified in the leading ideology.[6] Nevertheless, the latter quite precluded notions of chronic conflict of interests and outlook between groups. Similarly, ideas about changing aspirations and increasing social complexity and mobility were quite alien. Yet by Langland's time the dominant ideology had to confront new economic forces, and newly emerging social groups.[7] Like others, however, Langland assumed the total relevance of the chief and traditional social model to his world and his poem, a fact which those critics who call him 'a traditionalist, if not a reactionary' have noted.[8]

In the Prologue to *Piers Plowman* it can be seen in the following passage:[9]

> The kyng and knyȝthod and clergie boþe
> Casten þat þe commune sholde hire communes fynde.
> The commune contreued of kynde wit craftes,
> And for profit of al þe peple Plowmen ordeyned
> To tilie and to trauaille as trewe lif askeþ.
> The kyng and þe commune and kynde wit þe þridde
> Shopen lawe and leaute, ech lif to knowe his owene.
> (Pr. 116–22)

The peasantry serve the rest of society without any tensions while everybody is certain of his own fixed role. What 'trewe lif' and 'lawe' demand seems quite unequivocal, and in this scheme contemporary crafts all exist without conflict as they simply slot into unambiguous places in the harmonious totality. As late as Passus XIX Langland returns to this model, attributing it to the Holy Spirit (XIX 225–57), and it conveys his wish for the coherent world depicted in the inherited organic ideology. Nevertheless, his Prologue actually shows us something very different, something which goes considerably beyond the criticism of 'deviations' found in the estates satires and sermons mentioned earlier.

Probably all Langland's readers have relished the poetic vitality of the first dream 'Of alle manere of men, þe meene and þe riche,/Werchynge and wandrynge as þe world askeþ' (Pr. 18–19). The vitality is grounded in an outstanding imaginative response to the teeming energies of his society, and these justly famous lines represent the Prologue's impact:

> Of alle kynne lybbynge laborers lopen forþ somme,
> As dykeres and delueres þat doon hire dede ille
> And dryueþ forþ þe longe day with '*Dieu saue dame Emme*'.
> Cokes and hire knaues cryden, 'hote pies, hote!
> Goode gees and grys! go we dyne, go we!'
> Tauerners til hem tolden þe same:

'Whit wyn of Oseye and wyn of Gascoigne,
Of þe Ryn and of þe Rochel þe roost to defie!'

(Pr. 223–30)

Here, as throughout the Prologue and many of the following passus, we are shown a mass of self-absorbed social practices in which there is no consciousness of any coherent order, organic unity or social *telos*, let alone a divine one. The participants, as in the Meed episode, appear to be discrete members of a mobile, fragmenting society revelling in processes of consumption and production which are an end in themselves. The poetic conviction communicating this state already encourages us to question the applicability of the leading ideological scheme to the culture Langland inhabits and scrutinizes – even as a normative paradigm against which deviations may be identified and corrected.

The place of king and clergy in the Prologue may also be early signs in the poem of how extrinsic the major ideology has become. The clergy and religious institutions are immersed in the secular culture. Religion is predominantly another commodity, or an evasion of work, or training for service in secular affairs (Pr. 46–99) its roots and branches quite incompatible with the received model of the clergy's social role. I shall devote the next chapter to the church in *Piers Plowman*, for the degree to which the church is absorbed in the fluid culture Langland depicts is most significant.[10] As for the king, we do not meet him until well into the Prologue (ll. 112 ff.), and no sooner have we noted the image of a harmonious distribution of power and responsibility than Langland relates the fable about belling the cat. While 'þe commune profit' is invoked (Pr. 148, 169), the fable presents the ruler as one acquisitive and violent interest among other similar ones. Neither in theory nor practice is it possible to identify 'commune profit' in the manner envisaged by the presiding social ideology. Whatever Langland's own attitudes to the mouse who advises quietistic resignation in the face of an irresponsible and predatory ruling group, he shows that political power is contended for by autonomous groups and individuals motivated by immediate economic interests. The mouse's acceptance of this state of affairs actually participates in the cool egotism that seems prevalent among both the predators and those thinking about resistance. His own motivation is an unprincipled self-preservation which does not care who else may be destroyed as long as his own carcass is safe (Pr. 185–208).[11]

Struck by the centrality of economic self-interest in the world of the Prologue, Will asks Holy Church who actually has the right to 'þe moneie on þis molde þat men so faste holdeþ' (I. 44–6). The generalized question gets an even more generalized answer. Holy Church quotes from Matthew 22 where Jesus tells the Pharisees' disciples to render the things that are Caesar's to Caesar, and the things that are God's to God, and she rounds this off with her own comment.

> For riȝtfully reson sholde rule yow alle,
> And kynde wit be wardeyn your welþe to kepe
> And tutour of youre tresor, and take it yow at nede;
> (I. 54–6)

This brief statement raises issues we shall meet again and in more detail, but it is perhaps already becoming apparent that the instructor's moral language is rather remote from the realities of Langland's world and their visionary creation in his poem. For instance, in the lines just quoted, the abstraction 'welþe' is treated as a static thing, a box of physical treasure, rather than as the symbolic manifestation of social practices and unstable relationships which preoccupied Langland and made Will ask the question about money. Presenting these activities as a manageable fixity disastrously simplifies the problems raised by the mobile, acquisitive society of the Prologue, and Holy Church unhesitatingly puts forward the abstractions 'reson' and 'kynde wit' as agents who can solve the problems. But *Piers Plowman* has begun to make us uneasy with such solutions. We are told that 'kynde wit' is to be warden of wealth, yet we are made to wonder what the case will be if the 'welþe' has been accumulated by, for example, the merchants or tradesmen of the poem. Their occupations are essential in Langland's society, but the poet shows us how their practices transform 'kynde', leaving us to ask whose 'kynde' and 'kynde wit', whose 'reson' is *now* to provide the criteria of reformation.[12] The poem takes these as serious questions, finding that such disembodied and conventional abstractions may actually be controversial and equivocal terms with little obvious application to the world of incarnate beings Langland contemplates. Even Holy Church's confident statement that he who works well and ends in truth will be saved (I. 130–3), is turned by the poem into something profoundly problematic.[13] Doubtless, Langland wished he could simply accept Holy Church's general assertion, for it fits well into the dominant ideology with its depiction of a static social order in which everyone's function is fixed and uncontroversial. But his scrupulous, vital and honest involvement with current developments will not allow him this comfort.

Passus I opened with Holy Church complaining that in Catholic England most people 'Haue þei worship in þis world þei kepe no bettre' (I. 5–9), and Passus II begins with a characteristic act of self-reflexivity. Through his Will the poet acknowledges his own complicity in the life he studies around the figure of Lady Meed: 'Hire array me rauysshed; swich richesse sauȝ I neuere' (II. 17). As the marriage of Meed proceeds, Langland's imagination is indeed ravished by the diverse energies of his society exemplified in the numberless 'route þat ran aboute Mede', in their exuberant journey to Westminster and their evasive action under attack which confirms the vigour of their existence.[14] He insists that 'alle manere of men' are involved:

> As of knyȝtes and of clerkes and ooþer commune peple,
> As Sisours and Somonours, Sherreues and hire clerkes,
> Bedelles and baillifs and Brocours of chaffare,
> Forgoers and vitaillers and vokettes of þe Arches;
> (II. 58–61)

As in the Prologue, Langland evokes self-absorbed drives and a social matrix so alien to the ideology he favours that any idea of reform within its perspective is coming to seem quite impossible. One may even suspect that the way Theology (II. 115 ff.) remains the personification of an abstraction lacking embodiment or followers in definite social location, unlike Meed's followers who represent particular occupations and groups (e.g. II. 162–77), could be intended to cast doubt on its anchorage in Langland's world.

The poet certainly offers an intense and substantial vision of a world dominated by a money economy, a dynamic Meed dissolving all traditional ties, personal and ethical. He singles out a group of small tradesmen for special attention:

> Brewers and Bakers, Bochiers and Cokes;
> For þise are men on þis molde þat moost harm wercheþ
> To þe pouere peple þat parcelmele buggen. . . .

Thei richen þoruȝ regratrie and rentes hem biggen
Of þat þe pouere people sholde putte in hire wombe.
For toke þei on trewely þei tymbred nouȝt so heiȝe,
Ne bouȝte none burgages. . . .

(III. 79–86)

He selects such activities at a number of points and this is no mere idiosyncrasy. They represent small-scale commodity production for an impersonal market as it pressed most openly on poorer groups, especially in its control of food and rents.[15] For Langland 'reson' (III. 91–2) was explicitly against developments which absorbed the necessities of life into a system of exchange centred on individual profit. He, like other moralists, assumed an economy where towns and commodity production for a market were peripheral, one governed by unchanging direct relations, just prices and the fixed social order deputed in the chief ideology. This provided no cogent legitimation for a set of practices becoming more and more important,[16] and which the poet attended to with fascination, his imagination filled by their seemingly anarchic energies. Conscience, here expressing Langland's conscious views, tries to resist the energies embodied in Meed's followers. He follows Holy Church by stating that God's eternal Meed will go to those who 'werchen wel' now, those that have 'ywroght werkes wiþ right and wiþ reson', supported the 'riȝtfulle' and eschewed usury (III. 230–45). The passage poses the same difficulties we found in Holy Church's advice, for its pattern of abstractions has no obvious application to the complexities of Langland's milieu. On usury, for instance, reiteration of traditional principles was accompanied by a growing flexibility, an ambiguity in interpretations which accepted 'commercial activity and the irrepressible desire for profit' in a world where there were few philanthropists content to give men capital or loans without considerable interest.[17] Conscience's terms assume a universe of fixed and secure boundaries, between reasonable and unreasonable works, between usurious and non-usurious loans, boundaries which were increasingly hard to detect.

However, Conscience continues by asserting a distinction between just and unjust payment (III. 246–83) which leads to the following judgment:

That laborers and lowe lewede folke taken of hire maistres
It is no manere Mede but a mesurable hire.

(III. 255–6)

The comforting coherence of this statement depends on a body of ideas in which relations between employer and employee are fixed and unproblematic, as they were presented in the dominant ideology Langland favours. Yet despite the many controversies among historians of the later Middle Ages, there is widespread agreement that the fourteenth century was a period of exceptionally fierce social conflicts in the country as well as in towns. R. E. Lerner and G. Leff are representative when respectively they write of the fourteenth century as one including 'some of the most bitter and destructive class warfare to be seen in Europe before the Industrial Revolution', 'perhaps more than any other, a period of class struggles'.[18] Conscience's bland statement about 'mesurable hire' and its straightforward distinction from Meed simply ignores these struggles, despite the manner in which both employers and labourers had reacted to changing circumstances during Langland's own life. It is interesting to contrast the Commons' Petition of 1376, complaining at the failure of the Statute of Labourers (1351) and all attempts to impose a wage-freeze on the working population:[19]

> although various ordinances and statutes have been made in several parliaments to punish labourers, artificers and other servants, yet these have continued subtly and by great malice aforethought, to escape the penalty of the said ordinances and statutes. As soon as their masters accuse them of bad service, or wish to pay them for their labour according to the form of the statutes, they take flight and suddenly leave their employment and district . . . they are taken into service immediately in new places, at such dear wages that example is afforded to all servants to depart into fresh places, and from master to master as soon as they are displeased about any matter. For fear of such flights, the commons now dare not challenge or offend their servants, but give them whatever they wish to ask, in spite of the statutes and ordinances to the contrary – and this is chiefly through fear that they will be received elsewhere. . . . But if all such fugitive servants were . . . placed in the stocks or sent to the nearest

> gaol . . . they would not desire to flee from their districts as they do – to the great impoverishment, destruction and ruin of the commons.

The aggrieved language of the dominant class witnesses to very real conflicts between competing social groups over the whole standard of 'mesurable hire', while the received ideology informing Conscience's argument continues to treat it as straightforward.

Langland, we shall find, was not to settle for Conscience's picture, although he has him develop it further:

> In marchaundise is no Mede, I may it wel auowe;
> It is a permutacion apertly, a penyworth for anoþer.
> (III. 257–8)

Trade is envisaged as a mutual exchange for use; exchange for profits and their exploitationary consequences (pointed out in Passus III. 79–86), just disappear. But Langland's own poetry prevents us from believing that the massive energies of Meed's followers, and the ethos they reflect, can be so simply contained. His own poetic context makes us suspect that the traditional ideology he values is either failing to locate new forces and problems or mastering them with misleading ease.

Langland himself felt the acute tensions between his ideological convictions and his imagination's insights, and this unhappy experience led him to the memorable apocalyptic writing at the close of Passus III (284–330). I shall return to this passage when I consider the overall development and meaning of the apocalyptic mode in *Piers Plowman* (chapter 3 below), but here I should note that Langland has chosen to use Isaiah in constructing a messianic age which not only obliterates social practices and occupations the author found obnoxious, but also undermines the orthodox social ideology to which he adhered. For example, the act of abolishing existing legal organization, making law a labourer and having 'but oon court' would entail the end of feudal hierarchy of control and jurisdiction central to his own ideology.[20] As strikingly, the demilitarization of the knightly class (III. 305–10, 323–4) would have removed the main orthodox legitimation of this ruling class, in the words of Thomas Wimbledon quoted earlier, 'to lette wrongis and þeftis to be do and to mayntene Goddis Lawe and hem þat ben techeris þereof, and also to kepe þe lond fro enemyes'.[21] Deprived of its alleged reasons for non-productive existence and possession of the means of violence in the culture, the class would also be deprived of the armed power which had always provided an essential framework for its extraction of labour and produce from the peasantry. The abandonment of the leading ideology at this point is an intuitive acknowledgment of its basic strains and inadequacies in the face of the reality the poet is exploring. The basic paradigm is being subverted, something that does not happen in conventional complaint and satire, but although the painful tensions we have been considering made apocalyptic visions and riddles attractive to Langland, he ultimately denied their peremptory closure of historical processes. This was not due to the challenge they offered his conventional social paradigm, but because such closures were an evasion of his own deepest imaginative preoccupation with the basis of all spiritual life in history.[22]

Passus IV moves back to power and violence in the poet's culture, but imposes a successful union between the Ruler (not the apocalyptic king of III. 289), Conscience, Reason, Kynde wit, Love and Leaute (IV. 157–95).[23] This may have seemed an attractive solution to the difficulties that had been troubling Langland since it avoided the obvious threat to orthodox ideologies posed by the apocalypse in Passus III. Yet it too demands a dissolution of the imaginative texture presenting Meed's permeation of the culture – a *dissolution* rather than an equally realized portrayal of practices and tendencies which might credibly supersede those developments Langland found so offensive. The question as to what social agents will materialize this triumphant union of abstractions is not confronted and this leaves a revealing conceptual and imaginative lacuna.[24] Langland himself, as he does so frequently, immediately indicates his sensitivity to such gaps and his dogged refusal to tolerate their evasions. At the end of Passus IV, Conscience admits that unless 'þe commune' as a whole assents to the overthrow of Meed and the forces she represents, reform is most unlikely (IV. 182–4).

Thus, we are pushed into 'þe feld ful of folk þat I before tolde' (V. 10) as Langland tries to imagine an attempt at reformation in his world. He uses the framework of the seven deadly sins to organize the first part of his return to 'þe feld ful of folk', and a host of readers have testified to the vitality with which he represents practices judged as vicious. One vice is especially relevant to the theme of the present chapter – Covetise (V. 188–95).[25] With this figure he refracts market relationships and values he had contemplated before the apocalyptic passage in Passus III. In the first occupation mentioned, apprentice to 'Symme atte Nok', the characteristic features of present society as Langland experiences it again emerge: the work is considered purely for its 'profit', and in the section as a whole trades seem to exist in a fragmented society where questions of communal needs and well-being are unlikely to be taken very seriously even if they were to be put. Langland's emphasis once more falls on small commodity producers and retailers, and the 'grace of gyle' seems an essential part of the competitive market rather than a corrigible aberration.[26]

When Langland moves on to usury (V. 237 ff.) he has in mind big and small credit financing quite integral to the late medieval economy, and shows his sensitivity to developments which he sees subverting both the dominant ideology and the traditional order it sanctions:

> I haue mo Manoirs þruȝ Rerages þan þoruȝ *Miseretur et commodat.*
> I haue lent lordes and ladies my chaffare
> And ben hire brocour after and bouȝt it myselue.
> Eschaunges and cheuysaunces, wiþ swich chaffare I dele. . . .
> (V. 243–6)

The poet believes that the economic difficulties of landowners are being exploited by a social group represented by the voice in the part of the passage just quoted. But the speaker's relish of such practices throughout the overt confession has the effect of evoking the irresistible strength of such psychological and economic forces as they permeate the social fabric, involving all social groups.[27]

Despite this, Langland takes the Vices' revelations as signs of a general urge for a change of behaviour. Accepting the revelations as confessions he shifts into the theological mode (V. 477–512). The ensuing prayer for grace is a powerful, sharply focused poetic meditation on the Christian history of sin and salvation, God's second creation of man, and concentrates on God becoming flesh. This stress on Incarnation is absolutely central to *Piers Plowman*, and the prayer evokes what the dreamer will only grasp by participating in the dramatic process which evolves through the rest of the poem.[28] Langland takes God's Incarnation so seriously that it reinforces his preoccupation with man's fully incarnate existence and encourages him to expect the second creation to have affected the whole human being, soul and body growing within and through social relations and institutions – 'A þousand of men þo þrungen togideres . . .'. I suspect that critics do not always appreciate how precisely Langland's particular theological approaches contribute to the characteristic and continual movements of his imagination back to the social world in time present. Piers's directions to the lost pilgrims in Passus V culminate in a marvellous image for the individual's discovery of God and charity within himself (V. 605–8), but the poet does not, certainly not here, use this to initiate a mystical and individualistic search for a way to God 'In þyn herte', placing a cloud of unknowing between self and world.[29] Far from it, Passus VI begins by placing the reader in the world of social labour without which there would be no human spirituality.

It is a world Langland again wants to organize with the traditional dominant ideology, fixing knight, clergy and peasant in static harmony. When discussing Conscience's comfortingly simple distinction between 'mesurable hire' and Meed, with its reconciliation of labourers and employers, I mentioned some actualities in Langland's world which we now need to recall and locate in a slightly wider context. Due to major demographic and economic changes during the period, seigneurial incomes were under severe pressure and after 1349 the knightly class faced a shortage of labour which strengthened the economic positions of peasants still further in relation to landowners. Lords of the manor, as we observed, tried to protect their position by wage freezes and labour legislation, while at the local level they intensified the struggle with assertive peasants over labour services, status, rents and fines. The peasants' rising, it seems, should be seen as the most concentrated and violent episode in a chronic fourteenth-century conflict over the distribution of the social product, a conflict which assumed many forms, non-violent and violent.[30] In this perspective Langland's re-statement of organic estates ideology at the beginning of Passus VI seems so traditional that the historian Rodney Hilton cites it as an example of the dominant ideology and its defence of feudal order.[31] Langland's Ploughman says to the Knight:[32]

> I shal swynke and swete and sowe for vs boþe,
> And ek laboure for þi loue al my lif tyme,
> In couenaunt þat þow kepe holy kirke and myselue
> Fro wastours and wikked men. ...
> Loke ye tene no tenaunt but truþe wole assente,
> And þouȝ ye mowe amercy hem, lat mercy be taxour
> And mekenesse þi maister maugree Medes chekes; . . .
> And mysbede noȝt þi bondeman, þe bettre shalt þow spede;
> (VI. 25–8, 38–40, 45)

The peasants yield up their labour and produce out of love for the landowners while the latter's jurisdictional and economic rights are unquestioned by human beings and by divine truth. There seems no possibility of incompatible versions of rights and truth, no possible irreconcilable disagreements over what constitutes harming a bondman, no fundamental antagonisms. However, discussion of the ideology through which Langland perceives his world and its potential order should not be isolated from the imagination's vision of social practice.

Throughout the Passus Langland's poetry evokes a sense of extraordinary vitality among the people committed to the essential work of producing society's subsistence. For example, threatened by hunger,

> Faitours for fere flowen into Bernes
> And flapten on wiþ flailes fro morwe til euen . . .
> An heep of heremytes henten hem spades
> And kitten hir copes and courtepies hem maked
> And wente as werkmen to wedynge and mowynge
> And doluen drit and dung to ditte out hunger.
> (VI. 183–4, 187–90)

The decisive verbs, the specificity of the work and its materials, the free flow of the verse, convey the impression of great vigour which characterize the Passus. Langland's imagination, as so often, is marvellously welcoming to this secular exuberance. Despite the reiteration of conventional ideology, with Piers's version of peasants surrendering their labour for love, we find that the fragmenting of society into self-absorbed groups, investing their energies in the competitive pursuit of economic interest, has extended to the sphere in which most people worked and lived – the agrarian.

In this vision frantic work leads to material sufficiency, but with this opposition to the dominant ideology and its demands on peasants becomes dramatically evident (VI. 115ff., 310ff.). One appropriate place to celebrate the exuberance we have been watching is the pub:

> Thanne seten somme and songen atte Nale
> And holpen ere þe half acre wiþ 'how trolly lolly'.
>
> (VI. 115–16)

Piers resists the drinkers in pragmatic terms (neither religious nor moral) but his intervention is still fiercely challenged:

> Thanne gan wastour to wraþen hym and wolde haue yfouȝte;
> To Piers þe Plowman he profrede his gloue.
> A Bretoner, a braggere, he bosted Piers als
> And bad hym go pissen with his plowȝ: 'pyuysshe sherewe!
> Wiltow, neltow, we wol haue oure wille
> Of þi flour and þi flessh, fecche whanne vs likeþ,
> And maken vs murye þerwiþ maugree þi chekes.'
>
> (VI. 152–8)

Given Hilton's commentary on the relatively elevated economic status of ploughmen in peasant communities,[33] one may well be justified in sensing that Langland was also registering his consciousness of a stratification among peasants leading to conflict rather than harmonious hierarchical order within the village itself. At any rate, the Breton sees the flour and flesh as belonging to Piers who appeals to a member of the knightly class to reimpose labour-discipline on those he labels 'wastours' (VI. 159–63).

Langland's imaginative receptivity to conflicts and social movement pushes the total context beyond the perceptual bounds of his traditional model.[34] He shows us an extremely powerful peasant resistance, in practice and thought, to the pressures of the knightly class and the dominant ideology. Like Piers, the knight and his 'lawe' (VI. 166) are immediately defied:

'I was noȝt wont to werche', quod Wastour, 'now wol I noȝt bigynne!'
And leet liȝt of þe lawe and lasse of þe knyȝte,
And sette Piers at a pese and his plowȝ boþe,
And manaced hym and his men if þei mette eftsoone.
(VI. 167–70)

Of course, the poet's conscious evaluation of this defiance is made obvious in his naming the knight's opponent as 'Wastour'. But, as I have argued, Langland's vision is not contained within the framework of the dominant ideology and estates satire: the poetry carries an energy and conviction in the 'wastour's' defiance which is not matched in the knight's response (VI. 164 ff.), or in any realization of the normative paradigm. Although the knight has been invoked by Piers to fulfil his role, he proves unequal to his divinely ordained task of maintaining a static and hierarchic society. It is not surprising that neither Piers nor the author adjust their ideas to entertain this development, for the task of generating new ideologies in changed conditions is collective and long-drawn. What is arresting is that they do not even criticize the knight's failure in moral terms. This contributes to an impression that imaginatively the failure has been accepted as irreversible, beyond the blame of individual knights, or the group as a whole.

The impression is reinforced by the disappearance of the knight from the scene. In the second rising against the established ordering of society (VI. 300 ff.) no one even mentions a knight, although Langland focusses on one of the major areas of conflict – wages. He begins the later passage by figuring the expanded material aspirations of peasants, something reported with great disapproval by many comfortably placed moralists and gentry (VI. 302–11).[35] Even landless labourers who depend entirely on selling their labour for wages – easily the most vulnerable rural group – share these self-absorbed ambitions:

Laborers þat haue no land to lyue on but hire handes
Deyneþ noȝt to dyne a day nyȝte olde wortes.
May no peny ale hem paie, ne no pece of bacoun,
But if it be fressh flessh ouþer fissh yfryed,
And þat *chaud* and *plus chaud* for chillynge of hir mawe.
(VI. 307–11)

Langland disapproves, yet his imaginative involvement with the labourers' lives and energies allows him to express their determination, the unabashed material particularity of their aspirations and their independence of the traditional social ideology and ethics he wants them to accept. Their demands for a larger share in the social product, realistic enough in the period, are made through wage claims and what Langland explicitly presents as a total rejection of the dominant ideology and its traditional religious sanctification:

> But he be heiȝliche hyred ellis wole he chide;
> That he was werkman wroȝt warie þe tyme. . . .
> He greueþ hym ageyn god and gruccheþ ageyn Reson,
> And þanne corseþ þe kyng and al þe counseil after
> Swiche lawes to loke laborers to chaste.
> (VI. 312–13, 316–18)

The labourers see the connections between God, Reason, existing laws and, in the next two lines, the Statute of Labourers. They see that these all serve the interests of their rulers, clearly opposed to their own, and so they reject them. The social order is experienced and perceived in terms of antagonistic interests which construct their own self-legitimating versions of religion, rationality and law. Hallowed abstractions are brought down to earth and their human constructors and beneficiaries unveiled. Far from notions of a benevolently stratified organic society, theirs is a radically dissenting attitude which could well prove responsive to alternative ideologies such as those attributed to John Ball in 1381.[36]

Be that as it may, after the knight's failure both Piers (VI. 171 ff.) and the author (VI. 319 ff.) invoke Hunger as the only way to confine the challenging energies he has met within the framework provided by the major ideology. Hunger images a reversion to minimal subsistence levels, enforcing a drastic freeze on economic drives whose psychological implications Langland did not welcome. The appeal to Hunger is a desperate and ironically quite amoral wish for nature to reverse processes the poet has shown to be deeply rooted in his world. It also has a further meaning. The social paradigm Langland cherishes, despite its universalizing and religious claims, is revealed in a fresh light: it is dependent on material facts like the perpetuation of a minimal subsistence economy, with a peasant population made obedient through living on the brink of starvation. In spite of its own claims, the ideology is disclosed as historical. The poem actually displays to us how, as certain material factors are superseded, the credibility of the orthodox ideology is gravely undermined.

If anyone were to defend and impose this ideology it would be the knightly class, as Piers knew, and the disappearance of the knight at such a crucial point has, I think, a historical significance. It is an example of the way Langland's imaginative integrity fused with a sharp social intuition to give a result incompatible with his own overt ideology. In accepting the logic of his imagination's response to his world, Langland symbolically reflects the gradual disappearance of the feudal knight and lord from the field of history. He seems to reflect what Hilton has described as the 'failing grip of aristocratic domination', the failure of the knightly class to impose a wage freeze successfully, to tighten controls over unfree people and to defend its economic position in the face of internal problems and 'peasant self-assertiveness'. He seems to mediate the fact that 'the long period of the successful and multiform exploitation of peasant labour ended, at any rate in most Western European countries, between the middle and end of the fourteenth century'.[37] The Passus leaves us with a vivid sense of an energetic peasantry in a society where economic and ideological conflict is of the essence. This is distinctly incompatible with the normative ideology used in his perceptual framework, and it illustrates how he was prepared and able to subject cherished patterns of belief to an intense imaginative engagement with realities which were discrediting and destroying those patterns.

Indeed, the strains in received social ideas may be further witnessed as the poet's attitude to the knightly class becomes more explicitly ambivalent. For instance, in Passus X (24–9, 59–89), instead of emphasizing the necessary place of upper-class abundance in the feudal order he wants, Langland finds it a cause of economic self-interest, graphically contrasting brotherhood among 'meene men' with lordship's rejection of the needy. Those are 'moost unkynde to þe commune þat moost catel weldeþ' (X. 29); and in that suggestion Langland implies more than the conventional complaints in sermons and estates satire about abuses among what *The Book of Vices and Virtues* depicts as 'wikkede lordes, be þei knyȝtes or oþere, þat pilen þe pore folke bi talyages and gabels borwynge and bi euele customes, and make hem paye gret amendes for litle trespas, and þretene hem to haue of here good for feer'.[38] Langland conveys that the very *kynde* of those in the possessing classes can be changed by their habitual social practices and status, an issue he has raised before and will return to much later.[39] In Passus XIX he provides another perspective on the conflicts between landlords and peasants mentioned in our discussion of Passus VI, for he has a lord express the attempt to make the peasantry bear the weight of the economic crisis affecting landowners (XIX. 460–4, quoted pp. 33–4 below). Needless to say, Langland is not satisfied with such developments and he reminds people able to give feasts that they should call 'þe carefulle þerto, þe croked and þe pouere', for Jesus 'In a pouere mannes apparaille pursueþ vs euere' (XI. 185–94). But the way the poem attends to practice and the historical present emphasizes the incompatibility of such gospel teaching with traditional aristocratic values and needs, grounded in an order Langland wished to preserve. The difficulty is not uncommon: a moralist may have wished to change behaviour which was actually a manifestation of social position and values that could not be changed without changing the social structure, the last thing advocated by most moralists.

Langland brings the difficulties well into the open as he appeals to the notion of Christian equality and brotherhood against the possessing classes. For instance,

> alle are we cristes creatures and of his cofres riche,
> And breþeren as of oo blood, as wel beggeres as erles.
> (XI. 199–200; see 199–211)

Should the idea that all are brethren of one blood, all as 'gentil men' (XI. 203), have an impact in the present? Or should it be kept as a pious formula applying only to practices in some safely remote celestial region? Langland wanted the idea to have an impact, yet he wanted to preserve an order antagonistic to such ideas. These ideas were part of a radical Christian tradition which surface in the Peasants' Uprising giving terms for an alternative ideology, and one may wonder how the poet came to invoke them at this point.[40]

The answer lies in his frustration at contradictions between his imaginative presentation of social practice and orthodox ideology.

These may have opened his imagination to sympathize with neo-revolutionary doctrines as the ones most likely to bring his ethic of love into the sphere that so preoccupied him – historical practice. Sympathy is evident when he asserts that 'cristene sholde be in commune riche' (XIV. 201), and has Holy Church state that necessary clothing, food and drink should be 'in commune' (I. 17–22).[41] It is not that Langland wanted to change traditional structures, but that the tensions outlined here turned him towards company he would not have wished to keep, and may suggest the attractiveness the poem held for at least some rebels in 1381.

The tensions I have been discussing and the reading of Passus VI offered above, cast some fresh light on the famously obscure Pardon scene.[42] Passus VII opens with a statement that Truth instructed Piers to plough his fields, and promised him, and all who helped 'a pardoun *a pena et a culpa*' (VII. 1–8). Ninety-seven lines follow, allegedly describing the contents of the Pardon. These lines reimpose the traditional ordering of society which opened Passus VI but was then so drastically undermined. The passage begins by giving Pardon to 'Kynges and knyȝtes þat kepen holy chirche/And riȝtfully in Reme rulen þe peple'. This summarizes the version of the knightly class's role expressed by Piers and repeats it as though nothing had happened since then to show its supersession. Similarly, the lines on labourers pick up issues raised in Passus VI, offering Pardon to

> Alle libbynge laborers þat lyuen by hir hondes,
> That treweliche taken and treweliche wynnen
> And lyuen in loue and lawe. . . .
>
> (VII. 62–4)

This assumes a straightforward distinction between just and unjust payment reminiscent of Conscience's bland statements in Passus III (255–8), a resolution which ignores Passus VI. There, we recall, the 'Laborers þat haue no land to lyue on but hire handes' joined with others to show that the notion of what constituted 'true' wages was, at least, highly problematic in a conflict-ridden society. Likewise, the lines on merchants ignore key elements in the poem's memorable presentation of merchants' activities, such as that in Passus V (242–53) describing how their trade and financial practices eroded the whole supposedly fixed feudal order. Now, however, the traditional ideology and its world is supposed to absorb and baptize the intense, individualistic and unstable economic energies of the merchants. Truth

> bad hem buggen boldely what hem best liked
> And siþenes selle it ayein and saue þe wynnyng,
> And make Mesondieux þerwiþ myseise to helpe,
> Wikkede weyes wightly amende
> And bynde brugges aboute þat tobroke were,
> Marien maydenes or maken hem Nonnes,
> Pouere peple bedredene and prisons in stokkes
> Fynden swiche hir foode for oure lordes loue of heuene,
> Sette scolers to scole or to som kynnes craftes,
> Releue Religion and renten hem bettre.
>
> (VII. 24–33)

The opening two lines of this quotation approve the qualities of ambition, mobility, and energetic pursuit of markets so abundantly evidenced in modern studies of the merchant class of the later Middle Ages. These studies show the merchants' thoroughly self-centred drive for political and economic power in towns, together with the aspirations to monopoly. They also document the commitment to accumulate property in town and country from what Langland calls 'þe wynnyng'.[43] In her classic study *The Merchant Class of Medieval London*, Sylvia Thrupp observes some signs that this social group was coming to evolve 'alternative views of the structure of society' to the hierarchical, static and organic ideology which was still dominant, ones which were more in accord with their own practices, 'the opposite of static', fluid and in many ways especially insecure.[44] Committed to the pursuit of economic gain:[45]

> The merchant achieved a very happy justification of his pursuit of wealth as approved by God. The wealthy were fond of texts and mottoes that expressed confidence of divine approval. A fourteenth-century citizen's wife encircled her seal with 'God help þat best man.' A lighthearted letter written by a mayor of Exeter, assuring his friends that an enemy's charge of impurity in his private life was false, adds, 'therefore y . . . sey sadly *si recte vivas*, etc., and am right mery and fare right well, ever thankyng God and myn awne purse.' Late fifteenth-century aldermen displayed such

> mottoes as 'I trust in God,' 'dextra Domini exaltavit me,' 'A Domine factum est istum.' Wills of the same period, drawn 'of such goodes of fortune as god hath sent me and lent me,' show confidence buoyed up by the doctrine of the stewardship of wealth.

Langland's passage, however, goes on to tell merchants that the justification for their vigorous economic activity is in their use of 'þe wynnyng'. They are to save their profits to invest in charitable works. The dreamer claims that at this prospect merchants were merry and 'manye wepten for ioye' (VII. 38). Given what we see of them in the poem, their weeping at this treatment of their profits seems likely enough – only not for joy.

Yet Langland was in contact with an exceptionally complicated position. For Sylvia Thrupp points out that the merchants she studied were also deeply affected by traditional social ideology and religious attitudes to a life centred on the accumulation of property and material goods. She shows how charitable bequests were indeed an important means of justifying their pursuits and the use of interest which was so hard to distinguish from usury:[46]

> Charity had thus a magic virtue. The only difference of opinion concerned the question whether a man should give alms throughout his life or could safely wait until the division of his estate after death. By long-standing custom it was usual for a man to assign from a third to a half of his movables to uses that would benefit his soul. It is significant that in London this custom was followed quite strictly and that there was a tendency to extend it to immovables, land often being sold for pious and charitable objects.

This concern reflects their own doubts about the status of their occupation and here Thrupp finds a revealingly mixed attitude to the poor. Merchants believed that 'The better people were the more honest, the wiser, the more prudent, and the more discreet. All these qualities were assumed to be present in maximum strength in the richest of the citizens, the best, the most sufficient, and to be at a low ebb among the poorer citizens.' Nevertheless, she illustrates how they desired the prayers of the poor and arranged for the distribution of many small gifts on their death to ensure this, for there was 'a feeling that the poor were somehow blessed', allied to 'uneasiness as to whether economic relations with the poor were really just'. What Sylvia Thrupp identifies is an increasingly influential social group whose 'curiously mixed' attitudes in these areas are one result of the way traditional social and religious theory could not incorporate the merchants' forms of existence.[47] This was at the heart of Langland's difficulties in the passage under discussion. The significant presence of merchants in Langland's world had been vividly refracted in the poem, yet the traditional ideology the poet wished to affirm could not integrate their practices and basic motivations. The attempts to fuse incompatible outlooks leads to a fantasizing reconciliation which the poem itself powerfully discredits.

Indeed, the ninety-seven lines of Pardon themselves have a subtly ambivalent status, one I attempted to acknowledge by stating that they 'allegedly' describe the contents of a divine Pardon. For when Piers unfolds the Pardon it actually contains only two lines from the Athanasian Creed – do well and go to heaven, do ill and go to hell. The long passage is thus presented as a subjective gloss on the lines undoubtedly from Truth, the Creed. It attempts to solve profound contradictions in the worlds of work, social theory, ethics and religion, contradictions dramatically enacted in the poem, by substituting comforting fantasies. Langland himself was sorely tempted to settle for such pseudo-solutions, longing for equilibrium and coherence in the present, but his responsiveness to diverse and conflicting forms of life constantly delivered him from temptation. So in Passus VII his own imagination exploded the ninety-seven line passage which expressed ideological reconciliations his peculiar poetic integrity drove him to reject.[48] Piers's 'pure tene' when challenged by the priest may also be seen more clearly in this light. It was Piers who introduced the orthodox estates ideology in Passus VI, and the alleged content of the Pardon seems to be his gloss, his fantasy.[49] His fragile 'solution' to the problems confronting him and his world-view has been destroyed, leaving him with the vision of antagonistic fragmentation in Passus VI. His 'tene' is very understandable.

It leads to another real and recurrent temptation, for many besides Piers. The temptation is to withdraw from the complex field of social practice to a supposedly transcendent spiritual individualism (VII. 122–35), a retreat which simply abandons the realm of human activity to whatever emerging forces can take possession, and assumes a split between body and soul which many forms of Christianity have resisted.[50] In fact, both Truth and Holy Church stress the primacy of work for man (I. 85–93, 128–33; VII. 1–2), and in the last resort Langland was to remain the poet of *incarnate* man, of the existence of individual spirit in the social and material world.

The relations I have attempted to identify, between the imagination's re-creation of the world and traditional ideology, continue to inform and energize the poem right through to its conclusion. Langland evokes some memorable visions of social love, as in Trajan's speech in Passus XI, replete with sentiments like the following:[51]

> And þat alle manere men, enemyes and frendes,
> Loue hir eyþer ooþer, and lene hem as hemselue,
> Whoso leneþ noȝt, lord woot þe soþe, . . .
>
> And euery man helpe ooþer for hennes shul we alle:
> *Alter alterius onera portate*. [Gal. 6:2]
> And be we noȝt vnkynde of oure catel, ne of oure konnyng
> neiþer. . . .
>
> (XI. 178–80, 211–12)

Langland is completely involved with this vision of brotherhood and love, but his own poetry has made us want to know how such general imperatives could be realized in the concrete activities and social organizations he has displayed. He himself has taught us that in a dynamic, fragmenting society, where markets hold an important place, judgments about 'vnkynde' and 'kynde', about what is natural in social relationships and the handling of 'oure catel', are genuinely problematic.[52] The tensions between Langland's poetic realization of energies at the root of the problems and his wish to affirm received ideology remains, and with this remains the temptation to dissolve the imaginative insights in favour of the coherence, stability and certainties offered in the traditional model of social order. Rather than trace this recurring movement in detail through the rest of *Piers Plowman*, I will discuss its presence in two major episodes from the second half of the poem, which some readers may have been persuaded by a body of scholarly opinion to treat as a journey inwards simply forsaking the external world of the 'fair feeld ful of folk'.

The first episode concerns Patience and Haukyn, and the ideology in question is a spiritual one, traditional enough, which would sanctify the kind of spiritual transcendence mentioned in connection with Piers's reaction to the priest who read out the 'two lynes' written 'in witnesse of truþe' (VII. 109–35). Near the opening of Passus XIII we are taken to dine with a master of theology, 'goddes gloton' as the dreamer is to call him. This brilliant scene gives an image of the church's institutional reality, and Langland's response shows characteristic movements. One strong tendency is to advocate, like Piers in his 'tene', love and patience which by-pass the essential material mediations of grace and doctrine (XIII. 119–210) – shown by the poem to be distressingly problematic. Patience is so enthusiastic about this path that he claims it does lead back to the social world, a universal elixir transforming all groups (XIII. 164–71). The transformation is expressed in very general terms, lacking any of the specificity we meet in Langland's engagement with both his own world and many aspects of Christian history and doctrine. Such a poetic mode, rather than a more concrete, time-bound one, may well indicate some fallaciousness in Patience's account of the recommended path. It does not take us back to the sphere of active men, and poetic imagination does not sanction this part of Patience's claim. The decadent divine is hardly an endearing witness, but his intervention should not be dismissed as the corrupt comment of despairing worldliness, though it is that too:

> 'It is but a dido', quod þis doctour, 'a disours tale.
> Al þe wit of þis world and wiȝt mennes strengþe
> Kan noȝt parfournen a pees bitwene þe pope and hise enemys,
> Ne bitwene two cristene kynges kan no wiȝt pees make
> Profitable to eiþer peple;' . . .
>
> (XIII. 172–6)

Patience claims the power to transform social life, and the divine reminds us of actual conflicts he must confront in Langland's world. His check on Patience is salutary and represents decisive aspects of the poet's imagination. Moreover, a certain impatience with Patience's speech is surely justified by his retreat into the much-exegized enigma at lines 151–6:

Wiþ half a laumpe lyne in latyn, *Ex vi transicionis*,
I bere þer, in a bouste faste ybounde, dowel,
In a signe of þe Saterday þat sette first þe kalender,
And al þe wit of þe wodnesday of þe nexte wike after;
The myddel of þe Moone is þe myght of boþe.
And herewith am I welcome þer I haue it wiþ me.

These lines have attracted considerable efforts from scholars assuming that the passage should be interpreted according to some common allegorical and liturgical tradition, treated as an enigma whose shell must be cracked so that an already well-known discursive kernel can be extracted.[53] Yet these efforts ignore at least one real possibility – that the image is not designed to be decoded like a conventional picture model in exegetical and homiletic practice.[54] It may be nearer to the kind of apocalyptic image Conscience used earlier (III. 325–7) where the general sense of urgency and crisis includes areas of deliberately opaque mystery as well as more tangible allusions. Patience breaks into this mode because he tries to carry us over the serious gaps in his account. The image is obscurantist, gesturing at profundities of regeneration which the speaker cannot grasp with any conceptual or imaginative precision. We need not attribute coherence to images which do not have it, especially when there is excellent reason within the particular contexts as to why they cannot have it: the path back to the world of active humanity is harder than Patience realizes, and his obscurity manifests his unresolved difficulties. Conscience is carried away by Patience's self-advocacy to make similar assertions about universal social remedy as he turns to Clergy:

If Pacience be oure partyng felawe and pryue with vs boþe
Ther nys wo in þis world þat we ne sholde amende;
And conformen kynges to pees; and alle kynnes londes,
Sarsens and Surre, and so forþ alle þe Iewes,
Turne into þe trewe feiþ and intil oon bileue.

(XIII. 206–10)

Conscience thus still approves and shares Patience's desire to change the historical world, giving his own expression to the poem's orientation to the existence of social man, but he fails to see the inadequacies in the statement of Patience which he echoes.[55]

Nevertheless, Langland does see the lacunae, and he leaves Patience's present remedies at this point because he knows that if Love is to 'dowel' it will be within the field of practices his poem has grasped so concretely, not in some supposedly transcendent realm reached by dissolving the field. So we move to a representative of these practices, Haukyn or *Activa vita* (XII. 220 ff.). In the following passage the poetic mode is very different to the one Patience used. It conveys the need and enjoyment felt for Haukyn's indiscriminate delight in the variety of consumers:

> For alle trewe trauaillours and tiliers of þe erþe
> Fro Mighelmesse to Mighelmesse I fynde hem wiþ wafres.
> Beggeris and bidderis of my breed crauen,
> Faitours and freres and folk wiþ brode crounes.
> I fynde payn for þe pope and prouendre for his palfrey.
>
> (XIII. 239–43)

Patience's spiritual ideology tended to construct a picture of virtuous man in fantastic isolation, and passages like this correct his approach by drawing our attention back to the world of essential human work – 'In the sweat of thy face shalt thou eat bread' (Gen. 3:19):

> For er I haue breed of mele ofte moot I swete,
> And er þe commune haue corn ynouȝ many a cold morwenyng;
> So er my wafres be ywroȝt muche wo I þolye.
> Al londoun, I leue, likeþ wel my wafres,
> And louren when þei lakken hem; it is noȝt longe ypassed
> There was a careful commune whan no cart come to towne
> Wiþ bake breed from Stratford; þo gonnen beggeris wepe
> And werkmen were agast a lite; þis wole be pouȝt longe:
> In þe date of our driȝte, in a drye Aprill,
> A thousand and þre hundred, twies þritty and ten,
> My wafres were gesene [scarce] when Chichestre was Maire.'
>
> (XIII. 260–70)

One notes the striking specificity of the imagination's loving engagement with the material conditions under which life had to develop, with daily responses and drives. These again include areas of work and trade intrinsic to Langland's culture in which 'vnkynde' (XIII. 355, 378) values and practices were central. The problem was met earlier, particularly in his treatment of merchants, and he inevitably reverts to their occupation now:[56]

> And if I sente ouer see my seruauntȝ to Brugges,
> Or into Prucelond my Prentis my profit to waiten,
> To marchaunden wiþ my moneie and maken here eschaunges,
> Miȝte neuere me conforte in þe mene tyme
> Neiþer masse ne matynes, ne none maner siȝtes;
> Ne neuere penaunce parfournede ne Paternoster seide
> That my mynde ne was moore on my good in a doute
> Than in þe grace of god and his grete helpes:
>
> (XIII. 391–8)

The depiction of psychic obsession symbolizes a transformation of personality, of 'kynde', caused by an occupation dependent on market practices and motivation, but necessary to Langland's society. In the way 'my good in a doute' is shorn of its ethical and self-critical potential by the speaker, we see how language itself will be reduced to service of the market, commodities and 'profits'. Langland's first realization of such processes makes it even harder to accept generalized solutions and abstract moral propositions such as Patience had put forward, doubtless with the author's sympathy.

For, as I have said, Langland definitely wished to impose such solutions on the materials he grasped so firmly, and in the next Passus (XIV) he first moves away from the dynamic world which includes production, zealous trade and consumption. The movement is by now familiar, but its literary form deserves comment. Haukyn, image of 'the active life', is to repent and turn from 'vnkynde' social practices. The setting invites comparison with the sequence after the general repentance in Passus V. There the poem kept us in the working world, confronting the poet's cherished ideologies with a sharply focussed vision of present energies, conflicts and confusions. Here, however, Patience again takes up his attempt to transcend this densely textured, complicated world:

> 'And I shal purueie þee paast', quod Pacience, 'þouȝ no plouȝ erye,
> And flour to fede folk wiþ as best be for þe soule;
> Thouȝ neuere greyn growed, ne grape vpon vyne,

All þat lyueþ and lokeþ liflode wolde I fynde
And þat ynogh; shal noon faille of þyng þat hem nedeþ
(XIV. 29–33)

Once more the form of transcendence is the magic kind – a wave of the wand dissolves the fundamental and essential worlds of work and human relationships, so vividly present in the poem and so perplexing. Certainly man does not live by bread alone (XIV. 46), but his incarnate existence and development as certainly involves labour and community. Patience merely *substitutes* figurative food for material food socially produced (XIV. 30, 47–54). When he does acknowledge the obvious need for material food, he has it met by around-the-clock divine miracles (XIV. 63–70). Through this combination, 'picture-model' allegory and continuous miracle, he thus evaporates historical existence and the complex life-processes the poem habitually engages with.[57] But Langland himself could not rest content with a spiritualism whose foundations rested on the evasory dissolution of major problems he had disclosed as intrinsic to being a human, incarnate individual. With St Augustine he must have often asked himself, 'how could the city of God . . . either take a beginning or be developed, or attain its proper destiny, if the life of the saints were not a social life?'[58]

Certainly, Langland does not allow Patience to follow procedures which dissolved historical existence for long, since his imagination turns again to a fuller version of human living – here, that of the poor:

Ac beggeris aboute Midsomer bredlees þei soupe,
And yet is wynter for hem worse, for weetshoed þei gange,
Afurst soore and afyngred, and foule yrebuked
And arated of riche men þat ruþe is to here.

Ac poore peple, þi prisoners, lord, in þe put of meschief,
Conforte þo creatures þat muche care suffren
Thoruȝ derþe, þoruȝ droghte, alle hir dayes here,
Wo in wynter tymes for wantynge of cloþes,
And in somer tyme selde soupen to þe fulle.
(XIV. 160–3, 174–8)

Such writing offers little encouragement to the figurative mode Patience deployed earlier, with its rather jaunty 'spiritual' comments about providing food 'þouȝ no plouȝ erye,/And flour to fede folk weþ as best for þe soule;/ . . . liflode wolde I fynde/And þat ynogh'. The speaker is again Patience but Langland has shifted his perspective to take the incarnate nature of human spirituality and suffering seriously.[59] The mode he now creates resists all attempts to dissolve concrete life-processes, whatever respectable ideology such attempts might represent.

The resistance does not, of course, mean the poet stops *trying* to impose traditional schemes on his disturbing materials. His treatment of Charity in Passus XV, for instance, has many elements in common with the shifting handling of Patience. The dreamer's instructor excludes it from trade, war and all concern for rents or riches (XV. 151–78). Despite claims about finding Charity (XV. 216–50) it seems without any possible manifestation in social practice and the speaker resorts to transcendentalizing solutions like Patience's, *substituting* figurative food and divine miracles for the problems of understanding and reforming incarnate man (XV. 179–94, 255–89). There seems no need to analyse these passages as they are close to the parallel ones in Passus XIV discussed above.

But it is worth emphasizing *both* such passages, with the correspondingly extreme internalization of Charity in response to the intractable society (XV. 156–62, 272–87), *and* the characteristic counter-movement back to the poem's dynamic social world and the institutions of incarnate people acting in time present (XV, 307 ff., 546 ff.). For what I have argued is that the poet's commitment to received ideologies *and* to the imagination's engagement with the present, generates creative conflicts which are absolutely vital to the poem's momentum and its genuine exploratory power.

From Passus XV his search for Charity focalizes the theological grounding of the poem in a passionate involvement with Christian history and the Incarnation. Elsewhere I have considered these magnificent Passus with such aspects in mind and here it must suffice to note again how emphatically Langland's theology centres on God's Incarnation, his commitment to human history.[60] He is not interested in detailed meditations on the torn flesh and bleeding wounds of the crucified Christ, a form so popular in the later Middle Ages, and his Christ has perhaps been most remembered as the powerful, triumphant figure who harrows Hell. Yet just as he had stressed the incarnation of Christ in magnificent passages in Passus I (147–62) and V (478–505), so in these Passus it is Christ's immersion in time and the present consequences of his acts that hold his imagination. We see Christ being taught by Piers, becoming man to learn existentially what it is to be a 'creature', to know human sorrow by suffering, and through this we perceive the theological and historical grounds for Langland's own special insistence on the brotherhood of men in Christ and the latter's presence as one of the contemporary poor.[61] The subtle and powerful visionary dramatization of the Christian version of history, the intersections of time past and time present focussing on the incarnate Christ, the outflow of grace from his acts, these still leave open critical issues about men striving for 'dowel' and Charity in the present society and culture where they gain their being and identity.

To these Langland returns in the final episode I shall now look at, the poem's last two Passus, where Langland concentrated on the human world as he saw it.[62] The dreamer's cry for grace with 'manye hundred' others (XIX. 209–12) includes an allusion to the scene in Passus V where the great passage on incarnation and salvation preceded the search for grace and truth in the world of living, working people (V. 478–516). Now the grace released through Christ's redemptive acts is seen in personal form organizing a Christian world.[63] Grace, the Holy Spirit, explicitly adapts Paul's teaching about the diversity of spiritual gifts in the Church fused in its mystical unity (1 Cor. 12: 4–31), and applies it to society as a whole.[64] Langland thus has him propagate the dominant social ideology we have so often encountered. Society consists of stratified estates, organically related in a divinely established harmony free from flux and change. Perceived like this, the poet can set down vocation after vocation without any sign of the deep antagonism and mobility the poem has mediated so impressively. For example,[65]

> And some he kennede craft and knonnynge of sighte,
> By sellynge and buggynge hir bilyue [livelihood] to wynne.
> And some he lered to laboure on lond and on watre
> And lyue, by þat labour, a lele lif and a trewe.
> And some he tauȝte to tilie, to coke and to thecche
> To wynne wiþ hir liflode bi loore of his techynge
>
> (XIX. 234–9)

We have seen how fully Langland's imagination engaged with traders' activities, showing how deeply problematic they were to his preferred social model; yet in this comfortable statement the grave difficulties of practising anything remotely resembling what Langland would accept as Christian morality in an occupation based on profitable exchange of commodities in a competitive market demanding dedicated energy – difficulties the poem itself has awakened us to – these are simply ignored while the occupational activity persists.[66] Likewise with the labourers: the material and ideological conflicts intrinsic to agrarian relations in Langland's day and so vividly mediated in Passus VI, vanish into bland generalizations about 'a lele lif and a trewe'. Indeed,

> alle he lered to be lele, and ech a craft loue ooþer,
> Ne no boost ne debat be among hem alle.
> 'Thouȝ some be clenner þan some, ye se wel', quod Grace,
> 'That al craft and konnyng come of my ȝifte.
> Lokeþ þat noon lakke ooþer, but loueþ as breþeren;
> And who þat moost maistries kan be myldest of berynge.
> (XIX. 250–5)

The myth of divine institution thus confirms the existing social order in its orthodox ideological version. However, as with the preceding references to contemporary vocations, this can only be present in a form which eschews all imaginative specificity and engagement with the dynamic activities realized throughout the poem. The absence of particularity, the choice of generalized repetition ('ech a craft loue ooþer . . . loueþ as breþeren', 'Ne no boost ne debat be among hem . . . noon lakke ooþer'), these are signs of a reconciliation which is unconvincing because it only functions at an ideological level.[67]

And, as we have come to expect, Langland's imagination does not rest here, but re-engages with the social and economic world the poet hoped to contain within the received ideologies. Instead of the reassuring integration of merchants' practice with these structures, it now seems that 'pride' is justified in commenting that Conscience will not be able to judge of any kind of 'marchaunt þat wiþ moneye deleþ/Wheiþer he wynne wiþ right, wiþ wrong or wiþ vsure' (XIX. 348–50). Changing and more complex socio-economic practices are thus undermining received ethical categories and their received ideological framework. Not for the first time in *Piers Plowman* the figure who represents the nexus of commitments Langland finds so intractable is a brewer, one of the determined commodity producers met before:

> 'Ye? baw!' quod a Brewere, 'I wol noȝt be ruled,
> By Iesu! for al youre Ianglynge, with *Spiritus Iusticie*,
> Ne after Conscience, by crist! while I kan selle
> Boþe dregges and draf and drawe at oon hole
> Thikke ale and þynne ale; þat is my kynde,
> And noȝt hakke after holynesse; hold þi tonge, Conscience!
> Of *Spiritus Iusticie* þow spekest muche on ydel.'
> (XIX. 396–402)

This is a stunning contrast to the bland statement made by Spirit in which buying and selling were uncontentious activities taught by Grace, and it mediates the market practices of his own world. In its concreteness and strenuous rhythms the poetic mode once more registers the shift from ideological assertion to an imaginative grasp of those tremendous cultural energies so alien to Langland's received world-view but so important in the history of the later Middle Ages and Renaissance. Like the values of many groups in *Piers Plowman*, the brewer's are so deeply individualistic and market-oriented that once more Langland reveals how social practices can transform human nature, 'my kynde'.[68] He does not explicitly comment on the relation of this to his own assumption that there is an unchanging human nature – a universal 'kynde' known to us all and supplying a standard we can all use to assess 'unkynde' attitudes and behaviour, whatever our occupations – but it certainly strengthens our consciousness of cultural fragmentation and relativity. Again, Langland's poetry goes beyond the criticism of deviancy found in conventional satire and sermons, for he discloses how a view of human morality and nature, assumed in traditional paradigms, is in danger of being subverted by actual social practice.

The Passus drives home the fact that the brewer is representative of currents so strong that they include groups who should be defenders of the received ideology Langland wanted to affirm. He shows a knight saying:

> 'I holde it riȝt and reson of my Reue to take
> Al þat myn Auditour or ellis my Styward

> Counseilleþ me bi hir acounte and my clerkes writynge.
> Wiþ *Spiritus Intellectus* þei toke þe reuses rolles
> And wiþ *Spiritus fortitudinis* fecche it, wole he, nel he.'
> (XIX. 460–4)

This provides an interesting final perspective on the knightly class appealed to by Piers in Passus VI, and confirms the fundamental place of economic motivation, self-centred acquisitiveness and conflict at all levels in Langland's world. It also shows us how ideal abstractions ('riȝt', 'reson', '*Spiritus fortitudinis*', a cardinal virtue) are moulded by the material interests of particular groups and individuals in the culture. We see here how one powerful group's conception of what is desirable for itself is turned into a set of universals which function to generalize and legitimate its daily life and its self-interested goals. Even *Spiritus Intellectus*, Langland suggests, is appropriated and deployed by the leading group in its own interest. Fascinated by these historical processes Langland goes on to expose a classic statement of the organic social hierarchy, in terms of Paul's traditional metaphor, to a damaging image of its function. A king proclaims:

> I am kyng wiþ croune þe comune to rule,
> And holy kirke and clergie fro cursed men to defende.
> And if me lakkeþ to lyue by þe lawe wole I take it
> Ther I may hastilokest it haue, for I am heed of lawe;
> Ye ben but membres and I aboue alle.
> And siþe I am youre aller heed I am youre aller heele
> And holy chirches chief help and Chieftayn of þe comune,
> And what I take of yow two, I take it at þe techynge
> Of *Spiritus Iusticie* for I Iugge yow alle.
> (XIX. 466–74)

The corporate metaphor is appropriated by the ruler in defence of interests as egotistic and acquisitive as the brewer's or his fellow aristocrat's. Like the latter, he too demonstrates how abstractions supposed to be moral universals ('lawe', '*Spiritus Iusticie*', another cardinal virtue) are shaped by particular social and economic interests. Even Conscience now fails to oppose aristocrat and king, trying instead to use their own abstractions to hint at some vague qualification to their boundless self-interest (XIX. 477–9). As in Passus XX, Langland makes it clear that

Conscience too is immersed in specific historical practice, prone to defer before the powerful.[69] The 'Curatour' seems correct when he asserts the 'þe commune' will only use the counsel of Conscience or Cardinal virtues in so far as they tend to visible economic gain, 'somewhat to wynnyng' (XIX. 451–3). And Langland's poetry has just displayed that this will have profound effects on language, ethics, social ideology and 'kynde'. His own poetic vision, in Passus XIX thus mediates a culture evolving in ways which make the inherited ideologies he still cherished seem hopelessly inadequate.

Passus XX keeps us in this dynamic, fluid world, shifting the centre of attention to its absorption of the church, the mediator of Grace and doctrine. The poet abandons hope in his social ideology and constructs a parallel to its disintegration in Passus VI. As before, his vision of social and religious development leads to a call for *natural* disasters (disease, destitutions of age, death) to terrorize a world of people whole-heartedly opposed to Spirit's teachings (XX. 51–89). Jesus may well have told Satan that 'gile is bigiled and in his gile fallen':

> Now bigynneþ þi gile ageyn þee to turne
> And my grace to growe ay gretter and widder.
> (XVIII. 360–2)

But what Langland sees growing is very different:

> Antecrist cam þanne, and al þe crop of truþe
> Torned it tid vp so down and ouertilte þe roote,
> And made fals sprynge and sprede and spede mennes nedes.
> In ech a contree þer he cam he kutte awey truþe
> And gerte gile growe þere as he a god weere.
> (XX. 53–7)

We recall that in Passus II Gyle had been welcomed by merchants, while 'þe False' was embraced by friars (II. 211–17), and in his choice of agricultural imagery Langland obviously invited us to compare this scene with the actions of Piers and Spirit in Passus XIX, of Piers in Passus XVI and the cultivation of the half-acre in Passus VI.[70] Conscience's desperate resort to terror and physical afflictions (XX. 76 ff.) easily shows us the frailty of our lives, but cannot entail any particular set of moral values and social practices. Langland acknowledges this. Conscience asks

Nature to stop torturing men for a while, explicitly echoing Piers's request to Hunger (XX. 106–9; VI. 199 ff.). The result also mirrors the earlier episode, for as soon as the material threat is made less pressing the abundant energies we have got to know so well re-emerge in full vitality, as resistant as ever to the categories within which the poet would have liked to control them (XX. 109–64; see VI. 301 ff.). Conscience's only resort is yet again to summon physical terrors, closing the fruitless circle as Piers had done in Passus VI. Langland's re-enactment of this aspect of the structure of Passus VI invites the reader to draw related implications: there we found that the poet's desired ideological order could only be perpetuated by an economic freeze at subsistence level causing constant hunger (VI. 319–20). Now it becomes clear that the range of secular energies and values explored *negate* the organized Catholic Christianity Langland treasured, that in his culture the only motivation for entering 'into unitee', the church, is terror – at physical and material suffering (XX. 183–206). This is indeed a desperate position for a Catholic poet to reach, but it grows out of the integrity which constantly forced him to expose the solutions offered by inherited social and religious ideologies to his imagination's concrete engagement with alien energies and developments in his own world.

The closing lines of *Piers Plowman* maintain our focus on the consequences of the loss of Grace in the social fabric which has absorbed the church and subverted the poet's social ideals:[71]

> Conscience cryed eft Clergie to helpe,
> And bad Contricion come to kepe þe yate.
> 'He lyþ adreynt and dremeþ', said Pees, 'and so do manye
> oþere.
> The frere wiþ his phisyk þis folk haþ enchaunted,
> And doþ men drynke dwale [opiate]; þei drede no synne.'
> 'By crist!' quod Conscience þo, 'I wole bicome a pilgrym,
> And wenden as wide as þe world renneþ
> To seken Piers þe Plowman, þat pryde myȝte destruye,
> And þat freres had a fyndyng þat for nede flateren
> And countrepledeþ me, Conscience; now kynde me avenge,
> And sende me hap and heele til I haue Piers þe Plowman.'
> And siþþe he gradde after Grace til I gan awake.
>
> (XX. 375–86)

The poet whose vision consistently returns to the quest for individual salvation in its fully social and institutional context seems compelled, by his own poetic movement, to conclude with an individualistic pilgrimage which perhaps could indicate the total abandonment of the official church to the social and spiritual forces he has grasped so vividly and opposed so strenuously. Deprived of an ideological and institutional framework, the lonely Conscience is left to initiate a search for the lost Ploughman and the Grace he may mediate to the present world. This act of faith is a fitting symbol for the poet's own refusal to short-circuit the central dialectic between inherited ideologies and creative imagination, courageously choosing total engagement with the ambivalence and tensions his culture inspired, and evolving a form of writing brilliantly able to mediate and explore these in all their fluid complexity.

CHAPTER 2

Langland and the Church: Affirmation and Negation

And I awaked þerwiþ, witlees nerhande,
And as a freke þat fey were forþ gan I walke
In manere of a mendynaunt many yer after.
And of þis metyng many tyme muche þouȝt I hadde, . . .
And how þis Coueitise ouercom clerkes and preestes;
And how þat lewed men ben lad, but oure lord hem helpe,
Thoruȝ unkonnynge curatours to incurable peynes
Piers Plowman (B version) XIII. 1–4, 11–13

And siþþe he gradde after Grace til I gan awake.
Piers Plowman (B version) XX. 386

We shall now concentrate on the relationships between the ideas about the church which Langland wished to affirm and their place and meaning in the achieved poetic work which is *Piers Plowman*. The role of the church is central in the poem's anxious searching and had become an area of massive theoretical and practical controversy in the late Middle Ages. Accepting traditional ideas about the church, Langland envisaged it as a centralized, hierarchical community, led by its clergy, united by doctrine, sacraments which only the clergy dispensed, rituals and institutionalized structures of authority. He believed the established church mediated grace and doctrine to all Christians, while it should transcend the partialities and delusions of the present economic and material world. He wanted to follow the received orthodox ideology which located the salvation of the individual firmly within the official ecclesiastical framework – its sacraments, doctrines, authority – supervised by professional priests and religious quite distinct from lay people. The age-old dogma that there was no salvation outside the ark of the church had remained basic; the powerful official corporation, the Roman Church, was the medium for God's saving grace and revealed will: 'to reject it, or be rejected by it, was to reject God'.[1] With unwearied voice, preachers reiterated the essential mediation of officially accredited priests and their apparatus of confession and penance in the individual's attainment of salvation. As one of them puts it, 'ȝiff þou have þis womyte of þe sacrament of confession, Godes Sonne with-owten question dwelliþ þan wiþ þe and shall in thy dying resceyue þe to is blis'. They insist that without the official priests of the church, Christians are lost:[2]

> With-owten þer misterie oþur seruice þer is none helþe to none Cristen man. With-owten hem heþ no man perfitely þe sacrament of baptyme; withowten hem þer may no man resceyve is Saviour, þe blessed Sacrament. With-owte prestes who may be reconsiled to God . . . Lat vs þan all amend vs and shryve vs to þe prest, þat haeþ þis poure and dignite, and so shall we haue forȝeuenes of oure synnes and speke as þe children of God.

Langland would never wish to argue about the absolute centrality of the established church and its officers in the economy of salvation. Early in the poem Will falls on his knees before his vision of Holy Church, begging for 'grace', intercessionary prayers and doctrinal instruction which might enable him to fulfil God's will and save his soul (I. 79–84). At many points in *Piers Plowman* Langland explicitly stresses the decisive importance of confessors, together with the whole apparatus of confession and penance, while at the very end of the poem he concentrates attention on the significant role of the Catholic Church as Conscience falls 'Thoruȝ inparfite preestes and prelates of holy chirche'.[3] It seems reasonable to put forward Anima's insistence in the following passages as one that accords with Langland's own conscious judgment and received ideology:[4]

> As holynesse and honeste out of holy chirche spryngeþ
> Thoruȝ lele libbynge men þat goddes law techen, . . .
> Right so persons and preestes and prechours of holi chirche
> Is þe roote of þe right feiþ to rule þe peple; . . .

Iohannes Crisostomus of clerkes carpeþ and preestes:
Sicut de templo omne bonum progreditur, sic de templo omne malum procedit. Si sacerdocium integrum fuerit tota floret ecclesia; Si autem corruptum fuerit omnium fides marcida est. Si sacerdocium fuerit in peccatis totus populus conuertitur ad peccandum. Sicut cum videris arborem pallidam et marcidam intelligis quod vicium habet in radice, Ita cum videris populum indisciplinatum et irreligiosum, sine dubio sacerdocium eius non est sanum.
[As from the temple all good comes, so from the temple comes all evil. If the priesthood is upright, the whole church flourishes; however, if it is corrupt the faith of all is withered. If the priesthood is in sin, the whole people turns to sin. As when you see a tree pale and withered, you know that it has a disease in the root, so when you see a people undisciplined and irreligious, without doubt their priesthood is not healthy.]

(XV. 92–3, 99–100, 118)

These lines make the traditional importance of the official church in the individual's quest for grace and salvation absolutely clear. The emphasis on the images of root and growth of flowering plant or tree is again an emphasis on the primacy and essential role of priestly mediators in the Christian's ethical and religious development.[5] It is not surprising to find a preacher in the conventional collection of sermons, from which I have already quoted, turning to the same text as Langland:[6]

But swerynge of prestes is cause of many mo, and þer-fore seiþ Seynt Gregore in is boke, 'Ruina populi maxime ex sacerdotum et cleri est culpa.' Et Iohn Crisostimus seis, 'Si autem sacerdos in peccato fuerit, totus eciam populus ad peccandum conuertitur.' 'Cause o fallynge of þe pepull is most of þe preestes defaute, for and þe preeste be combred in anny opon synne, þan is þe pepull turned also to synne.'

In a similar way, whatever Ymaginatif's disagreement with Will's earlier views he and Will both see the priesthood's role as keepers of 'cristes tresor,/The which is mannes soule to saue, as god seiþ in þe gospel'.[7] From Passus XVI onwards Langland's visionary and dramatic meditations evolve around the incarnation and saving acts of Christ, his transforming power, and the means by which his acts can be efficacious in the present. Here Christ gives Piers power,

> be his pardon paied,
> To bynde and vnbynde boþe here and ellis,
> And assoille men of all synnes saue of dette one.
> (XIX. 188–90)

Piers, as I have attempted to demonstrate at length in an earlier work, functions as a developing means by which perceivers in the poem (especially Will of course) hope to be guided to salvation, embodying the saving power they can imagine and conceive at different stages of the quest, indissolubly linked to the knower's mode of perception and spiritual orientation.[8] Now Piers becomes the symbolic lens through which the effects of Christ's acts and his Spirit in history can be focused, and the locus for this turns out to be the construction of the church on earth. Piers is entrusted by Grace with the Gospels, authoritative instructors in orthodox doctrine, virtues which he has the power to sow in human souls, 'þe cros, wiþ þe garland of þornes'; Grace himself builds, 'þat hous vnitee, holy chirche on Englissh',[9]

> And when þis dede was doon Grace deuysede
> A cart highte cristendom to carie home Piers sheues,
> And gaf hym caples to his carte, contricion and confession,
> And made preesthod hayward þe while hymself wente
> As wide as þe world is wiþ Piers to tilie truþe
> And þe lond of bileue, þe lawe of holy chirche.
> (XIX. 329–34)

Here, then, Langland has envisioned the church of his ideology, an authoritative institution in every aspect, united, utterly reliable, freely mediating grace, doctrine and vital spiritual energy to the human world. The prominence of such ideology in the poem is enough to account for the common scholarly assumptions so lucidly voiced by A. C. Spearing:[10]

> It has been shown by Professor G. R. Owst that in its content *Piers Plowman* is extremely close to the sermons of medieval preachers. The ideas of the poem, even when they sound, as they sometimes do, most revolutionary, most closely related to the surge of revolutionary feeling that

> underlay the Peasants' Revolt and the Lollard movement, are in fact 'in perfect accord with . . . the most commonplace orthodox preaching of the times, indeed a perfect echo in every respect of the church's message to the world.' This can be taken as established.

Yet *Piers Plowman* demands a more complex account of the place such ideology holds in the overall movement of the poem as well as in its particulars. What Langland actually created here, we will find, was a dialectical process similar to the one discussed in our first chapter. To put the case concisely, while the informing ideology is indeed the received orthodoxy just described, his imaginative engagement with contemporary ecclesiastic realities acts in ways which go beyond conventional criticism of the *status quo* to undermine the very credibility of the ideology and organization he wished to preserve. His imaginative grasp of the church's committed practices as a vast vested interest, structurally incorporated in the contemporary political economic and social fabric at all levels, evokes an overwhelming sense of the inadequacies of the received paradigms he cherishes and of their supersession.[11] Even as they are affirmed, in the manner I have already noted, they are also negated within the poem itself. We must now attend to the negating moments of this dialectic as it concerns the church in *Piers Plowman*.

The Prologue soon shows us that the officials of the church are immersed in the dynamic social and economic world so marvellously present in the poem and which I described in chapter 1. Leaving aside the friars, to whom I shall return, the early passage on the pardoner preaching exemplifies what is at stake:

> Brouȝte forþ a bulle wiþ Bisshopes seles,
> And seide þat hymself myȝte assoillen hem alle
> Of falshede of fastynge and of Auowes ybroken.
> Lewed men leued hym wel and liked his speche;
> Comen vp knelynge to kissen his bulle.
> He bonched hem with his breuet and blered hire eiȝen
> And rauȝte with his Rageman rynges and broches.
> Thus ye gyuen youre gold glotons to helpe . . .
> Were þe Bisshop yblessed and worþ boþe his eris
> His seel sholde noȝt be sent to deceyue þe peple.
>
> (Pr. 69–79)

The pardoner's confidence, the people's total complicity and their shared assumptions that anything valuable must be a commodity – Langland's poetry discloses this with striking concreteness and zest. As we shall observe in discussing Chaucer's pardoner, it is important to remember that this figure had become an officially accredited, essential element in the practices of the late medieval church. That is precisely why Langland brings in the bishop who has licensed the pardoner.[12] It seems to me that the positive response writer and reader feel towards the energy of the successful pardoner in this scene pulls against the formal disapproval of his actions, disqualifying any simple moral judgment. We are made to feel complicity with the people, impressed with them by this figure. Even if some readers disavow any such complicity in their response to the poetry here, one point is, I believe, incontestable. In this image of people, pardoner and bishop, there is a unity of orientation which would offer little encouragement to those expecting to find the church in some recognizable relationship to the orthodox ideology we have recounted. If the poem were to elaborate many more images of this kind it would gradually discredit even ideas about reform of the institutions in accord with received ideology, for there seems to be no obvious place within the institutions, its officials and their attitudes, where reform would be welcomed, let alone instigated. As the passage continues this sense is strengthened:

> Ac þe parisshe preest and þe pardoner parten þe siluer
> That þe pouere peple of þe parisshe sholde haue if þei ne were.
> Persons and parisshe preestes pleyned hem to þe Bisshop
> That hire parisshe were pouere siþ þe pestilence tyme,
> To haue a licence and leue at London to dwelle,
> To syngen for symonie for siluer is swete.
>
> (Pr. 81–6)

Again the church is immersed in the values and assumptions of its secular milieu, and in the complaints of rectors and parish priests to their superior Langland conveys a tone which shows no scruples have to be overcome in making such a request; there is a sense that they are acting quite within their vocational rights and an unhesitating assurance that their stance is fully representative. After all, parochial incumbents mostly depended on glebe, tithes and various offerings for their living, held and cultivated land separate to church-rights, sold and bought produce, traded, and were as involved in the economy and its dislocations or opportunities 'siþ pestilence tyme' as anyone else, while unbeneficed priests depending on small wages might well find their position materially intolerable in their parishes and pursue better paid work as chantry priests in London.[13] Langland grasps all this and gives us a plausible glimpse of the outlook such pressures and forms of livelihood encouraged. The lines that follow emphasize how the priests' mentality is shared by their elevated superiors, 'Bisshops and Bachelers, boþe maistres and doctours'. They too are making for London and the sources of urban wealth at court and in the city, unambivalently absorbed in the financial and legal apparatus of the developing state or serving 'lordes and Ladies,/And in stede of Stywardes sitten and demen' (Pr. 87–96).[14] Already then, in the Prologue, Langland's poetry suggests that contemporary clergy can neither fulfil their role in the traditional social ideology looked at in my first chapter, nor provide any resistance to the total absorption of the church in the changing economic matrix. Readers may well begin to suspect that the official church, whatever Langland's own ideology, could well emerge as one no longer able to provide an environment capable of resisting the energies and tensions generated in the human practices of the secular world of which it was so important a part.

Such suspicions engendered by the Prologue are abundantly confirmed as the great poem continues its explorations. Instead of being content to impose conventional adverse moral judgment on stock images of clerical abuse, Langland's imagination continues the mediation of the very processes of laicization in the church's practice and outlook at all levels of its hierarchy. His imagination grasps and drastically enacts for us processes which are referred to in terms such as these by modern historians like Francis Rapp:[15]

> L'Église est insérée dans le siècle. Que celui-ci vienne à bouger et la vie chrétienne aussitôt ressentira les effets de ce mouvement. Or c'est bien le changement qui caractérise l'époque dont nous avons à parler. Dans le domaine de la production et des échanges d'abord: que nous admettions, avec la majorité des historiens, que l'Occident entrait dans une longue phase de stagnation ou qu'avec les marxistes, nous mettions l'accent sur l'apparition des structures

> nouvelles, celles du capitalisme naissant, le fait essentiel pour notre propos demeure. Après 1300, l'économie de l'Europe prit un autre visage. . . . Au XIVe siècle, introduit par la faim, la guerre et la peste, l'affaissement démographique, la baisse des prix agricoles et la hausse des salaires ébranlèrent les assises de la société, et plus particulièrement la seigneurie. . . . Ces ondes traversaient de bout en bout le monde sacré comme le profane. L'Église était une puissance financière, une force sociale, un appareil politique en même temps que la dispensatrice du savoir et de la sagesse. Toutes ses fonctions étaient touchées par la mutation que subissait la civilisation occidentale.

In my first chapter I observed how the forces of Meed represented developments whereby money, economy and market relations were becoming powerful enough to dissolve traditional personal and ethical ties, and now we must focus on the dynamic participation of the church which Langland realizes so impressively. It is typified in passages such as the following:

> Ac þanne swoor Symonye and Cyuylle boþe
> That Somonours sholde be Sadeled and seruen hem echone,
> 'And late apparaille þis prouisours in palfreyes wise;
> Sire Symonye hymself shall sitte vpon hir bakkes.
> Denes and Southdenes, drawe yow togideres;
> Erchedekenes and Officials and alle youre Registrers,
> Lat sadle hem wiþ siluer oure synne to suffre,
> As deuoutrye [adultery] and diuorses and derne vsurie,
> To bere Bisshopes aboute abrood in visitynge.
>
> (II. 169–77)

The apparatus of the contemporary church is made present in a way which conveys its total complicity in current civilization where Meed is central and the poet comments, 'I kan noȝt rekene þe route þat ran aboute Mede' (II. 62). The energies of those within the holy institutions are secularized as they ensure their survival and that of the institution they serve. Most of the offices Langland mentions here are familiar enough, but it is worth noting how he links the local branches of the church and the papacy in his reference to 'prouisours' who are to be used as horses in this symbolic marriage of Meed. Provisors were clerics holding a grant or promise of a benefice from the Pope. The historian R. W. Southern comments:

> There were, however, never enough vacancies to satisfy the host of competitors for the more lucrative benefices. These competitors were of many kinds. Most important of all were the many learned, acquisitive and under-endowed clerks who, in growing numbers from the mid-twelfth century, had business at the papal court. Very often they came as the representatives of important people, with money in their pockets to pay the many expenses of official business and to gain the goodwill of cardinals and officials.

The necessary use of money, gifts and expenses in the pursuit of benefices was a clear case of simony, as Langland stresses; but, and this is the most significant aspect of the case, such simony was not a peripheral abuse indulged by especially wicked people – it had become a fundamental element in the structure of the late medieval church. Southern makes some further observations about this particular simoniacal practice which are of interest here:[16]

> The clerk who obtained from the papal court the grant or promise of a benefice . . . had taken the first step towards getting what he wanted, but he still had a long way to go before he was put in possession; he was only at the beginning of a legal tussle in which he would have to defend his case against adversaries and objections as yet unknown . . . [the Pope] distributed no more than the right to enter the competition from a position of strength. Thereafter, success or failure depended on the resources of friends and money, and the staying-power that the claimant himself could muster. The pope simply laid down the rules of the competition and distributed the tickets; but in making this a main part of papal business in the later Middle Ages, the papal machine profoundly affected the whole history of the papacy.

I have quoted Southern at some length on this point because it helps us see the precise nature of the web of practices on which Langland's imagination dwelt, as well as the detail of his attention. It also shows how the ecclesiastic market was integrated with the secular one, calling for a similarly competitive outlook and energetic pursuit of all that would allow success in the market. Practitioners of civil law work with ecclesiastical officers of all levels in Langland's passage, and the speaker reveals how even the traditional categories of moral theology are absorbed in the quest for Meed, sin itself becoming a commodity in the markets of the institution – a nice parody of the teaching that Christ 'bouȝte vs on þe Rode' (II. 3; II. 174–7).

We shall find these simoniacal commitments play a major part in the poem's final passus, but before considering that I wish to offer just a few more representative examples of the vitality and orientation of the church as it is created in *Piers Plowman*. In Passus X, for instance, Langland makes a conventional attack on peripatetic and worldly monks. But the poetic form of the attack does not allow us simply to classify it as another illustration of the stereotype of monks in traditional satire.[17]

Whan fisshes faileen þe flood or þe fresshe water
Thei deyen for drouȝte, whan þei drie lenge;
Riȝt so by religion, it roileþ and steruеþ
That out of couent and cloistre coueiten to libbe. . . .

Ac now is Religion a rydere, a rennere by stretes,
A ledere of louedayes and a lond buggere,
A prikere on a palfrey fro place to Manere,
An heep of houndes at his ers as he a lord were,
And but if his knaue knele þat shal his coppe brynge
He loureþ on hym and lakkeþ hym: who lered hym curteisie?
(X. 301–4, 311–16)

Perhaps there is none of the subtle ambiguity of attitude Chaucer generates so carefully in his portrait of the Monk in the General Prologue, perceptively analysed by Jill Mann, but the poetry does disclose how the traditional ideal stated in the fish-out-of-water proverb, is now asserted in the face of activity which is so deeply entrenched in ecclesiastic and social organization as to be untouchable, let alone reformable.[18] The energy of the passage describing how the Monk rides about the country, a pack of hounds 'at his ers as he a lord were', presides over Lovedays and demands that his elevated social and economic status be recognized as befits a lord, subverts the traditional assertion, authorized by 'Gregorie þe grete clerk and þe goode pope' (298), that such monks die like fish out of water. Far from it, they thrive in the earthly element, secularized and dynamic members of society, sharing their orientation with most fellow-citizens:

> The mooste partie of þis peple þat passeþ on þis erþe,
> Haue þei worship in þis world þei kepe no bettre;
> Of ooþer heuene þan here holde þei no tale.
>
> (I. 7–9)

So while Langland affirms a traditional ideal and image, his imaginative openness to present practices (and, of course, the antagonism these inevitably triggered), negates the content of what he affirms. The poetic vitality itself embodies the vigour of the orientation and commitments the monk refracts, both socially and in individual consciousness. Traditional moralists could fulminate against monks, but as Jill Mann finds Chaucer asking, 'while monasteries are supported by manors, how can monks avoid acting like lords of them?'[19] Mostly they were drawn from dominant social groups, tended not to have abandoned the assumptions and expectations of their class on taking the cowl and, perhaps more importantly, were actually needed by the institutions they served to fulfil the economic and social roles they had been born to. For these institutions controlled land and property, traded, and offered members opportunity for secular advancement which would in turn benefit the monastery. As R. W. Southern showed, there were excellent reasons why the communities that were meant to be set apart from the world, in especial dedication to the contemplative life, should in fact 'become a mirror of the world in which they lived'.[20] It is one of the greatnesses of Langland's poetry that instead of merely adding another voice to the conventional moral attack it displays the internal and external forces which made such criticism still-born.[21]

It is in connection with his brilliant realization of the energies of churchmen immersed in the world of production, consumption and competitive exchange that his much-remarked preoccupation with the friars may perhaps be viewed in a fresh and relevant perspective.[22] For the growth of the friars was a phenomenon inseparable from the *urban* development of the later Middle Ages. R. W. Southern outlines the situation with customary clarity:

> Wherever there was a town there were friars; and without a town there were no friars. This was a necessary consequence of their way of life. A single beggar can survive in the countryside, but an organized community of beggars cannot. In order to survive, such a community, however small, needs a fairly large population of people who are not themselves on the verge of want. The friars therefore made at once for the towns. They would not have looked on themselves as men who were tapping a hitherto under-exploited source of urban revenue; but this is in effect what they did.

The friars' existence was thus intrinsic to the urban economy, on which they depended and in which they organized their base. Southern observes:

> Most of their income came from small gifts in money or kind, from legacies, and from fees for burials and masses for the dead . . . the public accessibility of the friars and their dependence on an urban environment was still obvious in the sources from which they drew their income.

Their poverty, by Langland's day, had certainly become a fable as they had corporate property, fixed incomes, and a sophisticated institutional apparatus able to play an important part in secular affairs. But their official way of life encouraged a particular set of vices as their institutionalization of begging 'led to a search for legacies and fees, and easily suggested a lenient treatment for penitents who were also benefactors'. Southern notes that their very vices 'required exertion', and that they always retained the marks of their urban origins.[23] Langland was thus reacting against an especially active group developed in response to new needs of new social groups emerging in the increasingly complex civilization of the towns.

Near the opening of the Prologue they enter the poem:

> I fond þere Freres, alle þe foure ordres,
> Prechynge þe peple for profit of þe wombe;
> Glosed þe gospel as hem good liked;
> For coueitise of copes construwed it as þei wolde.
> Many of þise maistres mowe cloþen hem at likyng
> For hire moneie and hire marchaundiȝe marchen togideres.
> (Pr. 58–63)

Ethics and exegesis are moulded to serve their pursuit of 'good' in the market, and the poem will evoke a sense that this march of their 'moneie and hire marchaundiȝe' is inexorable. When the king and Conscience attempt to check Meed and her numberless followers, the friars join with merchants and others to help the threatened carnival, and her own personal peripatetic confessor is a friar.[24] The Prologue had already told us that 'charite haþ ben chapman and chief to shryue lordes' (Pr. 64) and now Langland shows us the friar-confessor in action (III. 35–63). He adapts himself and religion to the orientation and commitments of the person he is confessing, for through this he gains a benefactor for the order, a necessary part of the institution's perpetuation. He asks for 'a seem of whete' and tells Meed about a new window they are having – 'Woldestow glaȝe þe gable and graue þere þy name/Syker sholde þi soule be heuene to haue' (III. 49–50). In return for this income, typical of the small gifts Southern reported, the friar not only absolves Meed but becomes her servant in the secular world, a dedicated participant in the market-place and the very last person to challenge values which sustain him and his order. And the commodities he brings are not only his verbal skill, his intellectual training, his exegetical skill and his knowledge of the world, but the sacrament of confession, the church's instrument for bestowing grace and the real hope of salvation (III. 49–50). This is an especially desirable commodity, and though he has competitors (famously, of course, the parish priests) he provides an array of services and a mobility few could match, allied to an encouraging sanctification of the market, 'moneie and marchaundiȝe'.

I have already noted the centrality of the sacrament of confession in Langland's ideology of the church, and in most of the appearances of friars in *Piers Plowman* they are seen exchanging this for the goods of the market and secular influence (e.g. V. 137–52; XI. 52–88; XIX. 221–2; XX. 228 ff.). Their own energy is abundantly realized in the poem, and Langland has Need offer a diagnosis which has significant elements in common with Southern's description quoted previously. As the friars press forward in the final passus of the poem, to which we shall return, Need tells Conscience that

þei come for coueitise, to haue cure of soules.
'And for þei are pouere, parauenture, for patrymonye hem failleþ,

They wol flatere to fare wel folk þat ben riche. . . .
For lomere he lyeþ þat liflode moot begge
Than he þat laboureþ for liflode and leneþ it beggeris.
(XX. 233–5, 238–9)

He is saying that their form of life is determined by their position in the economy, that their vices are an *inevitable* product of their way of gaining necessary subsistence. As a result of this diagnosis the poet wants friars to be given a fixed income. His poem has revealed their immense energy and mobility, but he hopes to protect the ideology he cherishes by confining them to a static and very limited place in the traditional ecclesiastic and social hierarchy. This is the meaning of the desire for friars to find 'a keye/Of Constantyns cofres þer þe catel is Inne' (X. 328–9), for them to stop expanding in numbers (XX. 253–70),[25] for them to cease competing with other groups (XX. 280–93), for them to have 'a fyndyng' (XX. 383). Could they *and* the forces they represent be frozen, the traditional feudal ideology and its order might be preserved, the longed-for stability and certainty attained. But Langland's imaginative integrity drives him to show the irresistible nature of the friars' energies, the way they are well suited to their social and ecclesiastic environment, leaving us with the conviction that however his ideology dismisses them or transforms them, they will neither be metamorphozed into some traditional ideal nor ejected from the world in which he writes.

Before we even reach the final two passus of the poem I believe Langland's poetic mediation of society, church and individual orientation, has made the very possibility of the hierarchic, stable, authoritative and thoroughly spiritual church of received ideology seem far-fetched, something irrelevant to the contemporary pursuit of holiness as his vision evokes it. The traditional ideology, from which I started this chapter (like the first one) has no positive presence, no imaginative realization in the poem's world, as the evidence which I have been examining makes clear. It is also made clear in some other respects I wish to point out before discussing Passus XIX–XX. It is striking that the poet never creates an episode in which any powers of self-criticism and self-transformation are revealed in the contemporary church. Initiatives towards reformation of individual and society come from a group of figures which conspicuously excludes the representatives of the church hierarchy, the estate of clergy and religious, in time present. The potential for reform in the early passus of the poem is associated with king, Conscience, Reason and 'a Plowman' who at *this* stage is perceived as a member of the third estate rather than as some allegorical image of an official, institutional priest.[26] In Passus VI, as we saw in chapter 1, the poet's mediation of contemporary orientation and antagonisms quite undermined the social ideology he favoured, but it also displayed another particularly important feature: the absence of the church as a moralizing and distinguishable agent. It is certainly mentioned, for Piers advises upper-class ladies to make 'Chesibles for Chapeleyns chirches to honoure' (VI. 12), reminds the knight of his traditional duty (in terms of the inherited ideology Langland favoured) of protecting the other two estates, 'holy kirke and myselue' (VI. 27), and arranges for his burial in the church:

> The kirke shal haue my caroyne and kepe my bones
> For of my corn and my catel he craued þe tiþe;
> I paide hym prestly for peril of my soule;
> He is holden, I hope, to haue me in mynde
> And mengen me in his memorie amonges alle cristene.
> (VI. 91–5)

Here the church appears as consumer, taking the tithe of all produce, and in return interceding to help the souls of the dead. Piers also insists he will only contribute to preachers licensed by the official church (VI. 148–51).[27] Yet despite these references it remains peripheral, contributing nothing. Even when Piers needs advice about the relationship between labour-discipline and Christian brotherhood ('for god bouȝte vs alle;/Truþe tauȝte me ones to louen hem ech one,/And helpen hem of alle þyng after þat hem nedeþ' (VI. 202–9)), still the church and its officials are absent. A reply comes from the personification 'hunger' who weaves together Old and New Testament texts in his reply before refusing to leave the field until he has been well fed (VI. 212–301). The poet's imagination has presented a vision where the official means of grace and authoritative instruction is irrelevant to the serious pursuit of social practices informed by the kind of moral consciousness Piers reflects in his puzzled questions to 'hunger'. Nor is this simply a defect in the perception of the visionary or of Piers, for the role of the church is precisely to act *within* the 'feeld ful of folk . . . werchynge and wandrynge' (Pr., ll. 17–19), as Christ and Grace will remind us in Passus XIX. When a priest does at last appear it is to challenge the long gloss Piers attaches to the two lines from the Athanasian creed (VII. 107 ff.). We examined this controversial scene in chapter 1, and here it is sufficient to make one observation:[28] the priest, representative of the church, mediator of grace and doctrine, proves quite unable to offer any positive guidance about the way in question, let alone to initiate and inspire the quest. This is typical of the institution he serves, at least as it is refracted in Langland's vision.

As typical is the manner in which the visionary poet is left to interpret the dream and its status as knowledge (VII. 144–206), wandering about, 'Metelees and moneilees on Maluerne hulles', alone. The responsibility of explication and judgment now rests with the individual consciousness. Will has to understand the scene without an authoritative exegete, without a satisfactory dogmatic handbook in which he can look up the answers to the problems and images he experiences. After all, the traditional source of authority, the priesthood and the church it serves, is precisely what has been made problematic.[29] Tentatively, at this relatively early stage of his search, Will makes a statement in which he firmly acknowledges the salvationary powers of 'pardon and penaunce and preieres' within the established church, while simultaneously expressing scepticism about their real efficacy, mocking the thought of sacks full of institutionally-issued pardons and double-indulgences at the Last Judgment, finding them absolutely worthless unless the individual's own good works help him (VIII. 179–200). Concluding the passus, he advises Christians to pray that God 'gyue vs grace er we go hennes,/Swiche werkes to werche, while we ben here': this advice actually allows the institutional mediations to be by-passed, the individual Christian praying for grace to enable him to do good works, 'er we go hennes', which will be accepted at 'þe day of dome' (VII. 201–6).[30] It would be quite wrong to abstract this as a definitive statement of the poet's views. We have seen his own conscious support of traditional ideology concerning the necessary role of the established institution in the Christian's salvation, as well as the ways his poem undermines such ideology, and the dialectical movement of the poem quite disallows the abstraction and exaltation of *one* moment. The dramatic and theoretical importance of this particular moment should not be missed, however, for it emerges coherently out of the movement we have been examining and sets Will off on the next stage of his search which continues without decisive institutional guidance or any signs of its authoritative presence in the world experienced by the poet.

Passus VIII opens with him roaming about to seek 'dowel', always asking for authoritative answers and directions. The difficulties of his situation in the face of the contemporary church are emphasized here, for the priest of Passus VII is followed by the friars, 'Maistres of þe Menours', who instruct him about 'dowel' (VIII. 6–61). Their glib claim, discredited by the poem, that 'dowel' dwells 'amonges vs' is capped by a bland exemplum which shows no grasp of the major psychological problems of habit and sin, and no grasp of the theological puzzles concerning 'free wil', grace and justification raised by their own speech.[31] Furthermore, the tone of calm assurance should not conceal the fact that 'dowel' is treated as the decisive agent in the commentary on their exemplum (VIII. 44–50) when they have quite failed to inform us about the location and availability of 'dowel' – which was the dreamer's opening question:

> þoruȝ þe fend and þe flessh and þe false worlde
> Synneþ pe sadde man seuen siþes a day.
> Ac dedly synne doþ he noȝt for dowel hym helpeþ,
> That is charite þe champion, chief help ayein synne.
> (VIII. 42–5)

How the person who habitually sins *can* 'dowel' while immersed in sin, how he could even want to 'dowel', this vital question the preachers beg.[32] Even their identification of 'dowel' and 'charite þe champion' does not help matters here, for it is subject to all the questions already begged. Where, for instance, do they locate this saving charity? In the corrupt will of the fallen individual, in the confessional and penitential apparatus of the church in which the friars, as the poem shows, played such a prominent part – or somewhere unspecified? We cannot tell, though we may suspect that as they claimed 'dowel' lives 'amonges vs', and as they now identify 'dowel' and charity, their order will be put forward in some manner as champions of charity, 'chief help ayein synne', ready to dispense the sacrament of confession. One remarkable fact here is the preachers' reticence about the figure who will emerge as incarnating 'dowel' and charity – Christ.[33] The latter only appears in their valedictory blessing and however pious this sounds its externality to their teaching and thinking should not be overlooked. The dreamer is admirable in his refusal to be satisfied by these pillars of the church, and modestly takes his leave (VIII. 57–62).

That these two inadequate preachers are friars does not detract from the representative nature of the scene, as I hope our discussion by now has illustrated. They follow the priest of Passus VII, the absence of the church as active guide in Passus VI, and, as I have said, the poem does not offer more impressive witnesses from the contemporary church. Will continues his dedicated search, and he continues it without the authoritative guidance and institutional framework provided by the church according to the inherited ideology the poet wanted to preserve and realize in his own day.

His explorations proceed through an all-encompassing range of important topics. These include contemporary theological problems which caused deep anxiety to those who reflected on their religion (predestination; free will; grace, works and faith), the viciousness of the upper classes, the brotherhood of all in Christ, the effects of bad clergy, the possible lay appropriation of ecclesiastical possessions, the place of learning and unquestioning faith in the pursuit of salvation, marriage, but there are many more (VIII–XV). He engaged with all of them in a poetry which is astonishing for its sustained critical passion, its boundless integrity and refusal to substitute conventional pieties and formulae for the taxing dialectical processes which exposed himself and his hopes to relentless scrutiny in the face of contemporary intellectual, ecclesiastic and social life. Here we will not follow him through these passus, for at this stage of the chapter it suffices to note that his explorations are undertaken with figures such as 'Thought', 'Wit', 'Study', 'Patience', 'Conscience', and that none of these represent the purportedly authoritative institution outside of which there was allegedly no salvation, nor are any of them part of its hierarchy. Even 'Scripture' enters into dialogue unmediated by the church which claimed a monopoly of correct learning, exegesis and dogmatics. M. W. Bloomfield comments that, 'Langland seems to be struggling to find an authoritative answer to the question of salvation and perfection, and by the multitude of his instructors, Langland in a sense admits his failure.' Bloomfield associates this 'failure' with the early disappearance of the 'louely lady' who had instructed Will in his first vision, calling herself 'Holi chirche' (I. 3, 75), and he is right to do so.[34] Yet in terms of the traditional ideology and the orthodox claims of the established church, the consequences are once again gravely subversive. For whatever its social and inquisitorial powers, the orthodox church would be deprived of the doctrinal, spiritual and moral authority it traditionally claimed, leaving the questing individual to pursue the Christian religion within the lights of his own vision and judgment outside its own institutional framework and instruction.[35] These, as I have reiterated, were not consequences Langland could welcome, but they are the product of his imagination's engagement with church and society, essential aspects of the poem's processes.

We began this chapter by illustrating Langland's affirmation of traditional ideas about the church on earth and the individual Christian's relations to the institution and its necessary officials who dispensed the sacraments, grace and revealed doctrine. Quoting from Passus XV we moved on to the poet's meditation on the building of this authoritative institution by Christ himself, his Holy Spirit and early Christians (XVI–XIX, pp. 39–42 above). The house called 'vnitee, holy chirche on Englissh', was endowed with the means of salvation created by Christ's redemptive acts, and within it the centrality of priesthood and the sacrament of confession were emphasized.[36] But that was in time past and Langland characteristically returns to time present and the contemporary church in the dynamic social world. We analysed this return at the close of the first chapter, but here will focus on the poet's concluding mediation of his church, and its implications.

The community, we recall, with its energetic practices and consciousness represented by the brewer, the landlord and the king, cares little for any counsel, 'But it soune, as by sighte, somewhat to wynnyng', transforming 'kynde' and language to fit the needs of market-success and self-interest.[37] The church and its officials, the poet's vision again discloses, are now as dedicated as their secular brethren in the pursuit of economic and social goods and power:

Symonye hym suede to assaille Conscience,
And pressed on þe pope and prelates þei maden
To holden wiþ Antecrist, hir temporaltees to saue.
And cam to þe kynges counseille as a kene baroun
And knokked Conscience in Court afore hem alle;
(XX. 126–30)

This is a continuation of the activity described in Passus II, where Simony was riding the 'prouisours' at the marriage of Meed in one of the images which suggested the structured unity between church and market, reminding us that in Langland's day, 'The papal court was now mainly a place where business was done.'[38] Langland, however, while his poetry displays this structured unity and shared orientation, cannot accept it as the modern historian does, and judges the hierarchy, 'þe pope and prelates', to be in league with Antichrist. We will come back to this judgment in a moment, but there is no doubt that the poet succeeds in disclosing, once more, the way economic individualism, secularized orientation and cash dominate the institutions of grace established by Christ, Holy Spirit and Piers. Prominent in Antichrist's army are 'Proude preestes. . . . In paltokes and pyked shoes, purses and longe knyues,' dedicated to the pursuit of economic success (XX. 217–27). Still convinced of the importance of the institutional church in the pursuit of salvation, Langland has Conscience cry out, 'I falle/Thoruȝ inparfite preestes and prelates of holy chirche' (XX. 228–9). But rather than magically reverse the movement of the passus, Langland now accepts it, telling us that when Conscience called out it was the friars who heard him and came to help (XX. 230).

The irony here is profound, for it points to a theoretical crux for Langland and his work, one we have encountered before: if 'þe pope and prelates' are in league with Antichrist, priests galore in his army, friars and the professional religious his worshippers and celebrants,[39] and if the established, orthodox institutional church is the decisive means of grace and salvation for men in the world, what can individual conscience do? The appeal is heard by the officials of the institution, but they turn out to be both product and cause of the outlook the poet identifies with Antichrist. And, as priests, they are also dispensers of the sacraments, including confession and penance:

'I may wel suffre', seide Conscience, 'syn ye desiren,
That frere flaterere be fet and phisike yow sike.'
The frere hereof herde and hiede faste
To a lord for a lettre leue to haue
To curen as a Curatour; and came with his lettre
Boldely to þe bisshop and his brief hadde
In contrees þer he coome confessions to here;
And cam þere Conscience was and knokked at þe yate.
(XX. 322–9)

As in the earlier passus, the friar is highly mobile, socially adept, officially so much part of the church that he is actually accepted, welcomed by the orthodox Conscience (XX. 356). His motives are thoroughly in keeping with the world he serves:

'In faiþ', quod þis frere, 'for profit and for helþe
Carpe I wolde wiþ contricion, and þerfore cam I hider.'
(XX. 332–3)

As religion is a commodity in this world, so the prophet becomes a profiteer, the official follower of the 'leche of lif' (XIV. 118) and spiritual healer, someone who appropriates the word 'helþe' to mean his own economic health, one whose 'faiþ' is faith to the market and its profits. His practice has been encountered before (eg. III. 35–63) but he is as unreformed as ever, trading the sacrament 'for a litel siluer':

And gooþ gropeþ Contricion and gaf hym a plastre
Of 'a pryuee paiement and I shal praye for yow
And for hem þat ye ben holden to al my lif tyme,
And make of yow *memoria* in masse and in matyns
As freres of our Fraternytee, for a litel siluer'.
Thus he gooþ and gadereþ and gloseþ þere he shryuþ
Til Contricion hadde clene foryeten to crye and to wepe.
(XX. 363–9)

So important is this to Langland that he picks it out as the especial cause for the way men in this community 'drede no synne'. The institution which was endowed with the means of grace and doctrine, now fully incorporated in the contemporary world, has become the means of individual profit and collective vice. Instead of the visionary journey into time past and the historical origins of the church providing legitimation for the present church (through continuity and authority of revered tradition), it has contributed to the criticism of the organization and practices of the contemporary church, undermining its status still further.[40] In a similar way, the poet's imaginative and theological engagement with the incarnate life of Christ, which we pointed out in the previous chapter, provided a memorable nexus of images and ideas which could only challenge the norms of the late medieval church, the powerful and wealthy secularized corporation the poet had re-created in his own meditations:

> For oure Ioye and oure Iuel, Iesu crist of heuene,
> In a pouere mannes apparaille pursueþ vs euere,
> And lokeþ on vs in hir liknesse. . . .
> Many tyme god haþ ben met among nedy peple,
> Ther neuere segge hym seiȝ in secte of þe riche.
> (XI. 185–7, 243–4)

The self-sacrificing fraternity of the Christ in *Piers Plowman*, proclaimed by himself and others, could only form a terrible indictment of the contemporary church, in vision and reality.[41]

The present Catholic church did not seem to provide a hold for Langland's traditional and orthodox ecclesiastic ideology, and it is in this perception that the poem comes to identify 'þe pope and prelates', priests and religious with Antichrist. Only a small remnant resists the forces of Antichrist (XX. 61). Now it is doubtless true that Langland would have resisted any attempt to align his visionary images of the church under the influence of Antichrist with heretical claims that the visible, hierarchical and very worldly church was indeed the church of Antichrist, while the true church was the remnant of believers, the group defined by the powerful orthodox institution as a pestiferous sect.[42] His explicit ideology affirmed a different view altogether, as we have repeatedly noted. Nevertheless, his imaginative mediation of the church in *Piers Plowman* negates his ideology and quite coherently pushes towards a position which had marked affinities with heterodox dissent, although he obviously never articulated this movement as an alternative ideology in anything like the way many Lollards did. That too would have been a renunciation of the poem's own dramatic processes, its replacement by a very different literary, imaginative and psychological outlook.

Yet despite these necessary qualifications, conscience *does* set out alone at the end of the poem, leaving the institution called 'vnitee, holy chirche on englissh' (XIX. 328; XX. 245–6; 380–5). Both Piers and Grace have disappeared from the field of present perception and practice, and there is just no help available in the inherited holy institution and its orthodox ideology. Conscience thus decides to give an answer to the question I put above, asking what he could do if the institutional means of grace and salvation seem under the sway of Antichrist: he can take up an extra-hierarchical pursuit, just as we saw Will having to do. This individualistic act I commented on at the conclusion of chapter 1, and in the context of this chapter it seems worth remarking that however much this choice undermines inherited patterns of thought and feeling about the church, and whatever problems it leaves about the realization of such a choice, it is a manifestation of the poet's imaginative integrity, and probably can also be related to developments in late medieval religious sensibility and thought. For there now seems abundant evidence to support the view that the later Middle Ages witnessed growing individualism in the face of traditional ecclesiastic authority and the established religious order, itself impaired by the Great Schism and the persistent questioning about the identity of the true church in the present world. Much spirituality in the later Middle Ages expresses a movement away from the church's mediation of grace, doctrine, salvation and the presence of Christ to an extra-hierarchical pursuit of holiness and Christ. Although the church resisted this strenuously, and violently, it could not stifle the development in theoretical or practical spheres of life.[43] In Gordon Leff's lucid words:[44]

> What is so striking about these different responses to the same desire for spiritual renewal is that they cut across the different divisions between reformer and heretic, mystic and ecclesiastic, that recur again and again between the twelfth and the fifteenth centuries. And what distinguishes the later Middle Ages spiritually is the pervasiveness of those responses in a growing recognition, implicit and explicit, that the existing balance of Christian life was wrong. The attempt to restore it carried those involved beyond the sacramental boundaries of the church in search of a spirituality that they

> could no longer find within the church or in the established religious orders. That was the new development. The failure of the later medieval church and its institutional forms . . . was a spiritual failure to meet the demands of a new spirituality that could no longer be contained within the existing structures and was not permitted new outlets under the latter's aegis. The consequences were precisely either a turning away from the church in the proliferation of extraecclesiastical groups and individuals devoted to their own religious experiences, or the demand for the church's own spiritualization by restoring it to its apostolic poverty.

Langland's great poem itself contains a complex set of responses which flow across the divisions Leff mentions. As we have seen, he wished to criticize and reform society and church within the framework of the traditional ideology and authority he often affirmed; yet his poem's intense imaginative and intellectual engagement with his world embodies a vision whose total movement and minute particulars negate and subvert this ideology, one which as Leff and others have shown, was proving less and less satisfying to many of his contemporaries. As we follow Conscience out of Holy Church in his quest for Piers and Grace, we are participating in an exit from the visible church and a flight from its traditional claims to be the sole, essential and universal mediator of the means of grace, the ordained channel between individual and God. This wonderfully coherent and honest conclusion to the poem, as I noted in the last chapter, is a remarkable one for a Catholic poet to choose, and it is replete with significance for the future of the church and Christian spirituality.

CHAPTER 3

Langland, Apocalypse and the *Saeculum*

> We give a much more unlimited approval to their idea that the life of the wise man must be social. For how could the City of God . . . either take a beginning or be developed, or attain its proper destiny, if the life of the saints were not a social life?
>
> St Augustine, *City of God*, XIX.5

More than a decade has passed since M. W. Bloomfield published his study of *Piers Plowman as a Fourteenth-Century Apocalypse*, and it now seems that the thesis expressed in its title has not convinced most readers of Langland's great poem, however willing they have been to acknowledge that Bloomfield's learned work 'does the poem a good service by refocussing attention on the prophetic element'.[1] Bloomfield himself tended to push his thesis to its limits, sometimes merging Langland with such unequivocally 'apocalyptic thinkers' as Joachim, Peter John Olivi and Angelo Clareno, 'men who stressed social perfection and the attainment of the kingdom of God on earth. The world must become a paradise fit for unfallen Adam. But man must create his own paradise with God's help; and to Langland this would be impossible without the reformation of the world, and in particular of the friars as the apex of the Church Militant.' Indeed, '*Piers* is first of all socially oriented – that is apocalyptic in its perfection', Langland had an 'apocalyptic frame of mind', and 'like all millenarians, was an optimist'.[2] Along with this thesis, which included the unquestioned assumption that apocalyptic beliefs and a commitment to society in history are one, went claims about detailed influence of Joachim's ideas on *Piers Plowman*, especially his views about the three ages.[3] Langland's poetry and ideas actually resist Joachite schema,[4] and this fact may well have discouraged further discussion of apocalypse in *Piers Plowman*. This is unfortunate, for few would deny that there are definite 'apocalyptic elements' in the poem, and I now wish to attend to these elements in a very different framework from Bloomfield's. I think that close scrutiny of the main apocalyptic passages provides important insights into some of Langland's central problems, his cast of mind and theological developments within the poem.

Before all else, we need to address ourselves to the basic question about the place of the main apocalyptic passages in the poem: when do such passages emerge and is there any common factor in their appearance? In the B version of *Piers Plowman*, edited by Kane and Donaldson, the relevant passages are the following: Prologue 64–7; III. 284–330; IV. 113–35; VI. 321–31; X. 322–35; XII. 150–6; XV. 546–67; XX. 51 ff. All these passages come in contexts where the poet has reached an impasse which is central to his work. The impasse at issue is caused by seemingly insoluble conflicts between the poet's chief social or ecclesiastical ideology and his powerful imaginative presentation of human commitments and practices in his world. Such conflict is fundamental to the organization, energy and honesty of the poem, and while we have explored this theme in the previous chapters, its relevance to the kind of apocalypticism in *Piers Plowman* is striking and seems not to have been noticed. We can agree with Donaldson, Bloomfield and the others who have stated that Langland was wedded to that traditional ideology which presented society as a static fixed hierarchy of estates (usually tripartite – knights, clergy, peasants), organically related, mutually beneficial and harmoniously ordained by God – like the diverse members of one human body.[5] Nevertheless, to summarize the burden of the last two chapters, major developments in late medieval society (economic, political, ideological) made the model less and less illuminating. We find that despite his ideological convictions, Langland actually presents us with a powerfully realized version of these developments, against which his received social scheme turns out to be a most fragile barrier. He clearly exhibits a world where Lady Meed is the dominating presence, her values fully internalized by the participants. With great force the poet embodies dynamic forces, economic and psychological, which were both dissolving traditional forms of life and heralding an increase of market values and practices.[6] We also showed how the same structure of conflict is evident in his ecclesiology, where he constantly stresses the primacy of traditional ecclesiastical institutions and hierarchy, as the necessary forms for mediating grace and instruction, yet he also shows the total and seemingly irreversible immersion of these institutions in an alien, utterly secular economic fabric. When this tension, between an imaginatively grasped historical present and a cherished frame of ideas received from the past, becomes unbearable to the poet he often attempted to resolve it apocalyptically. In examining how this happens in detail, we may also hope to establish whether such apocalypticism relates to the social and historical orientation in the way Bloomfield assumed.

In Passus III the conflict outlined above leads into the first passage we shall consider, III. 284–330. Conscience has been struggling to impose the ideology Langland cherished on to Meed and the world she permeates, deploying notions about unequivocally just prices for labour and a commerce based on exchange with no profit motive.[7] Yet these venerable ideas are not matched by any answering reality in Langland's version of his own world. One possible way of bridging the great gulf was through apocalyptic violence:

> And riȝt as Agag hadde happe shul somme.
> Samuel shal sleen hym and Saul shal be blamed
> And Dauid shal be diademed and daunten hem alle,
> And oon cristene kyng kepen vs echone.
> Shal na moore Mede be maister on erþe,
> Ac loue and lowenesse and leautee togideres;
> Thise shul be Maistres on moolde trewe men to saue.
> And whoso trespaseþ to truþe or takeþ ayein his wille,
> Leaute shal don hym lawe and no lif ellis.
> Shal no sergeant for þat seruice were a silk howue,
> Ne no pelure in his panelon for pledynge at þe barre;
> (III. 286–96)

In this vision, characteristic of apocalyptic modes, as Bloomfield showed, the way the seer deals with the perplexing present is well represented by his treatment of historical agency – a vital issue to which we shall return more than once. The use here of the passive tense, without agency being specified ('Dauid shal be diademed'), and abstract nouns acting as historical agents ('loue and lowenesse and leautee', with 'Leaute shal don hym lawe'), are both generally revealing grammatical features. They allow a writer to convey a sense of purposive human actions and processes while he fails to provide vital information about the agents enacting the processes – who will crown David? Who, precisely, will do what to whom? This is a point of the greatest importance, especially pertinent to the problem of the relation between the apocalypse and its social-historical orientation. The allusions to Samuel and Saul (I Reg [I Samuel] 15 and 16) may encourage comments like J. A. W. Bennett's: 'Samuel will represent the spiritual authority of the church, Saul the temporal power that must be chastened if necessary.'[8] But the *Visio* clearly shows that the church lacked any 'spiritual authority' and we shall see from later passages that in so far as Langland could focus his mind here he tended more towards Wycliffite views about the necessary relations between lay powers and the church in the present situation. Still, the present passage is undeniably shifty over this crucial and topical issue, perhaps illustrating a mode of grammar widespread in apocalyptic writing.[9]

As the passage unfolds we note linguistic features similar to those just described. The passive tense again works to hide tricky questions about agency, here in relation to judgment, so blurring issues of social power and responsibility in the reformed society:

> Alle þat beren baselard, brood swerd or launce,
> Ax ouþer hachet or any wepene ellis,
> Shal be demed to þe deeþ but if he do it smyþye
> Into sikel or to siþe, to Shaar or to kultour:
> *Conflabunt gladios suos in vomeres etc.*
> Ech man to pleye with a plow, Pykoise or spade, . . .
> Huntynge or haukynge if any of hem vse
> His boost of his benefice worþ bynomen hym after. . . .
> Al shal be but oon court, and oon burn be Iustice,
> That worþ Trewe-tonge, a tidy man þat tened me neuere.
> Batailles shul none be, ne no man bere wepene,
> And what smyth þat any smyþeþ by smyte þerwiþ to deþe:
> (III. 304–9, 313–14, 321–4)

The existence of a firm authority structure, one which carries out capital punishment indeed, is quite evident, yet we cannot possibly tell who the concrete judging agents are to be, how they become judging agents and how they relate to the judged. When the speaker does name a judge he uses an abstraction, as we saw him doing earlier ('Trewe-tonge', 1.322) and with the same effect.[10] The poet's language conveys a strong sense of conviction with the clear and certain resolution of key conflicts, but once more the drastic cost of this is a concealment of basic social difficulties – drastic because concealment is antithetical to genuine resolution and transcendence. Perhaps it is worth reminding ourselves at this point that the issues under discussion were not just castles in the air, for in a real enough sense Langland's period was what Mollat and Wolff's study showed, 'clearly the age *par excellence* of popular revolutions', from England to Italy, to the Netherlands, to Bohemia.[11] In Bohemia, we recall, a movement originating in orthodox criticism of ecclesiastical practices developed into a Wycliffite programme for disendowment and reform of the church under traditional lay rulers and led to the establishment of a communistic congregation at Tabor, undeniably 'a new kind of society'.[12] Indeed, the issues raised here were germane, in various forms, to the different reforming aspirations of peasants and Lollards in the poet's own society.

With these contexts in mind it is striking that despite the lack of focus and the concealments I have outlined, we can make out enough features of the reformed society envisioned by Conscience to perceive many elements in common with the most revolutionary visions and programmes expressed during the Peasants' Uprising which occurred very soon after Langland completed his B-text.[13] Summing up the implications of lines 284–330 we observe the following: (1) The traditional legislative and jurisdictional order, which of course protected the interests of the dominant social groups, will be utterly demolished – one court replaces all the manorial and central courts, and 'lawe' will be made into 'a laborer'.[14] (2) With the realization of Isaiah's millennial vision the aristocracy, the land-controlling militaristic ruling group will also be disarmed, thus ending the power-basis on which the present social order rested, a power-basis soon to be directly threatened in reality.[15] (3) Irreligious priests will have their benefices removed. While the summary again reflects the constant evasion of crucial questions about agency the passage's extremely revolutionary aspiration is manifest. Yet we saw in our first chapter how this conflicts with Langland's commitment to the traditional tripartite ideology and feudal order. The apocalypse was stimulated by deep contradictions, and these now drive Conscience on to the final apocalyptic riddle in the passage:

> And er þis fortune falle fynde men shul þe worste
> By sixe sonnes and a ship and half a shef of Arwes;
> And þe myddel of a Moone shal make þe Iewes torne,
> And Sarȝynes for þat siȝte shul synge *Gloria in excelsis etc*,
> For Makometh and Mede myshappe shul þat tyme;
> (III. 325–9)

Bloomfield, commenting on the popularity of such 'enigmatic prophecies' in 'a time of crisis', claims that 'To men convinced of their truth, they make sense out of the current miseries of history.' And as usual he aligns such writing with orientation towards 'redemptive history'.[16] Yet our own examination of the apocalypse in Passus III has shown how it arises specifically out of grave contradictions between the writer's ideology and his admirably honest perception of the contemporary situation, how it comes as a desperate attempt to transcend anguished frustration, how its revolutionary dimensions clash with traditional social ideas the poet would not consciously reject, and we noted the profound evasions over human agency throughout the passage. It seems reasonable to suggest that such writing constitutes a dramatic failure of the poet's normally powerful grasp of social and historical reality. If history is 'redemptive', then the mode deployed here may best be seen as a wilful and impatient attempt at premature solution, an enticing but misleading shortcut.[17] Or, in other terms, it may be seen as a romantically revolutionary evasion of complexities which the poem, as a whole, explores with heroic scrupulousness and energy. This judgment does not, of course, deny that apocalyptic writing has often expressed the aspirations and rage of subordinate social groups responding in a revolutionary way to various social changes, opportunities and pressures.[18] But we should not let such generalizations distract us from scrutinizing the genesis, precise meaning and coherence of each piece of such writing in its particular contexts, internal and external. Langland was certainly attracted to the mode, hoping that it might offer an immediate way out of social, religious and intellectual difficulties. But, as we will see, in the last resort he was highly critical of the mode, and finally himself judged it as an unilluminating subversion of his genuine engagement with human beings in time. Even in Passus III the apocalyptic riddle changes nothing as Meed and Conscience continue their struggle and we return to the norms of violence and rule by sheer power in his own world (IV. 47 ff., 149 ff.). This return is common to all the apocalyptic passages in the poem, and constitutes an essential comment on them.

The next apocalyptic piece I wish to mention occurs at the end of Passus VI (321–31). Since I have discussed this Passus at some length earlier, here I shall just point out how a similar pattern to the one in Passus III emerges. After making an explicit assertion of traditional ideology (VI. 21–56) the poet's engagement with the dynamic world of contemporary agricultural conflicts led him to portray the total discrediting of this ideology.[19] The process culminates in the rejection of the ruling establishment's version of reason, law and religion by dissident elements of the peasantry:

> He greueþ hym ageyn god and gruccheþ ageyn Reson,
> And þanne corseþ þe kyng and al þe counseil after
> Swiche lawes to loke laborers to chaste.
>
> (VI. 316–18)

Langland disapproves but he has grasped the authentic tones of some radicals who found voice in 1381.[20] Once again the poet's ideology, by his own demonstration, has been negated, this time by concretely realized historical developments and human agents. In his frustration he reacts as he did in that part of Passus III when he turned to what Bloomfield called 'enigmatic prophecies':

> Thoruȝ flood and foule wedres fruytes shul faille,
> And so seiþ Saturne and sente yow to warne.
> Whan ye se þe mone amys and two monkes heddes,
> And a mayde haue þe maistrie, and multiplie by eiȝte,
> Thanne shal deeþ wiþdrawe and derþe be Iustice,
> And Dawe þe dykere deye for hunger
> But if god of his goodnesse graunte vs a trewe.
>
> (VI. 325–31)

It would be wrong to try and pin the saying down by treating it as a 'picture model' allegory to be decoded, for the obscurities are a direct result of the baffling antipathy between the poet's ideological framework and the alien social reality he confronts so openly. The introduction of such apocalyptic riddles is again a flight from history, a loss of faith in what Bloomfield called, probably too comfortably, 'redemptive history' and a withdrawal from the intricacies of real human struggles.[21]

The apocalyptic passage in Passus X (322–35) is one of the most famous. The Passus begins with an immensely energetic and substantial critique of the dominant groups in Langland's world (X. 13–116). Indeed, it is pushed to the point where all secular power is seen to be in the hands of the corrupt and blasphemous, and where the only charity is among 'meene men' (X. 24–9, 54–68). Along with the critique of lay powers Langland as usual shows us that the secular order has thoroughly absorbed the official church (especially X. 72–80, 282–318). This is one of the central preoccupations of *Piers Plowman*, and our understanding of its intractability has been enhanced by many recent historians who have detailed how the official church had become a massive secular institution fully incorporated in the political and economic fabric of medieval society. Meditating on this predicament Langland focusses on its deeply disturbing implications, disclosing how the means and institutions of grace, and instruction, have become corrupt.[22] His passionate desire for reform of these institutions combines with his complete frustration and ineffectiveness to inspire the famous prophecy Bloomfield called 'the apocalyptic vision in all its glory':[23]

> Ac þer shal come a kyng and confesse yow Religiouses,
> And bete yow, as þe bible telleþ, for brekynge of youre rule,
> And amende Monyals, Monkes and Chanons,
> And puten hem to hir penaunce, *Ad pristinum statum ire*;
> And Barons wiþ Erles beten hem þoruȝ *Beatus virres* techyng;
> Bynymen that hir barnes claymen, and blame yow foule:
> *Hij in curribus et hij in equis ipsi obligati sunt etc.*
> And þanne Freres in hir fraytour shul fynden a keye
> Of Constantyns cofres þer þe catel is Inne
> That Gregories godchildren vngodly despended.
> And þanne shal þe Abbot of Abyngdoun and al his issue for euere
> Haue a knok of a kyng, and incurable þe wounde.
> That þis worþ sooþ, seke ye þat ofte ouerse þe bible:
>
> (X. 322–33)

In the rather general terms of intellectual history we may agree that the king here is 'a saviour-king' recurrent in apocalyptic writing.[24]

But given the contexts in which Langland was thinking we should go beyond the generalized account to acknowledge the affinities here with well-publicized Wycliffite hopes, expressed so clearly in the master's works of 1378 (*De Ecclesia* and *De Officio Regis*) and soon to become central strands in Lollard programmes, certainly before the defeat of Oldcastle. The effect of Wyclif's theological and political argument was to encourage the lay power to act against the ecclesiastical establishment, disendow it and appropriate its temporalities for themselves. The clergy must be forced to return to Christ and apostolic poverty, and the church compulsorily freed from lordship, possession and the secular world.[25] Leff makes a comment on Wyclif's programme which is extremely pertinent to the present study:[26]

> By making its implementation depend upon the lay power he turned an indefinite aspiration into an immediate programme; in place of the prophetic expectations of the Franciscan Spirituals and Joachists, which he explicitly rejected, he put political action. It was this which made him an heresiarch where they remained primarily heterodox. Unlike them, his conception of Antichrist as a palpable presence at work within the church called forth palpable measures for its destruction; where they looked to a new spiritual order and the end of the present age, Wyclif looked to the strength of the secular arm and the consummation of the existing state.

The distinction Leff makes here is very important. When we come to Passus XV we will see that Langland has moved still closer to advocating feasible political action, yet even in the undeniably 'apocalyptic vision' of Passus X we note that it is not just a mystical king whom Langland invokes, but 'Barons wiþ Erles' (1. 326). These titles show that Langland had the contemporary lay lords explicitly in mind, and the political relevance of the appeal in the late 1370s would have been obvious enough.

This commentary might seem to suggest that here we do have a passage which works in the historically and socially orienting way Bloomfield claims for apocalyptic writing in general. However, the context Langland establishes in Passus X makes this suggestion most questionable. Having noted how Langland, in the very same Passus, clearly showed the immersion of the church in a corrupt and quite un-Christian secular state, we must ask why he now suddenly expects Satan to act against Satan as conscious agent of Christian regeneration. It is characteristic of the poet's imaginative honesty and range that his work forces us to face this question, one which seems not to have been squarely confronted by Wyclif writing at the same time. For Wyclif, Leff writes:[27]

> The king was God's vicar and he stood apart from the rest of men, who were his servants. To resist him was to sin. Even tyrants were ordained of God . . . [Wyclif] attributed to him virtually limitless powers over his kingdom . . . as its spiritual overseer, he could ban evil priests; withdraw alms; sequestrate church property; correct the priesthood; demolish churches in an emergency. . . . Not only was the entire church, including the Pope in matters such as patronage, subject to the royal power, but so even were the predestined during their sojourn in this world. Whereas Wyclif effectively denuded the church hierarchy of any authority, he insisted upon universal submission to the king and lay lords.

So Wyclif yoked a genuinely revolutionary programme concerning the church with an extreme social conservatism. In his recent study of *Medieval Heresy,* M. D. Lambert summarized the position well:[28]

> Wyclif never lost faith in the lay lords as potential reformers and thus, somewhat oddly, at the end of his life combined a stark ecclesiastical egalitarianism with a profound belief in the just authority of the civil powers. . . . In secular politics Wyclif remained profoundly conservative; in ecclesiastical matters he became a near anarchist. This juxtaposition of viewpoints might well be criticised as unrealistic, for few would agree that the abuses of the late fourteenth century sprang so exclusively from the ecclesiastical side.

Langland, as we noted above, goes beyond Wyclif in driving us to consider the contradictions of an appeal to lay lords in a project for Christian regeneration. Nevertheless, as his frustrations explode into the apocalyptic mode his hope is placed in these lay lords ('a kyng. . . . And Barons wiþ Erles'). The stark incoherence of the hope as it emerges in Passus X is highlighted by a noteworthy omission: he does not appeal to the strand in the lay corruption he had depicted which was the most realistic element and major strength of a Wycliffite–Lollard programme – namely the naked economic self-interest of the secular possessing classes.[29] Given Langland's own religious aspirations the omission is understandable, but the leading social groups he had shown us in X. 13–116 are not the basis on which to build hopes for a *disinterested* religious reformation, *ad pristinum statum*! This, we shall see, he came to acknowledge.

Given these overwhelming problems, it is not surprising that at line 334 Langland suddenly defers his radical and apocalyptic reformation:

> Ac er þat kyng come Caym shal awake,
> Ac dowel shal dyngen hym adoun and destruye his myȝte.
> (X. 334–5)

The event is still expected within history, but the seer has now inserted a further stage to precede the radical renewal. However, what social and religious manifestations of Antichrist ('Caym') the poet has in mind, precisely how he relates him to the secular and ecclesiastical present with which the passus is preoccupied, all this is left completely vague. Furthermore, instead of the 'Barons wiþ Erles' of line 326 we have the highly problematic generalized abstraction 'dowel' acting with extreme violence at what seems to be some vital turning-point.

We presume the action is both individual and social, physical and mental, but there is such a lack of imaginative and intellectual precision that we have no means of being sure. We have again met apocalypticism dissolving history rather than engaging with concrete human processes.

The dreamer has attended closely to the apocalyptic vision and comments, 'Thanne is dowel and dobet . . . *dominus* and knyȝthode?' (X. 336). Far from offering an ultra-literalistic or foolish response, the dreamer has seized upon the role of the lay ruling groups in the apocalyptic vision and noted that no other human agents of reform are mentioned. He therefore concludes that the agents who will 'do well' and defeat Antichrist are those named in the vision. He has also responded to one of the convictions permeating so much of *Piers Plowman* that individual and social failings and reform are dynamically interrelated.[30] So he explicitly draws our notice to the significant vagueness about key actors contained in the active abstraction, 'dowel'.

Scripture, like some readers, refusing to give the dreamer credit or admit serious problems in the vision, shifts ground and assures him that 'Kynghod and knyȝthod . . . Helpeþ noȝt to heuenward' (X. 338–9). The apocalyptic passage is left behind and the shift tends towards an individualistic moral plain where individuals and their salvation could be considered in rather misleading abstraction from the living social-ecclesiastical whole within which the poet habitually explores individual existence. The shift, as usual, proves temporary, and the Passus concludes by exalting the path to salvation open to a particular social group – 'poure commune laborers' (X. 460–81). This is a very understandable reaction to the critique of the possessing classes with which Passus X opened, and one that accords well both with much in the Gospels and important aspects of late medieval piety.[31] Yet while we will all feel the passion and the power in the poet's expression of these feelings, we will still have to admit that his own poem forces us to detach ourselves at some stage and temper our participation with critical awareness.

For his own sixth Passus, referred to earlier in the study, shows us that the version of 'pouere commune laborers,/souteres and shepherdes; swiche lewed Iuttes' at the end of Passus X is an over-generalized idealizing wish. After all, we recall how the actual pressures and divisions of his world, so impressively grasped in Passus VI, led the labourers into a series of conflicts culminating in Langland's comment that the labourer, 'greueþ hym ageyn god and grucccheþ ageyn Reson,/And þanne corseþ þe kyng and al þe counseil after/Swiche laws to loke laborers to chaste' (VI. 316–18). The misleading, one-sided idealization at the end of Passus X is both a direct produce of the abstractionism referred to earlier in this paragraph and an acknowledgment that the apocalyptic vision has not illuminated the present, or the future.

So once more we find how the apocalyptic mode springs from unresolved social and ecclesiastical tensions at the heart of the poem, and how inappropriate it is for grasping the complex historical and moral issues with which Langland is preoccupied. Its blurring of historical agency is a good indicator of the ways it dissolves the terrestrial city and its history, thus only contributing to confusion and, ironically, the very frustrations which generated the mode. As St Augustine remarked, in the passage used as the epigraph to this chapter, 'how could the City of God . . . either take a beginning or be developed, or attain its proper destiny, if the life of the saints were not a social life?'

The next passage I wish to examine comes in Passus XV (539–67). In Passus XV Langland is still pursuing many of the problems of Passus X, and he pays especial attention to the institutions for mediating grace to individual pilgrims, to their disastrous incorporation in the economic fabric and ethos of the society (eg. XV. 76–139, 307–43, 419–23). His firm conviction both about the absolute necessity of traditional institutions and that 'out of holi chirche all yveles spredeþ/There inparfit preesthode is, prechours and techeris' (XV. 94–5), again seems to be pushing him towards apocalyptic visions involving the most radical ideas of ecclesiastical reform found in his period. The continuingly intractable problems of the total commitment of ecclesiastical institutions and staff to secular values and practices will soon be solved, as 'þe tyme approcheþ faste' (XV. 547). The sense of urgency and imminence in the phrase is certainly common enough in apocalypses, and Bloomfield describes Passus XV in general as 'an apocalyptic picture of the times'.[32]

Now when discussing the prophecy in Passus X we found it necessary to go beyond generalities about apocalypticism and comment not only on the detailed working of the passage in question, but also on its relation to contemporary Wycliffite hopes. The present passage guides us in just the same direction:

> When Constantyn of curteisie holy kirke dowed
> Wiþ londes and ledes, lordshipes and rentes,
> An Aungel men herden an heigh at Rome crye,
> '*Dos ecclesie* þis day haþ ydronke venym
> And þo þat han Petres power arn apoisoned alle.'
> A medicyne moot þerto þat may amende prelates.
> That sholden preie for þe pees, possession hem letteþ;
> Takeþ hire landes, ye lordes, and leteþ hem lyue by dymes.
> If possession be poison and inparfite hem make
> Charitie wer to deschargen hem for holy chirches sake,
> And purgen hem of poison ere moore peril falle.
>
> (XV. 557–67)

I have already mentioned that this passage occurs in a context which bears marked similarities to Passus X, and the portentous voice from heaven, the sense of a need for immediate action 'er moore peril falle' and the invocation of the lay powers, all encourage one to see it in the same mode as the earlier apocalyptic vision we discussed. However, there are fundamental distinctions here that must be registered. Instead of appealing to an apocalyptic king to be revealed in a future time after a vaguely imagined uprising and defeat of Antichrist, we actually have a direct invocation of the present lay ruling class to act now in a specific way against a specific group – 'Takeþ hire landes, ye lordes, and leteþ hem lyue by dymes' (XV. 564).

There is no blurring or ambiguity here about the agents involved in the desired events, nor about temporal dimensions. The realism of the passage is strengthened by the covert appeal to lay self-interest, whose absence we remarked in Passus X – 'Takeþ hire landes, ye lordes', advice given without any qualifications about the uses of such land or need for spiritual regeneration in lay rulers. As in Wyclif, the existing social structure is to continue without any threats to existing lay power and order (unlike the apocalypse of Passus III). The combination of church disendowment under the lay power with the continuation of tithes for purged priests was another aspect of Wyclif's programme which was not unrealistic. Furthermore, the retention of tithes emphasizes the continuity of the present social order.[33] Most striking too is the way advocacy for specific action in the passage is made without conjuring up any millennial expectations: there is no indication that lay powers will usher in a final state or a Utopia. These factors encourage us to recall the distinctions made by Leff in a passage already quoted (above on page 70). There he noted how Wyclif explicitly rejected prophetic expectations of Franciscan Spirituals and Joachists, substituting palpable measures of political action by the existing secular arm. It seems to me that the movement between the passages we have discussed so far in this essay invites us to see the one in Passus XV in the terms Leff establishes. Despite certain similarities we have mentioned, Langland has moved outside the apocalyptic mode and its treatment of historical processes.

Nevertheless, the movement beyond apocalypse still leaves one of the main anomalies we noticed earlier. This is the way Langland was entrusting the Christian reformation he so earnestly desired to a state power which, by his own account, was quite lacking in any Christian charity or commitment to reform. The anomaly was most prominent perhaps in Passus X, but it appears in a related form in

Passus XV too. For while he may have good reason to trust the self-interest of the lay power to expropriate the church, his unexamined assumptions about the effects this would have on the spirituality and consciousness of ecclesiastics are startling. He assumes a totally economistic solution to problems which involve whole human beings and their full range of activities. That is to say, he assumes that a total transformation of consciousness will occur within the clergy once they are disendowed by an economically-motivated laity who will then be spiritually transformed by the transformed priesthood. The laity will undergo this regeneration, it seems, without any economic or social changes to their order (XV. 568). One may wonder what would happen to his versions of reformation if Langland acknowledged the importance of the anomalies and confusions so sharply manifested here. I think the final Passus of the poem confronts such speculation most impressively.

Passus XIX concluded with a picture of the leading members of the possessing classes which leaves us in no doubt about the way they unself-consciously shape ethical and metaphysical language to serve their own material interests (XIX. 459–76, pp. 33–5 above). This, we saw, is another manifestation of the way Langland's imagination relentlessly exposes his own most cherished ideologies to the history of his culture and society as he so sensitively grasps it. Quite in accord with the movement of the poem, Passus XX presents the overwhelmingly powerful cultural, social and spiritual forces his poem has embodied as the attack of Antichrist, a common feature of apocalyptic writing already briefly encountered in Passus X. For the final time in *Piers Plowman* we see the church fully immersed in the energetic secular pursuits of the poet's society:

> Symonye hym suede to assaille Conscience,
> And pressed on þe pope and prelates þei maden
> To holden wþ Antecrist, hir temporaltees to saue.
>
> (XX. 126–8)

These lines, representative of the Passus, show how the institutions of grace, established by Christ and Piers, have become unambivalently incorporated in the market nexus, members of the church hierarchy being firmly aligned with Antichrist in defence of their economic wealth and power. Even the sacrament of confession, on which Langland lays enormous weight, is thoroughly corrupted as Antichrist and his values triumph in church and society.[34] The constant echoing of scenes and images in the unregenerate field of the poem's first six passus, especially Passus VI, carefully stresses the recurrent failure of the Christian dispensation (so powerfully imaged in Passus XVI–XIX) to penetrate consciousness and practice of men in time.

Bloomfield takes such echoes and the presence of Antichrist as evidence that we have here another 'apocalyptic vision', an example of Langland's 'apocalyptic mind' and the way in apocalypses 'The miseries of the world are the strongest evidence of a coming renewal.'[35] But these claims seriously misrepresent the attitudes to such issues in Passus XX. While, as Bloomfield maintains, Langland stressed the social dimensions of salvation, and while he devoutly believed in the necessity of traditional institutions of grace and ecclesiastical organization (unlike the Waldensians and Lollards), we have found that his engagement with his world led to a poem which actually shows the absence of traditional means of grace and authority – an absence which cannot be handled simply as a corrigible deviation from an unproblematically available norm. This fundamental absence informs Passus XX, and Langland could certainly have responded to the situation outlined in our previous paragraph by trying to take an apocalyptic leap beyond its bafflements. We saw the attractions such a leap held for him, though we have also seen how the apocalyptic leap was one which evaded the real problems of current historical processes and went against the scrupulous exploratory methods the poem habitually deploys. We also found that the apocalyptic mode actually failed to transcend the most disturbing contradictions it was supposed to comprehend. Now, at the end of his great poem, I believe we should acknowledge how Langland absolutely refused all the temptations of apocalypticism and the hopes of millenarian renewal, even though he envisaged the present as involving a massive defeat for Christianity.

It may be fruitful to focus this refusal as it relates to the question of lay power. We discussed the Wycliffite role given to lay lords in Passus X and especially XV, but what is most striking now is the contrasting absence of any role for them in any reform movement. Indeed, no mention of them is made.[36] This is a most significant change and has not received the emphasis it deserves. It reveals a *repudiation* of the Wycliffite hope that existing secular forms and rulers would enact the necessary reformation, that consciousness and practice could be transformed in such ways. It also reveals a rejection, however unwilling, of the traditional Catholic conception of a sacral society so dominant in medieval orthodoxy. In this conception the existing state is God's chosen instrument for unfolding his providential plan for man's salvation, Christianizing and ordering society to its final cause. Instead of this, the final Passus concludes with Conscience setting out yet once more for grace in search of the lost vision, Piers Plowman – and alone. With church and society dominated by the forces of Antichrist the pilgrimage here is emphatically extra-institutional, individualistic, participating in most significant trends in late medieval religion and psychology.[37] Now the secular order is not mentioned as Langland has come to believe that all institutions and orders are as infected as the ecclesiastical and there can be no especial hope placed in any particular human group. The immediate moral task and quest in an inescapably conflict-ridden and confused present must suffice. This is not a recipe for individualistic withdrawal or apathy. What it eschews is not search and aspiration but the temptation to offer apocalyptic and ultimate resolutions to history, with all their exhilarating claims to total clarification, and all the inevitable blurring of agency these involve.

Here the poem's final development may have many interesting elements in common with the *later* work of St Augustine as he came to reject the conception of a Christian state and empire based on hellenistic notions of cosmic order, secular kingship and the ruler's sacral role. It seems he moved towards a complex neutrality to secular institutions, a sense of the radical ambiguity of all human states and institutions, a sense well described by R. A. Markus:[38]

> The possibility of securing it [God's order] through the government of wise men, or of men perfectly dedicated to God, is dismissed as an illusory option. . . . Tension, strife and disorder are endemic in this realm. There can be no resolution, except eschatologically. Human society is irremediably rooted in this tension-ridden and disordered *saeculum*.

The search for grace, the search for Piers and the struggle for reform, the re-writing of *Piers Plowman* itself, these all continue, but with the knowledge that there will be no millennial resolution of the confusions and contradictions Langland was exploring and living. Finally there is the portentous fact that a great Catholic poet, committed to the traditional institutions and social organizations of the Catholic church, has concluded his poem with a vision of that church which drives him to a lonely and individualistic pursuit of grace *outside* the traditional institutions. These are now apprehended under the overwhelming domination of Antichrist, who is also the prince of this world – news that would hardly have surprised the authors of the Gospels, but which had disturbing implications for the orthodox Christianity of the Middle Ages.

CHAPTER 4

Chaucer: Reflexive Imagination, Knowledge and Authority

al that evere is iknowe, it is rather comprehendid and knowen, nat aftir his strengthe and his nature, but aftir the faculte (that is to seyn, the power and the nature) of hem that knowen.

Boethius, *Consolation of Philosophy*,
tr. and glossed by Chaucer, V. pr. 6

Thanne Scripture scorned me and a skile tolde,
And lakked me in latyn and liȝt by me sette,
And seid '*Multi multa sciunt et seipsos nesciunt*'.
Tho wepte I for wo and wraþe of hir speche
And in a wynkynge worþ til I weex aslepe.

Piers Plowman (B version), XI. 1—5

The man replied, 'Things as they are
Are changed upon the blue guitar.'

'The Man With the Blue Guitar'
Wallace Stevens,

Despite the extremely important differences in social situation and intellectual concerns, Chaucer gained his identity and developed his imagination in the complex, diversified and dynamic world which inspired and baffled Langland. In this world a writer could easily join the hosts of homilists and didactic poets devoting themselves to reiterating received ideas and conventional pieties, as though these remained totally viable and quite unproblematic. As Langland's own Ymaginatif reminds him:

And þow medlest þee wiþ makynges and myȝtest go seye þi sauter,

> And bidde for hem þat ȝyueþ þee breed, for þer are bokes ynowe
> To telle men what dowel is, dobet and dobest boþe,
> And prechours to preuen what it is of many a peire freres.
> (XII. 16–19)

But this mass of commonplace materials just did not prove adequate to Langland's experience of his world, as we have seen, and so the poet goes on writing his own thoroughly exploratory and profoundly critical poem, knowing that his puzzlement and range of insights have not been met by the conventional writers he knew so well. Chaucer himself was no more willing or able than Langland to confine his imagination and intellect within the received and still dominant paradigms which constituted official 'authority'. This is becoming better appreciated as critics pay more notice to the diversity and conflicts of fourteenth-century culture and society, for this has had the effect of freeing critical abilities to work much more closely with Chaucer's poetry than was possible for commentators who believed they possessed an unquestioned dogmatic code, governing all areas of life, which all 'medieval' writers (from the fourth century to the eighteenth) expressed in direct or allegorical fashion.[1] More recently, such critics as Charles Muscatine, Sheila Delany, Jill Mann and Donald Howard have shown the relevance of 'social and cultural changes . . . and individual conflicts' to a poetry which is seen to involve 'turbulence and multivalence', committed to 'exploring tensions and contradictions' both internal and external.[2] Like Langland, Chaucer intimately knew the authoritative and dominant traditions still being perpetuated by writers in his day, and was deeply involved in examining them, not in simply reiterating them. The rest of this book is concerned with some central aspects of Chaucer's engagement with different areas of his culture, including both ideology and social practice.

The present chapter is addressed to one outstanding characteristic of Chaucer's imagination in relation to knowledge and authority, its reflexivity. While I rely on the following discussion of Chaucer to establish what this means in his work and milieu, a few prefatory remarks about the quality I have in mind are probably necessary. Briefly then, the reflexive imagination grasps the way human beings actively constitute the world, the way they are agents in creating ideologies, dogmas and all that is known, not merely passive recipients of reality and impersonal verities. It subverts assumptions that human beings have access to an absolute viewpoint, it subverts the inquisitorial mentality which has been a recurrent feature of our civilization. Constantly showing us the relevance of our incarnate nature and historicity to the kinds of knowledge we can attain, the reflexive imagination discloses the processes by which authority is constructed, its grounds in individual and social consciousness and practice. It resists what Alvin Gouldner has described so well as 'the pressure to secure our speech, to make it seem certain, which in turn invites the speaker to obscure his own presence in his speech'. The pressures are as evident in Chaucer's world as our own:

> For if his presence is visible, if it is clear that what he calls the 'world' . . . are *statements* that he makes and speeches *he* utters, it then becomes evident that the world's structures are *attributes*, not 'properties', and have all the chancy contingency and problematicity of any 'subjective' pronouncement. 'Objectivism', which conceals the presence of the speaker in the speech, thereby conceals the contingent nature of that speech and the world to which it alludes. Reflexivity, however, makes the contingency obvious. It inhibits the feeling of conviction so necessary for the high and sacred moments of practice. . . . We seek to be sure of what we want and to be sure of the world in which we pursue it. From the standpoint of normal politics, however, reflexivity is the 'pale cast of thought' that slackens the finger on the trigger.

Or, one might revise the allusion, that slackens the fervent hands of the inquisition, that impedes the priestly minds dictating 'objective' codes against which all humanity is to be judged. The reflexive imagination is a powerful dissolvent of what Gouldner calls 'objectivism', discourse which,[3]

> one-sidedly focuses on the 'object' but occludes the speaking 'subject' to whom it is an object; objectivism thus ignores the way in which the spoken object is contingent in part on the language in which it is spoken, and varies in character with the language – or theory – used.

Reflexive imagination returns reified texts and authorities to their human speakers, disclosed with their inevitable limitations and partial interests. And I hope our chapters on *Piers Plowman* have shown that Chaucer's historical context was not unfavourable to the development of reflexive and critical imagination in those for whom a crisis in the authority of traditional paradigms and institutions could not be met by simple reiteration of received ideology. Indeed, from some perspectives such a crisis could be at least cause for some celebration, besides the inevitable anxiety. For it might disclose new and rich viewpoints for regarding a human world containing a multiplicity of forms and ends, a fascinating diversity in which a certain kind of artist might enjoy the possibility of showing how traditional rules, ideas and practices were actually problematic in hitherto unnoticed ways. To such an artist, awareness of tensions and new insecurities in traditional culture could be a great stimulus to develop reflexive imagination in attending to the role of historically specific human beings in constructing truths, values and the world, now no longer perceived in 'objectivist' fashion. Certainly this could have some affinities with fourteenth-century philosophy, where the focus of attention moved to 'the divergent conditions of natural knowledge and revealed truth', to the contingency of the world, knowledge and the order of salvation, for it seems that in more than one area of the culture the grounds of discourse and speculation were being called into question, made problematic.[4] And to this situation Chaucer did indeed respond most positively.

The development of the reflexive imagination could be followed through Chaucer's work from the early poem, *The Book of the Duchess*,[5] but limitations of space necessitate a more modest scope to the chapter, and besides, it is hoped that once the characteristic in question has been identified its pervasiveness will be recognized, with its immense significance.

The *Wife of Bath's Prologue* will re-appear in our discussion of Chaucer's treatment of love and sexuality, but here we will look at some examples of how the poetry invites readers to de-sublimate authoritative texts, to humanize texts that have become fixed as 'auctoritee'. The Prologue also foregrounds the fact that texts only have a continuing cultural life and importance in the conscience of particular readers, drawing out implications which are unpalatable to those who assume an absolute viewpoint offering access to truths which they envisage as outside all historical processes, impersonal and unambiguous. Although we shall later consider the text's critique of the anti-feminist tradition, we can isolate a passage which is especially relevant to the present chapter. The Wife of Bath comments:[6]

> By God! if wommen hadde writen stories,
> As clerkes han withinne hire oratories,
> They wolde han writen of men more wikkednesse
> Than al the mark of Adam may redresse. . . .
> The clerk, whan he is oold, and may noght do
> Of Venus werkes worth his olde sho,
> Thanne sit he doun, and writ in his dotage
> That wommen kan nat kepe hire mariage!
>
> (*W of B Pr.*, ll. 693–6, 707–10)

Suddenly the authoritative, allegedly impersonal doctrines propagated in a dominant ecclesiastical tradition are revealed in a perspective that brings their ground into consideration. They are returned to history, presented as products of human individuals and human groups inextricably bound up with particular interests and prejudices. As with the treatment of historiography and nationalism in the third book of *The House of Fame* (ll. 1419–519), the passage both foregrounds the specific human agents who make traditions and authorities and also suggests that our own understanding of the issues at stake will be much fuller if we try to retrieve the viewpoint of those the dominant culture of discourse has excluded from its own formation: 'if *wommen* hadde writen . . .' – a retrieval which is precisely one of the many facets of the *Wife of Bath's Prologue*, the product of a *man* with quite exceptional powers of reflexivity. The wife argues that psychological factors too are relevant forces in the construction of the authoritative traditions she is challenging. The product of a very limited social group (male, clerks), it is also now depicted as the product of sexual repression and frustration, self-righteousness and comically unself-conscious fantasy about female sexuality rooted in the individual male's own sexual existence. Once we begin to see 'auctoritee' as the product of inevitably limited and partial 'experience', we are in a position to stop 'objectifying' texts and traditions with the claims to certainty that habitually accompany such reification.

Even her curiosity about the individual authority's sexuality contributes to this. For example, when she is discussing St Paul's high valuation of virginity she comments, 'I woot wel that th'apostel was a mayde' (l. 79), and later, acknowledging that Christ and many saints lived in chastity, she observes, 'Crist was a mayde, and shapen as a man' (l. 139). The choice of the word 'mayde' to convey male virginity is here followed by a phrase which expresses her incredulity and amused prurience, 'a *mayde*, and *shapen* as a *man*'. Of course, the angle she takes is part of her own preoccupations, but Chaucer has at the very least led the reader to move through her perspective, at least momentarily to view Paul and the incarnate Christ through her eyes. Similarly another humanizing viewpoint on 'auctoritee' is provided by the poetry's gloss on Paul's statement that 'It is good for a man not to touch a woman' (1 Cor. 7:1):

> He mente as in his bed or in his couche;
> For peril is both fyr and tow t'assemble
> (*W of B Pr.*, ll. 88–9)

The gloss takes up St Paul's negation of sexuality and makes more explicit what he has almost euphemistically lodged in the word 'touch'. In doing this the Wife undoubtedly exhibits her own orientation. Yet she also suggests how ascetic authorities who preach about and against sexual enjoyment are more touched by what they condemn than they themselves admit, and that this will emerge in their language (and often elsewhere too, as Shakespeare's puritan Angelo reveals). People who preach vehemently against sexual contact display a being in which such matters are very much alive, in however unself-conscious a manner. The Wife's use of possessive pronouns, '*his* bed', '*his* couche' adds to the impression, for 'his' refers back to 'th'apostel' himself, although Paul's text makes a depersonalized reference to 'a man'. It is, of course, not a question of a definitive psychoanalytic interpretation which we must either accept or reject *in toto*: rather, we are again being presented with a perspective which foregrounds the fully incarnate nature of human beings who have been sublimated into rather abstract and timeless 'auctoritee'. It is in this framework that we can perhaps most relish and understand the Wife's famous handling of Bible texts (especially ll. 47–162). This has earned her much righteous chastisement from a host of scholars, but her orthodox aggressors have lacked awareness of the implications Chaucer brings out here. She starts off from the use of the New Testament made by a revered Christian 'auctoritee' to support his own violent antagonism to marriage and love that involved the whole incarnate person.[7] Now the standard practices of medieval exegesis included the sustained pulverization and fragmentation of Biblical texts, the utter dissolution of their existential and historical meanings, and the imposition of pre-determined dogmatic propositions. I have described these procedures in detail, illustrating some of their disastrous theological and literary consequences, in an earlier book, and here it must suffice to refer the reader to analysis and documentation offered in that study.[8]

In so far as the poet was mocking the Wife's methods of interpretation, he was, however discreetly, mocking the official and august tradition from which she, 'noble prechour' (l. 165), has learnt. What the Wife does add is a different combination of ideas to that deployed by St Jerome and his successors, and as I shall discuss these ideas in chapter 6 here it is enough to observe how she points out that conventional exegesis is the product of *males*, '*Men* may devyne and glosen, up and doun' (l. 26). This may seem so obvious as to be hardly worth saying, yet it plays a real part in the Prologue's exhibition of the partiality (social and psychological) of those responsible for a dominant and institutionalized tradition about women. It contributes to the desublimation of authority and its texts, reminding us that the texts have been appropriated and 'glosen' (in all its senses) by exegetes who, far from being the impersonal conveyors of impersonal 'auctoritee' are very human, male and high prejudiced in their hermeneutic activity. Bearing in mind the social partiality, it is a finely alert and delicate criticism to introduce Christ's teaching on poverty and perfection in this context:

> Virginitee is greet perfeccion,
> And continence eek with devocion,
> But Crist, that of perfeccion is welle,
> Bad not every wight he sholde go selle
> Al that he hadde, and gyve it to the poore
> And in swich wise folwe hym and his foore.
> He spak to hem that wolde lyve parfitly;

And lordynges, by youre leve, that am nat I.
(*W of B Pr.*, ll. 105–12)

A reader's first reaction may be to laugh at the Wife's startlingly candid rejection of Christ's and Paul's councils of 'perfeccion', whether in sympathy or the righteous indignation she has elicited from certain scholars. Yet readers should not leave the lines with this reaction, for they imply some interesting points of identity between the Wife and the ecclesiastical institution she seems to oppose. In her open self-interest she makes it clear that she will pick and choose among Christ's or Paul's sayings until she comes out with something that is at least tolerant of her desires. She makes no claims that her readings are definitive and final, only that they are plausible legitimations of her practices. Now the authoritative ecclesiastic tradition, with its avowedly definitive and impersonal exegetical tradition and its supporting inquisitorial apparatus,[9] lacks such modesty. And these lines work obliquely to raise questions about this tradition. For they remind us that the thirteenth and fourteenth centuries were marked by well-known and bitter conflicts within the church over evangelical poverty in which Pope John XXII proclaimed that it was heretical to assert that Christ and the Apostles did not own property and made the possession of earthly rights and lordship superior to the renunciation of them. As Gordon Leff sums up, 'Having withdrawn material poverty from any part in evangelical perfection, and transferred its divinity to property, the pope then proceeded to associate possessions with Christ and the Apostles.'[10] With this the Wife's lines remind us of the wealth and power of the late medieval church and its hierarchy, an issue we considered in chapter 2. Thus reminded, we see the continuities between the approaches of official authority to Christ's councils ('Be ye therefore perfect. . . . If thou wilt be perfect, go sell what thou hast and give to the poor' (Matt. 5:48; 19:21)), and the Wife's. Far from being an impersonal and 'objective' response to Christ's words, the official choice among texts and counsels is seen to involve some self-interest. The 'auctoritee' of the church, embodied in clerks supposedly celibate, could comfortably exalt texts aligning virginity and perfection, using allegorization to muster further support for this emphasis.[11] But when it came to texts dealing with wealth and poverty, with social and economic power, texts which dissidents of all kinds used in their attacks on the late medieval church, then the official practice, hermeneutic and socio-economic could indeed be summarized in the Wife's comment quoted above (ll. 107–12), denying that Christ demanded extreme economic renunciation.

Once more then, as we see the 'auctoritee' concentrating on sexual rather than economic renunciation, its human mediators are uncovered and all pretensions to an absolute and final viewpoint in the exegesis of texts, an essential fact of the traditional claims of the church, are greatly undermined. When this happens, the time is ripe for other, conflicting interpretations and views to be heard – such as the Wife's. She has even contributed to loosening the stranglehold of orthodox exegetes on the living words of scripture, and we must again acknowledge that her own polemical readings make no claims to a new priestly certainty. As in the passage just quoted, she displays a self-conscious individualism in her treatment of texts, combined with an equally self-conscious sense of play and 'fantasye' (ll. 190–2), of imaginative activity in the hermeneutic practice through which all texts, even those sacred in the particular culture, lead their risky, fluid but vital existence.

Chaucer's works contain many examples of the de-sublimation of reified discourse, retrieving the specific human speakers who have become occluded, but there is one particularly concerned with exegesis which I would like to mention. It is typical of Chaucer's procedures that a Biblical text used by authorities as an important exegetical rule is made decidedly tricky. St Paul's statement that the letter kills but the spirit gives life (2 Cor. 3:6) had been wrenched out of its context and appropriated by exegetes in defence of traditional allegorizing practices. Chaucer's imagination, engaged with his own world, including its hermeneutics, gives the authoritative text to a grasping ecclesiastic, in a tale told by another official of the church, as he explains how his sermon was,[12]

> Nat al after the text of hooly writ;
> For it is hard to yow, as I suppose,
> And therefore wol I teche yow al the glose.
> Glosynge is a glorious thyng, certeyn,
> For lettre sleeth, so as we clerkes seyn.
> There have I taught hem to be charitable,
> And spende hir good there it is resonable;
> (*Summoner's Tale*, ll. 1788–96)

Without directly challenging the orthodox use of Paul's text in exegetical practice, the poem reminds us how rules are used and composed by specific human beings with specific interests. We are reminded how 'we clerkes' have considerable stakes in glorifying the glossing/glozing which is our trade (our living and our pleasure) and a professional desire to protect our mystery by asserting the incompetence of all but officially accredited authorities to explicate 'the text' whose naked 'lettre' will surely kill. We should also notice how 'charity' and 'reason' become terms to sanctify the exegetes self-interest – just as the 'resoun' expounded by the goose in the *Parliament of Fowls* was the 'parfit resoun of a goos' (rather than of a sparrowhawk, or of any other of the competing groups, *PF*, ll. 562–9). None of this necessarily means that 'we clerkes' ever gloss texts in a fashion guided by self-interest, nor does it necessarily mean Paul's text has been misappropriated and abused by the church to serve economistic and self-glorifying ends, nor does it necessarily mean that this particular officer of the ecclesiastical institution is representative of 'we clerkes'. These are merely made very real possibilities. The perspective in which the authoritative text of authoritative exegetes is placed makes it problematic. Instead of accepting it unreflectively, we are persuaded to start asking questions about the grounds of interpretation of the basic rule, to consider the possible role of personal and group interest in its deployment and to wonder what criteria people actually do use for distinguishing between the different forms of glorious 'glosynge' (St Jerome's, the Wife's . . .). Langland too was openly troubled at the issues here as he found official preachers of the church 'Prechynge þe peple for profit of þe wombe;/Glosed þe gospel as hem good liked'.[13] But perhaps what Chaucer's poetry most brings out is the *inevitably* complex and active role of human consciousness and circumstances in creating 'legitimate' exegesis and 'auctoritee'. We are not allowed to indulge any simple sense of superiority to the glossing ecclesiastic, for the poetry shows us the deeply problematic nature of the issues involved and persuades us to reflect on our own immersion in them, 'we clerkes'.[14]

One could accumulate further examples in abundance of the procedures I am illustrating, but I will turn to the *Pardoner's Prologue*, an astonishing exhibition of the poet's reflexive imagination which joins religious, social and psychological dimensions, as well as conducting a meditation on reflexivity itself.[15] The Pardoner has been requested by the 'gentils' in his audience, to tell 'some moral thyng, that we may leere/Som wit' (ll. 323–6), an appropriate enough request to an official of the church, the ark outside of which there was, Christian dogma insisted, no salvation.[16] As he answers this by giving an account of his preaching, followed by a sermon, it is worth recollecting the importance attached to it in much Christian thought in the later Middle Ages, orthodox as well as heterodox. In a treatise on preaching Humbert of Romans, Master-General of the Dominicans, declared that 'preaching gains entry for souls into heaven' while it 'prevents their fall into hell', and indeed, 'Without preaching, which scatters the word of God like seeds, the word would be sterile and produce no fruit.' As for preachers themselves, 'they resemble Christ' and they are the necessary organs of the universal holy Catholic church – 'the Book of Canticles says: "Thy lips are as a scarlet ribbon" (Cant. 4:3) – a reference to preachers who, as the gloss holds, are the lips of the church.' (How Chaucer's preaching friar would have applauded this, 'Glosynge is a glorious thyng, certeyn.') Furthermore, they are the eyes, teeth, bowels, neck and breasts of the church, the very 'heavens' adorned by the Spirit.[17] The preacher, ideally, is thus an impersonal 'auctoritee', certainly an essential organ of the authoritative church which, in orthodox eyes, had a monopoly of sound doctrine and the means of grace.

Chaucer's preacher appropriately starts from an authoritative text (1 Tim. 6:10), his office 'in chirches whan I preche', and his official credentials from Pope and Bishop for carrying on a particular function within the church's overall organization (ll. 329–43). The poet then immediately sets out to desublimate the discourse of preachers disclosing the processes that may very well beget discourse and office. This particular 'mouth of the Lord', as Humbert calls preachers, displays the preacher's essential concern with his speech:

> 'Lordynges,' quod he, 'in chirches whan I preche,
> I peyne me to han an hauteyn speche,
> And rynge it out as round as gooth a belle
> (*Pardoner*, ll. 329–31)

Depicting this necessary self-concern, Chaucer sets about focalizing the human agent who actually makes discourse taken as authoritative in the culture. The very idea of a 'good' sermon, as the numerous *artes praedicandi* witness, includes its skilful construction. But the far reaching implications of this were not usually grasped in the way Chaucer reveals in the Pardoner's Prologue. Attending to the human activity of construction he displays its concrete institutional contexts and the preacher's specific psychological movements, encouraging us to cast aside conventional inhibitions about examining the grounds of officially authoritative discourse – a process which once instigated will probably go far beyond the one particular case in his fiction.

Furthermore, through this Pardoner's reflexivity about his own discourse Chaucer evokes the analogies between accredited preaching and the making of poetic fictions. Readers have always enjoyed the Pardoner's own relish of verbal and rhetorical crafts essential to good preaching, his self-dramatization before an audience of whose presence he is acutely aware, his consciousness that his *raison d'être* and his livelihood are inseparable from his ability to impress his audience through his language and overall performance. (Some readers may remember Izaac Walton's admiring memory of John Donne, whom he had known as vicar of St Dunstan and during the end of that preacher-poet's life: 'A Preacher in earnest; weeping sometimes for his Auditory, sometimes with them: alwayes preaching to himself, like an Angel from a cloud, but in none; carrying some, as St *Paul* was, to Heaven in holy raptures, and inticing others by a sacred Art and Courtship to amend . . .'.)[18]

These features, integral to the preacher's calling rather than mere idiosyncratic deviations, are obviously shared by poets like the Pardoner's own creator. In Donald R. Howard's view, the Pardoner is 'like a grotesque mirror-image of Chaucer himself. Like Chaucer he possesses enormous gifts of rhetoric, of impersonation and dramatic flair. Like Chaucer he role-plays himself, and in an ironical spirit. And as with the role-playing Chaucer we get a sense of the man himself behind the role.'[19] This is well put, but the poetry goes still further in that it prevents us making the reassuringly clear distinction between 'the role' and 'the man', between, in terms relevant to the religious function of the Pardoner, the authoritative office and the individual incumbent, the sacrament and the individual celebrant.[20] The presence of the constructing person is *in* the ecclesiastical office, not safely 'behind' it or dissolved into some impersonal power.

We have already quoted the opening of his Prologue, where he describes his concentration on the delivery of the sermon, and his elaboration of this is impressive and meaningful:

> I stonde lyk a clerk in my pulpet,
> And whan the lewed peple is doun yset,
> I preche so as ye han herd bifoore,
> And telle an hundred false japes moore.
> Thanne peyne I me to strecche forth the nekke,
> And est and west upon the peple I bekke,
> As dooth a dowve sittynge on a berne.
> Myne handes and my tonge goon so yerne
> That it is joye to se my bisynesse.
> Of avarice and of swich cursednesse
> Is al my prechyng, for to make hem free
> To yeven hir pens, and namely unto me.
> (*Pardoner*, ll. 391–402)

There is a marvellous energy both in the reflexive, very particularized depiction of the performance, and in the sacred performance itself.

The Pardoner also understands full well the Christian audience's own relish of the preacher's exhibition, their aesthetic response to his own, inevitable, aestheticization of religion in the arts of communication, rhetoric and drama. He enjoys them enjoying him doing his 'bisynesse' in such brilliant style, and we too are drawn into this performance, with delight – delight at his act and his self-consciousness, perhaps also, as Donald Howard has claimed, at being with the preacher, above 'the lewed peple' whom he converts with his powers of speech and dramatization.[21] Chaucer, so reflexive about his own and others' discourse, shows us the presence of creating *self* and the centrality of aesthetic dimensions in the discourse of the church's preachers. In embodying this, however exaggerated the form, he was articulating what should be a major problem for preachers, religious 'auctoritee' and its audiences. By foregrounding the activity of individuals in creating the discourse he establishes a detachment from authoritative instruction which was likely to deprive accredited teachers and authorities of the kind of assent they had traditionally required and received, based on their office or institutional role. Those who responded thoughtfully to the Pardoner's self-awareness about the aestheticization of religion in his vocation, watching him describe his actions in the pulpit, turning the symbolic dove into the nodding preacher perceived as a barn-dove firmly bound into the world of matter, these people would respond far more questioningly when they heard preachers proclaim that like '"eagles" which swoop down on carcasses . . . preachers in much the same way, search from afar the souls dead in sin'.[22] Similarly, when they next heard a preacher using Latin tags and phrases in his sermon, a common device, looking up at the individual in the pulpit they would have been encouraged by Chaucer's text to detach themselves from the speaker's discourse and their own very subordinate position as lay men ('doun yset'), to recall the Pardoner's comment:

> in Latyn I speke a wordes fewe,
> To saffron with my predicacioun,
> And for to stire hem to devocioun.
> (*Pardoner,* ll. 343–5)

The preacher is foregrounded as a kind of poetic cook, subtly deploying spices to make the audience swallow his dishes more enjoyably, but also to conceal the real materials they are being served. Instead of the Latin confirming the preacher's impersonality and superior knowledge, it encourages the listener to speculate about the motivation of the individual exalted in the pulpit, for he now views the language as a self-centred drama, a this-worldly performance. Such detachment is not likely to lead to what the institution which employs the Pardoner, and a host of more specialized preachers, would welcome as 'devocioun'.

We certainly must not underestimate the range of the poetry here, for it involves processes which enter into the structure and meaning of all religious discourse, raising fundamental questions about the role and effects of selfhood, aesthetic delight in relation to religious devotion, and economic factors we shall duly consider. (Some of these major difficulties were to cause George Herbert, another exceptionally self-conscious poet and preacher, much trouble as he consistently returned to the ones enacted in the 'Jordan' poems – the more he strove to create an aesthetically appropriate form for his religion, 'So did I weave my self into the sense', 'Jordan' II, 1.14.) Chaucer's own reflexivity, here bestowed on his preaching Pardoner, makes religious discourse, devotion and certainty problematic topics, in a manner quite alien to conventional religious poets and preachers of his day and later.

Among the chief problems raised by the *Pardoner's Prologue* is the role of the authoritative institution we considered in the second chapter. Chaucer's imagination attended to the social and economic dimensions of the problems we have just been discussing, and it is probably fair to say that much commentary has weakened the force and scope of the text by treating the Pardoner as an individual deviant whose existence posed no serious problems to the holy institution which employed him, or to orthodox ideologies about the necessary role of the established church in the order of salvation (illustrated in chapter 2). However, in an article published many years ago, A. L. Kellogg and L. A. Haselmayer argued that 'Chaucer's satire is not directed against false pardoners or against pardoners of any particular establishment, but against the state of institutional decay which made the existence of the pardoners possible.' They documented the *practice* of contemporary pardoners and how they had become important and official financial agents of the church, although, 'Like the usual professional collector, the Pardoner's interest in his duties is limited to what those duties yield him in cash and negotiable commodities.' Their essay demonstrated that except for the open sale of false relics, 'In practices as well as moral principles, he [Chaucer's Pardoner] is typical.'[23] This was the situation Langland was wrestling with at the same time, the absorption of the orthodox church in the economic fabric and values of secular society. Chaucer enacts his own meditations on this state of affairs through his Pardoner, granting him a reflexivity which lays bare not only the grounds of his own discourse but the foundations of the institution which licenses his activity, and gains from it. He understands his truly representative nature and rejects the comforts offered by conventional double-think in this sphere, expressing his own motivation in a passage which includes a rather witty use of line-endings:

> Of avarice and of swich cursednesse
> Is al my prechyng, for to make hem free
> To yeven hir pens, and namely unto me.
> For myn entente is nat but for to wynne,

> And nothyng for correccioun of synne.
> (*Pardoner*, ll. 400–4)

Moving through the condemnation of avarice and such vice we come to the final cause of his preaching – 'for to make hem free'. Here the line ends, and the reader naturally pauses on 'free' before moving his eyes back and on to the next line. The emphasis on 'free' may well seem to invite thought about stock Christian ideas concerning liberation from sin, recalling comments such as, 'If therefore the Son shall make you free, you shall be free indeed' (John 8:36). But as the line falls over into the next one any such ideas are swept aside by the contemporary reality, 'free/To yeven hir pens'. The Pardoner's knowing acceptance of the material organization and basis of the institution he serves is clear. Christian liberty has acquired a new meaning, one firmly institutionalized, as Langland's poem too suggested. As much as the sharpest critic of the established hierarchy the Pardoner's stance discredits conventional self-indulgent compromises which allow individuals to avow a set of values deriving from Jesus (preaching and following a path of poverty and extreme self-sacrifice), while leading lives immersed in economic pursuits and the acquisition of material comforts. Only he acknowledges and accepts his own complicity in the dominant institution, the attitudes and values it shares with the secular world. Accepting this, he then sets out to cash whatever he can bring to the thriving social market, be it pardons, 'pigges bones' (*General Prologue*, l. 700), his poetic skills or his learning. So he continues his commentary:

> Thanne telle I hem ensamples many oon
> Of olde stories longe tyme agoon.
> For lewed people loven tales olde;
> Swiche thynges kan they wel reporte and holde.
> What, trowe ye, that whiles I may preche,
> And wynne gold and silver for I teche,
> That I wol lyve in poverte wilfully?
> Nay, nay, I thoghte it nevere, trewely!
> For I wol preche and begge in sondry landes:
> I wol nat do no labour with myne handes,
> Ne make baskettes, and lyve therby,
> By cause I wol nat beggen ydelly.

I wool noon of the apostles countrefete;
(*Pardoner*, ll. 435–47)

Chaucer again uses the Pardoner's self-reflexivity to unmask the dominant practices and values of the orthodox institution which claimed a monopoly on the means of grace and correct doctrine. Here it is worth illustrating the way scholarship has tended to obscure the critical, social and economic dimensions of the text by referring to one of the most influential articles on the Pardoner, R. P. Miller's 'Chaucer's Pardoner, the Scriptural Eunuch, and the *Pardoner's Tale*'.[24] Discussing this passage Miller takes up the Pardoner's explicit reference to Ephesians 4:28. Paul advises Christians to 'put on the new man, who according to God is created in justice and holiness of truth', and goes on to say, 'He that stole, let him now steal no more: but rather let him labour, working with his hands the thing which is good, that he may have something to give to him that suffereth need.' Miller comments, 'To Paul's exhortation . . . the Pardoner retorts, "I wol nat do no labour with myne handes", and engages rather in thievery of spiritual offerings.' To me this seems too cosy a reading. It comes from a one-sided concern with moral treatises by Augustine, Lombard and other theologians, dead long before Chaucer's world emerged, and a failure to attempt to give scholarly and imaginative attention to the social and religious world within which Chaucer thought, met his problems and wrote. For in fact the Pardoner's attitude is perfectly orthodox in asserting,

I wol nat do no labour with myne handes,
Ne make baskettes, and lyve thereby

Had R. P. Miller gone about Chaucer's and Langland's world preaching (without licence, of course, unlike the Pardoner) that friars, pardoners, abbots, many monks, priests living off tithes, priests legitimately absent from their benefices, clerics in the universities, and indeed all officials of the church at all social levels should be manual labourers according to the letter of Ephesians 4:28 and the example of apostolic poverty, he would soon have been arrested as a Lollard, a Waldensian, a seditious person. One suspects he would soon have seen the error of his ways and recanted, for it takes immense courage and conviction to stand against authorities ready to invoke state powers, including prison, torture and a most terrible form of death. The fact is, literary scholars like Miller too comfortably ignore what comes out so clearly in the studies on late medieval dissent and heresy by historians such as Leff, R. E. Lerner, and M. D. Lambert – namely, vociferous dissatisfaction with contemporary practices of the clergy and hierarchy or extra-institutional pursuit of holiness and poverty very easily aroused the church's opposition and charges of heresy. For heresy was basically defined by the established church as obstinate opposition to its authority and its interpretation of what constituted an appropriate way of life and belief for Christians, lay and clerical. In his inquisitorial notebook Bernard Gui, with typically unreflexive circularity, wrote, 'one is presumed to be a heretic from the very fact of striving to defend error', defined, of course, by 'loyal, learned sons of the church'. He acknowledged that sometimes 'low and uncouth persons' may seem to overwhelm the learned officials of the church in argument, but this is treated as bad publicity for the Inquisition and orthodoxy, not as possible signs that the heretic's grasp of Scripture and apostolic life may possibly have more to commend it than the establishment's. If those being questioned are suspect to the orthodox, they are 'to be kept in prison until they have confessed the truth'. Bernard Gui reminds his followers, 'in order to elicit the truth, he [the suspect] may be constrained in various ways: limited in food, held in prison, or chained; or he may even be put to the question [i.e. tortured]'.[25] The institution's entrenched power and its rejection of reflexivity is clear, not something a man would take on lightly. Furthermore, as we noted earlier in connection with the Wife of Bath's observations on poverty and perfection, the whole meaning, relevance and application of apostolic poverty, which Miller assumes to be so straightforward, was actually an area of fierce controversy in theory and practice.

In fact, like Langland's work, the subtly reflexive speech given to the Pardoner opens out on to profound contradictions and anomalies in the theory and practice of the orthodox church. Besides those already mentioned, it suggests disturbing questions about the interpretation and application of Scripture in the present, and about the relations between the contemporary church and Scripture. Whose interpretations of texts about apostolic life should count, the Lollards' or Pope John XXII's and the officials of the church, those Bernard Gui called the 'loyal, learned sons of the church'? Whose views about the relative authority of tradition, Scripture and contemporary ecclesiastic practices should count, Wyclif's or those of orthodox theologians who condemned him?[26] Chaucer's mode is far removed from Langland's direct and dogged encounter with the issues that worry him, but in his own way Chaucer has obliquely raised major problems about authority and hermeneutics, through the Pardoner's reflexivity. The text he created refuses us the comfort of reified authorities (Paul or anyone else), subverts simple reverence for official authority and exposes his reader to a host of disconcerting problems about knowledge, authority and the pursuit of grace in his world. As Donald Howard wrote, the Pardoner, 'makes us question all cultural values and . . . throws into relief not only the Christian institutions involved with pilgrimage and pardon, but the realms of civil, domestic and private conduct.'[27] This radical questioning of the grounds of discourse, values and conventional practices, this sustained reflexivity is very much part of the vision of the man who created the Pardoner. And he was, as we shall point out, aware of its risks.

After the Pardoner has practised the art which is part of his 'auctoritee' (l. 387), he completes his performance by acting out his official calling as a licensed Pardoner (ll. 919–45). This stunning conclusion has fascinated readers, naturally attracting a wide range of interpretations, to which I intend to add one that emerges from the perspectives of the current discussion. It seems to me that the Pardoner's highly developed self-consciousness has not been abandoned at all. He concludes his performance by deliberately alluding to the Prologue. There he encouraged multifaceted meditations on preaching, authority, the church and the mediation of grace and doctrine. He, or rather the controlling intelligence and imagination of the poet, led us to appreciate the interactions between individual outlook and institutional setting, between individual religious consciousness and the social contexts in which religious meaning is made and given. From lines 904–15 he frames his calling as a Pardoner within the bounds of what is overtly the recollection of a 'moral tale. . . . Which I am wont to preche for to wynne' (ll. 460–1). This allows the pilgrims to treat what is happening as another tale, another aesthetic performance – which it is – emphasizing again the deep continuities between Christian preaching, poetic games, tales told on the road to Canterbury. But because the Pardoner's discourse is aesthetically framed, the audience *can* protect themselves from what it discloses about the institutions in which they all trust for the means of grace and the hope of salvation (none of them being, as far as we know, 'heretics' rejecting the Roman church), and from what it discloses about their own complicity in the current state of affairs. They *can* protect themselves, although neither they nor Chaucer's audience need do so. At this point the Pardoner (and, of course, the creator, Chaucer) decides to deny them the possibility of such self-protection. He deliberately steps into his official vocation as a licensed pardoner, on the road to Canterbury, institutionally approved goal of countless pilgrims 'from every shires end', an important and workaday representative of the particular Christian church to which all the pilgrims adhere (like most of Chaucer's audiences). His reflexivity becomes mocking, and the passage cannot be shortened:

> I have relikes and pardoun in my male,
> As faire as any man in Engelond,
> Whiche were me yeven by the popes hond.
> If any of yow wole, of devocion,
> Offren, and han myn absolucion,
> Com forth anon, and kneleth heere adoun,
> And mekely receyveth my pardoun;
> Or elles taketh pardoun as ye wende,
> Al newe and fressh at every miles ende,
> So that ye offren, alwey newe and newe,
> Nobles or pens, whiche that be goode and trewe.
> It is an honour to everich that is heer
> That ye mowe have a suffisant pardoneer
> T'assoille yow, in contree as ye ryde,
> For aventures whiche that may bityde.
> Paraventure ther may fallen oon or two
> Doun on his hors, and breke his nekke atwo.
> Looke which a seuretee it is to yow alle
> That I am in youre felaweshipe yfalle,
> That may assoille yow, bothe moore and lasse,
> Whan that the soule shal fro the body passe.
>
> (*Pardoner,* ll. 920–40)

The mockery, as so many readers have felt, is extremely

complicated. Putting it in summary form, its targets include, at least, the following: the authoritative institution which gives him pardons to sell; his orthodox self-seeking Christian audience whose bizarre (yet thoroughly normal) combination of materialism, magical religiosity,[28] fear and uncritical deference for authority (when it brings them security) makes them such gullible objects in his habitual trade; himself, dependant and employee of institution and audience both of which he holds in contempt, both of which he continues to serve. As he reaches into the passage his imagination (his author's too) is fired by the utter mechanization and materialization of the means of grace and forgiveness in the *practice* of the Christian church he serves. The lines telling his audience that they can take pardon all new and fresh every mile are marvellously sharp comedy, obviously appropriate to this particular fragmented, competitively quarrelsome, holy journey from pub to pub via Canterbury Cathedral. They are also most appropriate to the contemporary church mediated throughout the Pardoner's prologue, refracted in his existence and sponsoring pilgrimages and the marketing of pardons, the more the better. On top of this, they capture a striking aspect of the official trade in pardons and the legitimating ideology, which related them to the treasury created by Christ's sacrifice and entrusted to the church, and the whole apparatus of compulsory confession and penance supervised by the institution's officials. This is its role as a constant stimulator of detailed moral and religious *anxiety* which can only be alleviated by constant payment of the institution which monopolizes the means of salvation; the institution's careful cultivation of guilt, with the insistence that people were accountable not only to God but also to the men who mediated his binding and loosing, re-stimulated anxiety which drove people back to the controlling institution . . . and so the cycle continued, with the institution gaining control over the minds and purses of its adherents, waxing fat on their anxiety and the materialization of religion. Part of the Pardoner's comedy is due to his precise and detailed grasp of this cycle and his role in it – a 'seuretee' who stimulates anxieties about the minutiae of conduct in a way which will fill the coffers and keep the audience dependent. The web of issues here has been overlooked, as far as I am aware, by literary critics, but is important within the text and the culture. Nor were these issues to be resolved within the late medieval church.

('Therefore it is impossible for men who want to provide for their salvation through the Law, as all men are inclined to do by nature, ever to be set at peace. In fact, they only pile laws upon laws, by which they torture themselves and others and make their consciences so miserable that many of them die before their time because of excessive anguish of heart. . . . This is shown by the innumerable *Summae* that collect and expound such laws. . . .' Thus the record of psychological anxiety encouraged by the system in the words of an intensely religious renegade from this church – Martin Luther.)[29]

The long quotation above, from the concluding moments of the Pardoner's display, also reveals the completeness with which religion could be made into a commodity. The free sacrifice of Christ, the gifts of grace, individual renewal, all is turned into the currency of Mammon, the life-blood of the institution the Pardoner works within. Even the potential of language is reduced to a financial frame of reference as 'goode and trewe' become merely measures for monetary quality. In the given circumstances where the Pardoner has to live out his life, the multi-faceted mockery is a thoroughly intelligible reaction. There were others, but this was *one*, an exceptionally aware response to an institution and culture marked by profound contradictions and tensions. However distorted we may find his vision, in the last resort, we should not miss the profound penetration of the culture his author has bestowed on him.

As the quoted passage comes to its close we remember the Pardoner's earlier statement that he does not really care what happens to his clients when they are dead (ll. 405–6; 939–40). His detachment from his employer, from his clients and from the common ideological ground between them is almost complete. Almost, but not quite. He still *needs* to express his reflexivity and his critical insights. The need is a product of his humanity, as St Thomas Aquinas notes 'the companionship of his fellows is naturally necessary to man . . . nature has destined him to live in society . . . dividing the labour with his fellows'; or, in the charged words of Donne, a preacher-poet already mentioned: 'Solitude is a torment which is not threatened in hell itself . . . God himself would admit a figure of society, as there is a plurality of persons in God, though there be but one God; and all his external actions testify a love of society, and communion. . . . No man is an island, entire of itself. . . .'[30] The creation and comprehension of discourse, the most intimate forms of introspection even, take place within the processes of wider social intercourse, however much these processes themselves are made the object of critical attention. The inescapable need for 'the companionship of his fellow men', fused with the reflexive penetration of his culture and the practices of his employer and clients, have left him in a dreadful situation, needing what he despises. It is in his full grasp of this that Chaucer presents the risks of self-reflexivity and finally transcends his own creation. The risks are that in its continuous unveiling, its continuous quest for the grounds of discourse and practice, one's own and others, it may unleash a reductive cynicism, the product of a total estrangement from self and others. In this state egoism seems to free itself of all illusions, all unexamined and blinding pieties or 'sentimentalities', only to be left with nothing. Nihilism, a spectral existence. The Pardoner penetrates the institution he serves, the role of clients and himself, together with the chains that bind them in a unity which is indeed a version of the mystical body the church has proclaimed itself to be. Yet because his penetration is not accompanied by the conviction or faith which would turn him into a heretical critic or a radical critic, trying to work from within the institution, he continues to earn his living through the degrading spiritual and economic apparatus for which he has nothing but contempt. His mental and physical labour serves to increase his alienation from his society, his religion and himself. The only pleasure remaining to him is critical reflection about himself and others. This has become an end in itself, rather than an essential moment in the constructive activity of imagination, which it always remained for his own generous creator. The poet has taken us far beyond the banalities of conventional moral condemnation of figures such as the Pardoner, disclosing the complicated and fluid interrelationships between social practices, contemporary ideologies and individual consciousness. The existence of the Pardoner is quite as central to the *Canterbury Tales* as Donald Howard argued. In the Pardoner's discourse and life Chaucer created an endlessly fascinating self-reflexive vision of one possible fate of reflexive imagination in his own world.

I shall conclude this discussion of the Pardoner with a few suggestions about the Host's violent reaction to the invitation he receives:

'I rede that oure Hoost heere shal bigynne,
For he is moost envoluped in synne.
Come forth, sire Hoost, and offre first anon,
And thou shalt kisse the relikes everychon,
Ye, for a grote! Unbokele anon thy purs.'
'Nay, nay!' quod he, 'thanne have I Cristes curs!
Lat be,' quod he, 'it shal nat be, so theech!
Thou woldes make me kisse thyn olde breech,
And swere it were a relyk of a seint,
Though it were with thy fundement depeint!
But, by the croys which that Seint Eleyne fond,
I wolde I hadde thy coillons in myn hond
In stide of relikes or of seintuarie,
Lat kutte hem of, I wol thee helpe hem carie;
They shul be shryned in an hogges toord!'
This Pardoner answerde nat a word;
So wrooth he was, no word ne wolde he seye.
(*Pardoner*, ll. 941–57)

Of the abundant critical commentary on this riveting scene, Donald Howard's should be singled out to precede any attempt to venture one's own reading: 'part of the realism of the passage lies in the fact that we don't know the Host's intentions any more than we would if we were there.'[31] That is a pertinent response to the text's silences, the brevity of the Host's outburst and the plurality of plausible psychological interpretations offered by Howard and many others. With this caveat in mind, we may nevertheless construct an account which shows the particular relevance of the religious and cultural implications we have been considering to the Host's reactions. The Host, we come to see through the journey, is a conventionally worldly, bourgeois Christian innkeeper, a 'fairer burgeys is ther noon in Chepe' (*General Prologue*, l. 754). He combines pious sentimentalism, a desire for 'myrthe or japes' (which he demanded from the Pardoner), domineering aggressiveness, a crude but typical form of male ego in which personal identity is perceived in terms of the 'manhod hym lakkede right naught' and for which he praises the Monk. His ego may occasionally be challenged by his wife (*Merchant's Tale*, ll. 2419–40) but this does not provoke any questioning about himself or his world. He leads the unexamined life with untroubled gusto. This, naturally, does not make him any less loyal a son of the orthodox church, as we see from his piety, his suspicion of one who might be 'a Lollere' and his readiness to let the 'povre Persoun' preach his 'Moralitee and vertuous matere'.[32]

The Pardoner's contrasting reflexivity and critical intelligence has stripped away veil after veil from the church he represents, undermining its claimed authority, its dispensation of grace and absolution, its holy relics, so profitable a source of income for many centres of grace as well as a sign of the institution's access to supernatural powers. He has taken his orthodox audience to the edge of what could well seem a terrible abyss, one which Langland himself viewed with anguish. If the institution they supported, with tithes, money, land and their presence, the institution on whose authority and system of penance and indulgences they relied for their salvation, if this institution was actually as the Pardoner presented it, where was their hope and trust to be placed? How were they to allay anxieties about their state 'Whan that the soule shal fro the body passe', where was their 'seuretee'? For Lollards the visible, orthodox church could be assessed in terms encouraged by the Pardoner's vision, while the individual could still be assured hat his relations with God and his salvation did not depend on the established hierarchy in any way. They were cultivating an alternative ideology to explain and manage their situation and responses to the religious practices and attitudes of the day.[33] But for the piously orthodox no such alternative was available. Here, I believe, is at least one of the grounds for the Host's violent abuse of the Pardoner. That 'noble ecclesiaste' has negated the institution the pilgrims rely on. After such knowledge about church officials, sacred objects, pardons and the mentality of preachers, on what can the Host and those like him depend? The reality disclosed to them seems to demand a terrible burden of continuous individual scrutiny and critical discrimination. The individual is faced with inner isolation and spiritual loneliness, one we mentioned in connection with the Pardoner and even saw signs of in *Piers Plowman*. The challenge the Pardoner offers is that the unexamined life, well supported by the official establishment, is an absurd and totally irreligious one which actually serves and sustains the economic interests of very earthly beneficiaries. His own examined life plainly provides no hope for living, but the Host is neither able nor willing to join the poet in a meditation on the

Pardoner's intellectual and psychological processes within an overall situation they all share.

Instead he seeks to preserve his own simple-minded certainties and pieties from the Pardoner's revelation, by turning him into a scapegoat, trying to destroy him and the effects of his speech. The Host's spontaneous, unexamined aggression cannot be concealed by the later claim that he spoke in play (l. 958), for the notion of play entails a level of detachment and self-control not in evidence. His violent language, as many readers have noticed, indulges 'images of excrement and castration' which unself-consciously yield additional insight into his own psychological organization and the nature of his attack on the sexually ambivalent Pardoner.[34] Confining the disturbing issues the preacher has raised to a purely personal matter which can be dealt with by an individual assault, the Host rejects any attempt at critical analysis of self, society and the religious institution of which he is a member, officially served by the Pardoner and his colleagues. In this response Chaucer dramatizes an all too common response to insecurities of various kinds. Psychological, intellectual and social difficulties or confusions are projected on to vulnerable individuals (or minority groups) who may then be abused and attacked as the cause of the problems at stake. The unexamined life and its bad faith must be preserved, the abyss must be veiled, the disturbing and disturbed individual silenced.[35]

In the assault on the Pardoner the preacher is silenced by the Host, the laughter of 'the peple' and the intervention of the Knight to whom the Host is 'so deere' (ll. 960–8). The Knight wishes to preserve the framework erected by the Host at the Tabard, where the pilgrimage is due to conclude, allowing the participants to 'laughe and pleye' as before the Pardoner intervened with his discomforting performance. He is as resistant to critical reflection as the Host, content with conventional assumptions and the established religious institutions.[36] In fact, no one on that pilgrimage is seen to welcome the Pardoner's form of discourse or his revelation about their church, and in their different ways they seek to repress his contribution. Yet in the most important sense, he has not been silenced. The voice created by Chaucer continues to undermine the unexamined life, 'to haunt us, to hover over our whole reading of *The Canterbury Tales*, to be central to its idea'.[37] The reflexive imagination of the poet was fully engaged in creating both the profound insights and the limitations of the Pardoner's own critical, reflexive discourse. Through it he explored central features of his own imagination and his cultural situation, and it is not Chaucer who invites us to hide with the Host, the laughing people or the Knight.

I shall conclude the chapter by considering the *Parson's Tale* and the 'retracciouns' in relation to the preceding discussion about reflexive imagination, joining those critics who have taken the contexts in which Chaucer placed this treatise with the seriousness his choice demands.[38] In *The Canterbury Tales* the treatise is approached as one pilgrim's attempt to teach, 'Moralitee and vertuous mateere', one pilgrim's attempt to give his version of 'the way' (*Parson's Prologue*, ll. 22–73).

At once Chaucer has the Parson, another official of the church, raise the issue of poetic fiction, human knowledge and instruction:

> 'Thou getest fable noon ytoold for me;
> For Paul, that writeth unto Thymothee,
> Repreveth hem that weyven soothfastnesse,
> And tellen fables and swich wrecchednesse.
> Why sholde I sowen draf out of my fest,
> Whan I may sowen whete, if that me lest?'
> (*Parson*, ll. 31–6)

After this strident declaration he assures his audience that if they listen to him they will hear 'Moralitee and vertuous mateere'. The speaker clearly aspires to some version of the discourse we earlier called 'objectivist'. He assumes that he has direct access to a totally impersonal and timeless truth. Quite unaware of the complex mediations through which human beings come into contact with existence he shows himself markedly unlike his maker. In fact he has no sense of the problematic nature of human knowledge, no consciousness whatsoever of his own presence in his discourse.[39] It is not surprising that for him religion and human knowledge are very simple, 'soothfastnesse' *or* 'fables and swich wrecchednesse', 'draf' *or* 'whete'. His contempt for fiction re-emerges later under the classification 'the synne of Ire' where he makes an unqualified attack on those who 'maken folk to laughe at hire japerie as folk doon at the gawdes of an ape'. He seems ignorant of the distinctions Langland tried to make between different sorts of minstrels and, predictably enough, manifests no awareness about the aesthetic and mimetic aspects of his own exempla and images. He never even takes account of the fact that he is allowed to perform by the Host and his audience in what is a game, providing what they see as an appropriate end to a series on the road from the Tabard to Canterbury (ll. 61–71).[40] Unlike the Pardoner, he forgets how he is, perforce, a performer. It is Chaucer's own reflexive imagination and the contexts he has evolved through *The Canterbury Tales* which help us to focus on the Parson's failures to examine the grounds of his discourse and alleged knowledge. The poet has constructed a one-dimensional and unself-conscious preacher whose ambitions are to 'make an ende' of discourse (ll. 46–7), to fulfil the aim of dogmatic and inquisitorial procedures to end dialogue, to possess a fixed and closed truth from a position no longer exposed to challenge and correction. And the poet has placed this enterprise within a work, whose reflexivity resisted all attempts to assert a final, absolute viewpoint, as did its form, open-ended and unfinished. Describing the ability of *The Canterbury Tales* 'to recreate the clash of experience with experience, to set one man's reality against another's', Donald Howard went on to suggest that 'the established idea of *The Canterbury Tales* as unfinished is correct . . . because he created a literary form and structure, a literary idea, whose possibilities were inexhaustible. The idea itself, which is complete, makes the work "unfinished".'[41] The 'literary form and structure', we might add, was itself a brilliant manifestation of the reflexive imagination and cognitive processes we have been exploring, ones that are antithetical to the Parson's.

From the verse prologue we move to the 'myrie tale in prose' which turns out to be translations, with some adaptation, of works on penitence, the seven deadly sins and their remedy.[42] Recently the work done on Chaucer's sources by S. Wenzel has been used to argue that Chaucer deliberately changed the sources to suggest a preacher (perhaps we should say a manual-composer) whose views on some matters were neither in the main-stream of fourteenth-century moral theology, nor, much more relevantly, Chaucer's own views. The claim is that Chaucer set out to satirize at least some of the assertions made so categorically by the Parson. This line of inquiry and argument is most promising and has already shed some light on Chaucer's detachment from the Parson and his views, but here I intend to look at a few representative examples of the Parson's form of discourse from the perspectives evolved in this chapter.[43]

The opening text of the treatise is taken from Jeremiah's account of God's wrath with Israel for the nation's oppression of others, their covetousness and their false dealing (Jer. 6:1–16). In this context the Jewish people are told to ask for the old paths, which is the good way, and refreshment for their souls (Jer. 6:16). The Parson assumes the text applies quite unequivocally to his late-fourteenth-century audience, quotes it and then announces that the one way 'which may nat fayle to man ne to womman that thurgh synne hath mysgoon fro the righte wey of Jerusalem celestial' is called 'Penitence', enacted, he goes on to show, within the orthodox church. J. B. Allen has argued that the Parson's application of this text to penitence 'cannot be found in the most popular exegetical collections of Chaucer's era, and is, in fact, explicitly denied in one of the most popular'.[44] Be that as it may, the sentiment and instruction is perfectly compatible with institutionally approved stress on the sacrament of confession and penitence under the control of its officers. What interests me, from the perspectives of the present chapter, is the way the Parson glosses the 'olde pathes' we should seek as 'olde sentences', assuming their unanimity, unequivocal meaning and reliability in the present. Yet this is just what readers of Chaucer's poetry, from the *House of Fame* onwards, have been made to doubt as the poet disclosed how 'olde sentences' were generated by many historical beings with partial and often conflicting viewpoints.

Furthermore, the authoritative traditions had to be continually recreated by the interpretative activity of other historical beings in changed and changing circumstances encouraging still different interests.[45] Chaucer's work invites us to see the Parson's statement as an unhelpful generalization which evades these major questions. (It even ignores the fact that the 'olde pathes' of the *Old* Testament were far from identical with those paths recommended to the 'new men' in the *New* Testament by Paul and his colleagues.) Moreover, readers of Langland and Chaucer will know that these poets suspected the state of the contemporary Church, made traditional paths of confession, penance and absolution tragically perilous – as we saw in our study of the Pardoner's performance and the place of the Church in *Piers Plowman*. The Parson's evasions of such fundamental issues are signs of a weakness of critical intelligence and imaginative engagement which we have no good reason for attributing to his creator.[46]

The Parson's ideas on love, marriage and sexuality have been well distinguished from Chaucer's by J. Finlayson and C. V. Kaske, and I now wish to follow their commentaries by discussing the literary and imaginative mode Chaucer bestows on the Parson when he is handling such areas of experience.[47] He writes at length about sexuality ('Lecherie' is the most interesting sin to him) and exhibits a hatred of the body and revulsion from all sexual delight which was perfectly orthodox but would have seemed 'rigorist' even among orthodox moralists.[48] His talk about the incarnate nature of humanity is characterized by the platonic-manichean metaphor of the body as the soul's prison, one he finds unambiguously horrible and shameful and attributes to St Paul in a mistranslation of Romans 7:24.[49] He proclaims that we are 'engendred of vile and corrupt mateere' and associates original sin particularly with the body, from which he seems to think the soul contracts it on arrival (ll. 332–3). What is particularly striking is that in these unqualified pronouncements he never pauses to reflect on the vital implications for his *own* vision.

We should certainly ask about the consequences of incarceration, the 'prisoun', on this man's vision, and we should ask about the effects of the 'vile and corrupt mateere' from which he was engendered, and, so he claimed, contracted original sin. The outcome of such questioning is in itself subversive of his confident assertiveness, for it focalizes fundamental problems about the status of claims made by those imprisoned in such corrupt matter. Why should this man feel entitled to make dogmatic utterances about 'soothfastnesse', morality and the sinfulness of *other* people when he himself must be immersed in the corrupt prison, his vision correspondingly distorted and unreliable? The answer is that he should not. Lacking all self-reflexivity he totally fails to bring the grounds of his discourse, and his own fallen state, into consideration. Unlike his maker, he fails to attend to the mediations through which knowledge and moral judgment are constructed. This is a grave and debilitating failure of imagination and critical intelligence.

We saw earlier too that Chaucer's own work explicitly invites us to meditate on the motivations of moralists, how they may condemn and abuse what they actually ponder and may even enjoy in the act of negation. John Finlayson quoting the Parson's attack on 'sexually titillating' fashion, finds a 'prurient fascination with that which it condemns', and he is surely right to do so:[50]

> the horrible disordinat scantnesse of clothyng . . . the shameful membres of man . . . . Allas! somme of hem shewen the boce [swelling] of hir shap, and the horrible swollen membres, that semeth lik the maladie of hirnia, in the wrappynge of hir hoses; and eek the buttokes of hem faren as it were the hyndre part of a she-ape in the fulle of the moone. And mooreover, the wrecched swollen membres that they shewe . . . semeth that half hir shameful privee membres weren flayne [cut off]. . . . Of the hyndre part of hir buttokes, it is ful horrible for to see. For certes, in that partie of hir body ther as they purgen hir stynkynge ordure, that foule partie shewe they to the peple prowdly. . . .

Overt disgust is unaccompanied by any self-examination about his own orientation, his own obsessions and his own participation in what he sees as the sins of fallen men. Throughout his discourse it just never occurs to him to join Chaucer and the Pardoner in wondering how subtly the self is woven into the senses.

The same lack of reflexivity is also plain in his treatment of other sinners. Whereas the Parson of the *General Prologue* is 'to synful men nat despitous' but always 'discreet and benygne' here we have someone whose vindictive aggression takes unself-conscious delight in some of the more appallingly violent retribution so lauded in the Old Testament.[51] He comments that 'Lecherie', which he defines to include any pleasure in love-making between married people, is 'ful displesaunt' to God and instinctively turns to 'the olde lawe' rather than to the New Testament:

> If womman thral were taken in this synne, she sholde be beten with staves to the deeth; and if she were a gentil womman, she sholde be slayn with stones; and if she were a bisshoppes doghter, she sholde been brent, by Goddes commandement. Forther over, by the synne of lecherie God dreynte al the world at the diluge. And after that he brente fyve citees with thonder-leyt, and sank hem into helle.
>
> (*Parson*, ll. 837–8)

The Parson's sheer relish for the grotesque and self-righteous male violence in these examples is utterly devoid of any self-awareness about the emotions he is indulging in himself and inciting in other males, supposedly Christian rather than the Jews of Israel. Although elsewhere he reels off traditional dogma asserting the superiority and natural rule of men over women, here he makes no mention of male responsibility and attitudes, while the male sinner is not even noticed. When he recalls God's own characteristically male violence in the Old Testament, he chooses to overlook the fact that God then decided to change his own fanatically rigid moralism and promised to 'no more curse the earth . . . no more destroy every living soul as I have done' (Gen. 8:21; 9:8–15). Furthermore, he has absolutely no sense that *he* (with his present audience) is *part of* the fallen humanity condemned and standing under God's judgment. In this he is antithetical to Langland and Chaucer.

Later the Parson does remember that most powerful and relevant example from the *New* Testament of Jesus' own treatment of one of the sinners the Parson and his like were so happy to condemn to hell.[52] Jesus was confronted by Scribes and Pharisees with a woman taken in adultery, in the very act, they gleefully report, and remind him of the Old Testament laws that such offenders should be stoned to death. Jesus' reply and its effect was recorded thus:

> 'He that is without sin among you, let him first cast a stone at her' . . . . But they hearing this, went out one by one, beginning at the eldest. And Jesus alone remained, and the woman standing in the midst. Then Jesus lifting up himself, said to her: 'Woman, where are they that accused thee? Hath no man condemned thee?' Who said: 'No man, Lord.' And Jesus said: 'Neither will I condemn thee. Go, and now sin no more.'
>
> (John 8:7, 9–11)

When the Parson does at last use this text it is in a most illuminating way. Having spent much time reviling adultery for its economic effects, in a vein very close to Januarie's concerns, as well as for more overtly theological ones (ll. 876–7, 883–4), he asserts in conclusion: 'And therfore, by the olde lawe of God, they sholde be slayn.' He now acknowledges the new dispensation and St John's account just quoted:

> 'Go', quod Jhesu Crist, 'and have namoore wyl to synne,' or, 'wille namoore to do synne.' Soothly the vengeaunce of Avowtrie is awarded to the peynes of helle but if so be that it be destourbed by penitence.
>
> (*Parson*, ll. 887–89)

Chaucer again makes the would-be impersonal and authoritative dogmatist disclose the very personal presence which the Parson tries to ignore. The selectivity and emphasis of the Parson patently transforms Jesus' subversive and apparently un-traditional and anti-institutional act into yet another bullying threat about 'the peynes of helle', pains which can only be avoided by carrying out penitence within the institution that employs the Parson and the Pardoner. Most strikingly, the Parson deletes Jesus' statements to the official authorities, 'He that is without sin among you, let him first cast a stone at her', just as he deletes part of Jesus' statement to the woman – 'Neither will I condemn thee'. Unhesitating in his casting of stones and condemnation of people to hell, the Parson rejects the extremely compelling invitation to self-scrutiny in Jesus' statements. He deletes aspects of the text which remind moralists to reflect on the various ways they participate in what they condemn, and to let this self-reflexivity inform their moralizing and their relationships with fellow humans. The Parson's response to Jesus is startlingly less adequate than the one the gospel attributes to the Scribes and Pharisees. Once more Chaucer shows us how even the most authoritative of 'auctoritees' is mediated through very particular and partial human consciousness, something the Parson quite fails to take into account.

One could continue this analysis of the monumental lack of reflexivity in the Parson's discourse, but rather than accumulating still further examples to illustrate the same limitations and distortions, I will conclude with a few related comments on some much-quoted judgments he makes about marital love-making. He insists that man can commit the sin of lechery with his own wife, and illustrates this commonplace dogma with a proverb, 'a man may sleen hymself with his owene knyf', recommending that a man should love his wife 'as though it were his suster' (ll. 858–60). Invariably these lines are quoted to highlight the un-Christian wickedness of Januarie, since that 'worthy knyght' believes that marriage legitimates sexual desires and pleasures, claiming that 'A man may do no synne with his wyf,/Ne hurte hymselven with his owene knyf' (*Merchant's Tale*, ll. 1835–41). We will return to this Tale (chapter 6), but for the moment it is the *continuities* between the Parson's attitude to human sexuality and Januarie's to which I wish to draw attention, for this seems to be invariably overlooked.

That they both choose the proverb about the knife is quite as important as Januarie's stupid misquotation of it. This reveals how they actually share a view of love-making which they both appropriately represent by an instrument of aggression and destruction. The Parson's imaginative and conceptual failure to incorporate love into the purposes and practices of even marital sex leaves the erotic as a degraded area where male activity is symbolized by the knife, apt image for the love-less genital assaults which are the only kind of sexuality the Parson can envisage and Januarie practise. Because the Parson so lacks reflexivity he could never begin an examination of his own language and the assumptions it carries. He does not even notice how he shares Januarie's thoroughly secular and class-bound obsession with marriage as a means of ensuring an heir with the male's family blood flowing in his veins, a fit inheritor, in the secular ideology, for the family property and a perpetuator of the male line: the explicit reasons for the gravity of adultery include the fact that it engenders 'false heires ofte tyme, that wrongfully occupien folkes heritages. And therefore [*sic*!] wol Crist putte hem out of the regne of hevene.'[53] He is quite unconcerned that he cannot produce texts of Jesus supporting the idea, that gentry property relations and family blood will be a major factor at the Last Judgment, but after his treatment of Jesus' statements to the Scribes, Pharisees and adulterous woman, this hardly surprises us. We again see the immunity of his speech from self-examination about its foundations and limitations.

It is Chaucer's poetry, its particulars and the total context created by the existing *Canterbury Tales* which encourage us to focalize the inadequacies of the Parson's 'objectivist' discourse, so representative of a major form of moral and religious indoctrination during the later Middle Ages. Chaucer's own work helps us see the Parson's discourse, so conventional in many respects, as devoid of all reflexivity – ignorant of its own complicity in what it condemns, most superficial in its assumptions about the modes and scope of human cognition, unaware of the speaker's presence in the interpretation and selection amongst authorities, altogether a hopelessly crude form for moral thought and the self-knowledge to which the reflexive imagination is central. Chaucer thus placed the *Parson's Tale*, as one very important form of conventional 'objectivist' discourse, within poetic processes where the reflexive imagination was prominent. In doing so, he gave readers the means to penetrate the disastrous limitations of such discourse and every encouragement to supersede its style of thought and the attitudes to self, others and religion that it reflects.

In manuscripts which have completed versions of the *Parson's Tale* it is followed by Chaucer's 'retraccioun'.[54] Without doubt this very brief prose passage shows that at the point of his life and in the mood in which he composed it, the productions of the creative imagination seemed of little importance to him. The engagement of his art with human living is viewed in a perspective which turns his work into 'enditynges of worldly vanitees'. Alfred David's response to this perspective, which he finds in writers as removed from Chaucer as Tolstoy and Kafka, has much force: 'The luxury of literature and the study of literature have never been easy to justify in a world torn by harsh necessity, wars, and relentless social struggle.'[55] Chaucer, however, does not quite reject art in the way David's terms suggest. Instead, his mind is overtly concentrated on the Christian *after*-life in which the person is eternally fixed in a state of bliss or torment, heaven or hell. In this perspective the human existence which his poetry had explored with such exceptional intelligence and insight is reduced to the narrowest version of the Christian pursuit of individual salvation. The self-image he now constructs, and prays to realize in his life, is of a thoroughly abstract individual obsessed with his own personal salvation 'at the day of doom' and thereafter, begging that from now on he may have:

> grace to biwayle my giltes, and to studie to the salvacioun of my soule, and graunte me grace of verray penitence, confessioun and satisfaccioun to doon in this present lyf, thurgh the benigne grace of hym that is kyng of kynges and preest over alle preestes, that boghte us with the precious blood of his herte; so that I may be oon of hem at the day of doom that shulle be saved.

All questioning has ceased. Yet there are great difficulties in this move, since the works Chaucer now claims to 'revoke' have taught the reader to ask at least some questions about performances such as this. One question concerns the peculiar temptations in constructing this sort of self-image in this language: does it not encourage the concealment of selfhood and the fact that, willy-nilly, this too is a self-image constructed by the fallen self – 'So did I weave my self into the sense' (George Herbert, 'Jordan', II)? Another question concerns the abstract version of the individual assumed here. All the complexly interacting relationships (intellectual, social, economic) within which individuals gain and develop their identity and language are magically dissolved. We studied the attractions of such strategies to Langland but continually saw his refusal to let it collapse the exploratory, and often most unhappy dialectic of *Piers Plowman* in which such solutions were superseded as understandable but faithless evasions of his particular imaginative engagement with individual, social and intellectual life as he experienced it. He refused to terminate his dialectic in what would have been a betrayal of his own visionary process. Where the poem does reach its formal conclusion the isolation of Conscience (and Will) is presented as the tragic outcome of religious and social developments the poet wishes to resist but finds overwhelming. The individualism here, we saw, thus emerged as the unhappy but coherent outcome of leading tendencies in the poem and the world it mediates. The case in Chaucer's 'retracciouns' is, in my view, very different, for they suddenly assert a model of the individual and his one-dimensional psychological simplicity which has no grounding in the poetic totality, the bulk of which is similarly rejected. This dogmatic rupture also turns away from difficult but relevant questions about the individual, the church and society raised by Chaucer, as well as by Langland: for instance, how will Chaucer's wishes for 'penitence, confessioun and satisfaccioun' fare in the institution explored in *Piers Plowman*, where penitence and confession were major issues, and in the *Pardoner's Prologue* and elsewhere in the *Canterbury Tales*? Langland's lonely conclusion confronted such issues, whereas Chaucer's retractions try to bury them.

These retractions are indeed an attempt at closure, the will to dissolve problems his own work focalized so memorably, and they are grounded in a thoroughly understandable fear about 'the day of doom.' It is this which led him to a belated attempt to collapse and terminate the reflexivity of his own poetic processes. (Not knowing exactly when he wrote these brief retractions we do not know what, if anything, he wrote 'from hennes forth unto my lyves ende' – we do not know if the fear of damnation finally silenced him and his creative imagination's outstanding and critical reflexivity.) In the mood and mode in which he wrote the retractions he would doubtless wish to affirm the Parson's 'objectivist' discourse against the totality of his own reflexive and genuinely exploratory poetry. Yet, as he must have known, and in this mood feared, the revoked poetry survives, and still has the power to energize many readers to pursue forms of thought and imaginative experience antithetical to the Parson's and his followers or admirers through the ages.

CHAPTER 5

Chaucer's Criseyde: Woman in Society, Woman in Love

> Retornyng in hire soule ay up and down
> The wordes of this sodeyn Diomede,
> His grete estat, and perel of the town,
> And that she was allone and hadde nede
> Of frendes help; and thus bygan to brede
> The cause whi, the sothe for to telle,
> That she took fully purpos for to dwelle.
>
> *Troilus and Criseyde*, V, ll. 1023–9

Anyone attempting to contribute to the understanding of Chaucer's achievement and meaning in creating the figure of Criseyde will be aware that, in reaction to much previous criticism, influential commentators in recent decades eschewed interpretations which might seem to treat medieval writing as though it held any affinities with the kind of 'naturalism' medievalists associate with nineteenth-century novels.[1] So in his important study of Chaucer it is not surprising that R. O. Payne praised modern critics who had evolved approaches to 'the patterns of characterization which remove it from the realistic and motivational-psychological categories in which earlier criticism had sought to define it'. He himself wished to demonstrate that there is no ground in the poem for any 'naturalistic reconstruction of "personalities"', nothing approaching 'individual psychologies'. In common with others, such as D. W. Robertson, Payne's treatment of *Troilus and Criseyde* assumed that all late medieval poetry was governed by the same unambiguous 'ultimate moral principles', while the past was viewed as a straightforward 'series of illustrations of intellectual abstractions'. The function of characters in art was to convey already known 'typical significances' through fixed symbols quite isolated from the contingencies of 'actual existence'. Criseyde, for example, 'is a way of saying something about the lovely vanity of human wishes'.[2] Thus, the multifarious and dynamic forms of human existence were transformed into a set of unproblematic abstractions and judgments as medieval art allegedly eliminated individuals in the service of clearly presented and static universals. However, as the previous chapters have suggested, such approaches blind us to central currents in both Langland's and Chaucer's poetry, and I now wish to show how, in creating the figure of Criseyde, Chaucer developed a social psychology which comprised a profound contribution to the understanding of interactions between individual and society. His astonishing achievement in making Criseyde included an exploration of the ways in which individual action, consciousness and sexuality, the most intimate areas of being, are fundamentally related to the specific social and ideological structures within which an individual becomes an identifiable human being. Far from either simply transporting his readers 'away from contemporary reality to a distant and romantic Troy',[3] or exemplifying unproblematic ethical and metaphysical universals, this exploration paid particular attention to the position of women in courtly society, ideology and literary traditions. Choosing Boccaccio's tale, placed in Troy, may have made it easier for him to engage in detailed and imaginatively sympathetic explorations of love, sexuality and female consciousness without constantly addressing himself to the dominant attitudes and judgments of conventional Christianity, but it did not entail a flight from the world of his own audience.[4] Quite the contrary, his treatment of Criseyde shows concern with women *in* the social group for which he wrote – the expectations they cherished, the manipulative pressures they had to accept and use, the contradictory self-images and realities with which they were presented. He also, as he would do later in the *Canterbury Tales*, showed great interest in women's complex mixture of opposition, accommodation and positive complicity in a situation where they were a subordinate group, at all social levels.

In much romance writing and courtly literature there is an attempt to remove love from the compromises, confusions and institutionalized miseries of the contemporary world. Instead of constructing utopian images and fictions which were made to encounter the present world in a critical and earnest examination of it, romances could be used to offer far more simple and comforting escape. The formula of an outstanding knight committing his existence to the devoted service of a woman fulfilled a psychological and perhaps growing need to create a more satisfying alternative to the real organization of Eros and marriage in medieval society. Customary practices and ideology (secular as well as ecclesiastic) demanded the subordination of women to men and to land, aristocratic marriages being primarily land transactions and family alliances. This is the context in which courtly literature evolved images and conventions in which the normal relations between women and men were inverted, the knight serving the woman, paying homage and devotion to her. The role of female patronesses in shaping such literature is no coincidence, and Eileen Power's suggestion that it served a psychological function for upper-class women not dissimilar to that served by modern romantic stories and magazines for working-class women may be plausible, for the image of women as goddesses worshipped by aristocratic males sorted very ill with their actual position.[5] It seems to me that Chaucer was fascinated by these contradictions and was not prepared to leave them peacefully coexisting. In *Troilus* he actually used the romance genre and conventions of courtly literature to explore the tensions between the place women occupied in society and the various self-images presented to them. He set out to imagine his way into the psychic cost for men and women in the situation he perceived so sharply, returning to society in his own art.

At the very opening of the poem Chaucer shows that he wants his audiences to take Criseyde's social situation seriously. He emphasizes her sense of isolation in Troy at this point in her life, her danger as the daughter of a traitor in a long war, and her immediate need for a male protector.

Chaucer reports the general view that not only Criseyde's father, but all his kin 'Ben worthi for to brennen', so her fear is most understandable:

> For of hire lif she was ful sore in drede,
> As she that nyste what was best to rede;
> For bothe a widewe was she and allone
> Of any frend to whom she dorste hir mone.
> (*Troilus and Criseyde*, I, ll. 90–1, 95–8)

Before critics venture any remarks about Criseyde's 'weakness' or 'slydynge of corage' they need to project their imaginations into this situation, following Chaucer. Her fear is justified and has specific grounds, her weakness is a genuine aspect of a social reality in which women are a subordinate group, and her feelings of isolation are a subjective registering of both the particular crisis she faces and a more general vulnerability and precariousness in the position of woman.[6] In these circumstances her chief asset, her leverage on the powerful, is her sexuality. She understands this well enough, so that although she is 'Wel neigh out of hir wit for sorwe and fere' (I, l. 108), she still approaches Hector, one of the most powerful men in the city:

> On knees she fil biforn Ector adown
> With pitous vois, and tendrely wepynge,
> His mercy bad, hirselven excusynge.
> (*T & C*, I, ll. 110–12)

This scene offers an interesting contrast to images of the male prostrate before the female, and it is significant that it precedes the enactment of these images by Troilus and the arch-manipulator Pandarus (III, ll. 183–4, 953, 1079–80). Yet even before he has introduced Troilus, Chaucer invites such contrasts by introducing her frightened act of homage with a very conventional description of her 'aungelik' beauty and her appearance as 'an hevenyssh perfit creature' (I, ll. 100–5). To survive in this culture the woman needs to make use of her sexuality and whatever courtly sexual conventions, fictions or male fantasies may serve her.[7]

She does so, and we should not miss the way Chaucer has opened his poem by placing the courtly forms of sexual relations and language in a setting which stresses the 'aungelik' female's subordinate position and her urgent need for male protection. It is Hector, responding to her beauty and helpless sorrow, responding to her as a woman, who guarantees her safety and 'hir estaat' (I, ll. 113–31). The esteem in which she is held by Hector and the royal family is very important to her, and during her first discussion with Pandarus in Book II she asks directly after Hector, the potentate whose goodwill and existence appears necessary for her own well-being and relative security within the community. Similarly, when later it seems that there is a threat to her property, the importance of the royal family as her patrons who can protect her is made clear

(II, ll. 1414–91, 1611–36). And being reliant on this group Criseyde is influenced by their opinions, whether about Troilus, when her mixed feelings are soothed by hearing these powerful people praise him (II, ll. 1583–94), or when she considers Troilus' proposal that they elope, a scene we shall examine later.

The first interview between Pandarus and Criseyde confirms Chaucer's interest in the processes of interaction between individual consciousness and various social pressures, manipulations and values, often bewilderingly conflicting (II, ll. 87–597). Criseyde's natural impulses and fears, her joys and her anxieties, are carefully situated in the context established in the first book. It is May, and Pandarus asks her to cast aside her self-possession and dance. At once Criseyde turns to one possible social role (in Chaucer's society) to protect herself from risks that could be involved in her uncle's invitation:

> 'I? God forbede!' quod she, 'be ye mad?
> Is that a widewes lif, so God yow save?
> By God, ye maken me ryght soore adrad!
> Ye ben so wylde, it semeth as ye rave.
> It sate me wel bet ay in a cave
> To bidde and rede on holy seyntes lyves;
> Lat maydens gon to daunce, and yonge wyves.'
> (*T & C*, II, ll. 113–19)

Criseyde may be playing with her uncle, but the game involves genuine and, as we saw, well-founded fears. Here she confronts them by using her widowhood, a state which allowed contemplative withdrawal from the threatening life of the world and the repression of natural instincts, with all the risks these carried. Of course, Criseyde does not claim this is what she wants, as her uncle knows, only that it would be a legitimate and decorous defence, one she has not yet been driven to. As we shall see, she can assess the potential of widowhood and its acknowledged values in yet another way.

In the ensuing gossipy conversation the war is the overtly central topic, another source of fear (II, l. 124) being used by Pandarus to bring Troilus into mind, until Criseyde consults Pandarus about her 'estat' and 'governaunce' (II, ll. 212–20). This focusses on his relationship to her as uncle, elder male relative and guide to subordinate female, and the gamesome quality in the exchanges should not conceal the authority relations here, for as the narrator notes, nieces should obey uncles (II, ll. 232–52, 295–8; III, l. 581). Pandarus uses his position in these roles to push Troilus' interest at her. Chaucer's handling of Criseyde's situation here is, as throughout this work, extraordinarily delicate. Its vulnerability has been stressed and Pandarus' circumlocutions both deliberately play on her fears and excite her (II, ll. 267–315). When he has done this, he introduces the core of his matter:

> Now, nece myn, the kynges deere sone, . . .
> The noble Troilus, so loveth the,
> That, but ye helpe, it wol his bane be.
> (*T & C*, II, ll. 316–20)

Pandarus emphasizes the social status of the lover, the king's son – the personal name only follows three lines after the identification of rank and power. He uses this as a bait, but also as a threat, for what would become of Criseyde if she should be held responsible for his sickness or death (II, ll. 320–50)? In a similar manner, Pandarus adds to the pressure by stating that if she does not acknowledge Troilus then he, her uncle, will cut his own throat (II, ll. 323–9). This added threat has a double force, for Criseyde is not only subordinate to him but fond of his company. She plays for time and seeks clarification, using the social roles Pandarus has elected for the moment – '"Now em," quod she, "what wolde ye devise?/What is your reed I sholde don of this?"' Her uncle's reply is unequivocal and recommends total fulfilment of Troilus' sexual desires (II. ll. 386–406). Criseyde tries to forestall this demand by appealing to his identity as her quasi-father (ll. 408–28). This tactic fails completely, for Pandarus renews his previous threats and gets up to leave. Her response is then carefully traced in the next three stanzas, emphasizing how she 'wel neigh starf for feere,/So as she was the ferfulleste wight' (II, ll. 449–69). Her fear has again been given a thoroughly sufficient social basis and there is no reason to treat it as a peculiar flaw. Thinking of her uncle's threats and their social repercussions, she thinks about her own social survival, the dangers for her if Pandarus and Troilus are in earnest, and her uncle's personal survival. Her comment (to herself) that, 'It nedeth me ful sleighly for to pleie', suggests how aware she is that her uncle manipulates her and uses the courtly forms of game as they suit him. She must try and out-play him and shifts to the area where, as we mentioned, convention allowed women a seemingly dominant role – 'love'. This allows her to assert that she cannot love anyone against her own will, and she takes a certain initiative in the role of powerful beauty able to bring even a king's son to woe (II. ll. 462–504). But the rules of the game were neither designed nor controlled by women, and Pandarus may well smile, for he sees her move as the concession essential to Troilus' gratification. By the time this interview between uncle and niece concludes, Chaucer has taken us far into one of the central problems he was exploring – the contradictions between aristocratic love conventions, in which woman was an exalted and powerful figure, and the reality in which she was a subordinate being to be manipulated and made serviceable to men.

We begin to see the ways in which the realities of the situation actually pervade these conventions in a subtle confirmation of the existing order and power relations. Furthermore he has shown us that he explores the problem concretely, as it was lived out in Criseyde's own consciousness and actions.

When Pandarus, sure of his success, leaves Criseyde, she withdraws 'into her closet' to examine her own feelings. But 'as she sat allone' and thought that to give or withhold love was something in which she was free, Troilus rides past her house in military triumph, almost presented as an event stimulated by Criseyde's meditations (II, ll. 599–647). The diversity and fluidity of her movements of consciousness are marvellously evoked by Chaucer as he expanded and changed Boccaccio's work here.[8] She responds to Troilus' presence, 'And leet it so softe in hire herte synke', part passive, part agent, a delicately realized 'process' which the narrator notes a few lines later when he comments that 'she gan enclyne/To like hym' but gradually his own being 'Made love withinne hire herte for to myne'. She tries to analyse his qualities and 'his estat', but while she does not try to repress her sexual feelings, we are reminded that she is 'allone' and fully understand her need to take into account her social circumstances and the psychological risks of loving (ll. 649 ff.). Her mind moves to the implications of any involvement with Troilus for her own social existence:

> Al were it nat to doone,
> To graunte hym love, ye, for his worthynesse,

It were honour, with pley and with gladnesse,
In honestee with swich a lord to deele,
For myn estat, and also for his heele.
Ek wel woot I my kynges sone is he;
And sith he hath to see me swich delit,
If I wolde outreliche his sighte flee,
Peraunter he myghte have me in dispit,
Thorugh whicch I myghte stonde in worse plit.
(*T & C*, II, ll. 703–12)

The opening two lines of this quotation imply grounds for not giving Troilus her love but at the moment they are vague and convey some confusion, easily sliding over into positive grounds for involvement, within legitimizing social conventions ('honour', 'honestee') themselves equivocal as to precise content. Having followed Chaucer's stress on her estate and its uncertain position, we appreciate with sympathy this blend of self-preservation and care of another, characteristically realized by a poet with a fine care for the complexity of motivation. Indeed, the complications increase within the quoted passage as Criseyde recalls that her 'estat' might not only be protected by 'my kynges sone' but could be threatened from two distinct directions. If she rejects him he could certainly undermine her position even further and she would be in a far 'worse plit' than at present, protected as she is by Hector. Her assessment is thoroughly realistic, as the court-poet well knew, and it again displays the real power relations underlying the forms and conventions of courtly and literary love. The second direction from which she envisages a threat is stated some lines later, and although very different is equally realistic in terms of Chaucer's own world: the threat of marriage. A widow in medieval society, a basic model for this fictional Trojan aristocracy, had a privileged position in relation to married women as long as she had adequate means of subsistence. As soon as she married the legal and economic rights she had as a widow were removed and her husband took total control of her and her lands. These are the factors Criseyde bears in mind when she thinks of the re-marriage:

I am myn owene womman, wel at ese,
I thank it God, as after myn estat,
Right yong, and stonde unteyd in lusty leese,

Withouten jalousie or swich debat:
Shal noon housbonde seyn to me 'chek mat!'
(*T & C*, II, ll. 750–4)

Doubtless this confident statement includes some idealization of her present state and its anxieties, an independence which is clearly dependent on Hector and other males. But it does bring out the unpleasant problems of having the male protector in the form of a husband who would destroy whatever measure of precarious independence she had.[9] Throughout the entire period before she commits herself to Troilus in bed, threatened as she is, she constantly expresses fears about losing the relative independence she has and becoming totally dominated, fears Troilus tries not to arouse as she becomes directly involved with him.

Finally she is aware that the relevant problems go beyond the issue of marriage and male domination to embrace the way any full and serious love for another person necessarily involves risking oneself, jeopardizing a self-possession often won with great pain and difficulty. The whole process of genuine commitment to another opens out the self and is experienced as both joy and taxing constraint. She puts these risks well:

Allas! syn I am free,
Sholde I now love, and put in jupartie
My sikernesse, and thrallen libertee?
Allas! how dorst I thenken that folie?
May I naught wel in other folk aspie
Hire dredfull joye, hire constreinte, and hire peyne?
Ther loveth noon, that she nath why to pleyne.
(*T & C*, II, ll. 771–7)

This fear is quite distinct in theory from the more material group previously discussed, but in practice it overlaps, and Chaucer once more discloses the inextricable connections between objective social factors and the individual psyche.[10]

Chaucer's preoccupation with the issues under discussion is manifest in the dream about the eagle which Criseyde has after the delicate and many-layered scene in the garden. She dreams,

How that an egle fethered whit as bon,
Under hire brest his longe clawes sette,
And out hire herte he rente, and that anon,

> And dide his herte into hire brest to gon,
> Of which she nought agroos, ne nothyng smerte;
> And forth he fleigh, with herte left for herte.
> (*T & C*, II, ll. 926–31)

This dream exhibits the violence and perils of loving concealed behind the traditional and cosy conceit of an exchange of hearts. Chaucer shows that although the dreamer feels no pain she perceives herself as passive in the face of an aggressive and dominating male. Her feelings are described in negatives ('she *nought* agroos, *ne nothyng* smerte'), and there is a striking absence of any tenderness, mutuality or pleasure. There is also an absence of security, for although the eagle inserts his heart, he actually flies on. True enough, this is a dream focussing Criseyde's fears rather more than her hopes, but the point here is that these fears are well grounded in the realities with which women had to cope, and the consequences these had for intimate areas of experience. It is in such terms, if any, that Chaucer creates the 'typical' and 'universal', a universal which does not dissolve the individual consciousness or particular social circumstances, a universal only apprehensible in and through individuals.

As the third book progresses, Troilus' behaviour gradually melts away Criseyde's fears as she comes to rely on him as one who, although her male social superior, is a loving protector willing to leave her identity and status free from domination by him (III, ll. 463–83). She remains subordinate to male initiatives and commands, but we also see that she may perhaps be using this submission while conforming. For example, she dutifully *obeys* her uncle, 'as hir ought' when he tells her to stay the night in his house (III, ll. 575–81); but Chaucer reminds us that we cannot have complete knowledge of a consciousness such as Criseyde's, even though he is the poet creating her for us, and he implies that she may be doing so for her own advantage (the possibility of seeing Troilus) without having to accept responsibility as initiator or decision-maker. Yet he only implies it by encouraging us to guess at 'What that she thoughte' when Pandarus denied that Troilus was in the house, even while he himself claims he does not know ('Nought list myn auctour fully to declare'). This interchange embodies the way that in noticing the possible uses of her subordination and imposed passivity, the poem does not allow us to go to the extreme of claiming that the woman is really the controlling manipulator, as some readers have asserted.[11] Even at this point, in a Book which contains one of the most powerful celebrations of fulfilled human love, of what Blake called 'the lineaments of gratified desire' and what Chaucer called 'the grete worthynesse' in love, we see that her final coming together with Troilus still needs the offices and presence of her uncle. This is especially noteworthy for it is a very different matter in Boccaccio's text, where his Criseida organizes the consummation, sends Pandarus to bring Troilo to her and needs no third party on the night.[12] Far from this version, Chaucer shows the effects of the pressures and the overall situation he has realized so fully, and we see Criseyde's real confusions, social anxieties, distress at Troilus' alleged jealousy, her sexual desires, all interacting to bring her to her 'wittes ende' and place her in Pandarus' hands, 'I am here al in youre governaunce'.[13]

However, once the uncle completes his offices by throwing the fainting Troilus into her bed ('O nece, pes, or we be lost!' – still playing on her fears as much as her erotic desires (III, ll. 1065–118)), Criseyde takes the sexual initiative, kissing and reassuring Troilus.[14] Once she has done so she delicately and trustingly hands over the initiative to him, in a transaction Chaucer describes with marvellous tact and insight (III, ll. 1177–83). Troilus, 'with blisse of that surprised', responds joyfully and the poet creates an atmosphere of mutual discovery and shared stimulation as a new serenity encompasses them which contrasts most strikingly with the manipulative but socially inescapable love-games played out previously.

Yet, even in this admirable transition, there are still images to remind us that the subordinate position of women leaves its imprint on this mutually satisfying and intimate relationship. The timorous 'mouses herte' Troilus, anxiously swooning at Criseyde's bedside (III, ll. 736, 1092), is transformed into a predatory bird not so dissimilar from the one in her own violent dream:

> What myghte or may the sely larke seye,
> Whan that the sperhauk hath it in his foot?
> (*T & C,* III, ll. 1191–2)

The power relations are again overt, the predatory nature of the sparrow-hawk undisguised. Well may the narrator muse about what the lark might say from this position. Chaucer leaves the lark and turns to the newly confident Troilus. Far from thanking Criseyde for bringing him to erotic life and so generously giving him the sexual initiative, he unreflexively starts thanking the seven planetary gods (l. 1203), and then addresses Criseyde in a conventional but revealing image. This also presents their relationship in terms of male hunter and female vanquished prey (ll. 1205–11), mirroring the sparrow-hawk/lark image. The effects of male domination and egotistic predatoriness, legitimized in social practice and ideology, are reflected even in the most personal acts where there is genuine love.

While this needs pointing out, it would be very wrong to leave the passage by emphasizing these aspects of what is a characteristically multi-faceted piece of writing. Despite the social and ideological forces Chaucer has evoked with such imaginative depth, and despite his refusal to make them just vanish away, he does certainly create a most powerful example of the way in which fulfilled Eros enables individuals to transcend social pressures, repressions and fears. Mutual love, involving the total person, is achieved, and in this mutuality we celebrate not only the triumph over adverse forces but the momentary and joyful abandonment of anxious selfhood as together they 'Felten in love the grete worthynesse'. The conflicts of power and the distortions of energy are transcended in an oasis of 'hevene blisse', the 'perfit joie' of a generous love which informs body, mind and affections (II, ll. 1219–414).

The final point I wish to make about the third book concerns the aubade (ll. 1429–70). Here the coming of morning symbolizes not some inquisitorial sun of righteousness against which the evil worldlings are in rebellion being damned by Chaucer, but the re-intrusion of day-to-day society into their lives, the society in which practices and ideas concerning women have the deforming and elaborately contradictory effects we have followed, a society fighting a war initiated by male aggression and the rape of a woman. It is a society which subordinates human relations and Eros to power structures and militaristic glory, with disastrous results – 'many a lovere hastow slayn, and wilt' (l. 1459). Nevertheless, although the lovers curse the day and promise an eternity of the kind of love they have just experienced, they do not yet question their own resumption of aristocratic life, accepting that 'it mot nedes be' (l. 1520), however antagonistic it is to their own love. They accept the society's downgrading of the magnificent human achievement that their love is, accept the claims of the society's values and the war. It will not always be thus for Troilus, nor should it be so for Chaucer's readers.

The Prologue to Book IV opens with the narrator castigating the abstraction 'Fortune' for causing the misery we are about to witness. This way of talking about events was traditional enough, and in fact here Chaucer is virtually translating the final stanza of part three in Boccaccio's *Filostrato*. Yet it is actually far less relevant to what Chaucer's own poem reveals than many readers, and perhaps even the author himself, have been prepared to admit. His work, as we have seen, portrays individual consciousness and the relationship between Criseyde and Troilus in a mode which incorporates relevant social and ideological dimensions, as different to Boccaccio's poem as to most medieval romances. It makes us unwilling to accept claims that 'Fortune' cast him out of Criseyde's grace, for Chaucer has concentrated so intensely on human processes that such statements come as evasory, pseudo-explanations, the irrelevant vestiges of a tradition which needed them to provide some sense of understanding about troubling, obscure and seemingly inexplicable events and changes. Book IV confirms this impression, for it carefully describes the prime importance of social organization and cultural values in determining what happens to Criseyde and the consequences of this in her relationship with Troilus. It too makes addresses to Fortune (and even more metaphysical speculations about destiny) seem an unnecessarily vague and mystifying discourse in which to grasp the events of the last two books, a discourse which can only conceal human practices revealed in the poetic processes Chaucer created.

Immediately the fourth book brings the crucial social contexts to our attention (ll. 29–231). First, Chaucer reminds readers that Troy had immersed itself in a long war (ll. 29–56), and we might be expected to remember that its origins lay not in 'Fortune' but in specific acts of male social aggression and greed leading to the present state of continuous legalized violence. Chaucer reports a day-long battle in which men fight with all kinds of weapon, 'And with hire axes out the braynes quelle' (IV, ll. 43–6). The Trojans suffer severe losses and seek a truce and negotiations with the Greeks for exchange of prisoners. At this point the sudden intervention of Calkas underlines a key element in the social structure: woman is seen as a passive object to be disposed of by a patriarchal ruling group. Calkas decides that he wants his daughter to join him, now blaming his cruelty in leaving her in a place he felt sure was soon to be destroyed. However strange such paternal care may now seem from the father who abandoned his daughter to face hostility and possible persecution when he left the city, no one questions his right to claim her, nor her right to be consulted (ll. 64–147). Although her alienation from her treacherous father is as complete as her wish to remain in her home (ll. 659–871, 1128–69), neither Calkas, Greeks nor Trojans consider that a mere woman is a being with needs, desires and choices to be honoured, even though she is close to court circles. Troilus sees this quite clearly, and he reminds Criseyde that her father will be able to marry her off as he sees fit, persuading her verbally or by using violence as he wishes.[15]

Chaucer highlights these issues for us as ones we should continue to take very seriously, and he moves us from Calkas and the Greek assembly to the Trojan 'parlement' (IV, ll. 141–217). The purpose of the parliament is to discuss the exchange of prisoners (l. 146), the Greek delegation's request for Criseyde and Toas in exchange for Antenor. The assumptions here are extremely revealing. Because Criseyde is a woman and a daughter without a husband (whose authority would replace the father's), she has no different status from that of a prisoner. We now see from yet another perspective how Hector's promise to protect the fair woman, the 'aungelik' creature of courtly convention, contradicted many major elements in existing social organization. Hector does have the integrity to remember his promise and speak out at the parliament:

> 'Syres, she nys no prisonere,' he seyde; . . .
> We usen here no wommen for to selle.'
> (*T & C,* IV, ll. 179–82)

This gets to the nub of the matter. Criseyde is not officially a prisoner, and once this is acknowledged then it becomes clear that the proposal under consideration is simply to sell her, to handle her as a commodity in a social market organized by and for male possessing groups. Parliament's decision to sell her is realistic enough and also acts as a symbol for the position of women in relation to men (fathers, husbands, rulers) in Chaucer's world as much as the fictional one of his poem. The Trojan Antenor is

'Daun Antenor . . . so wys and ek so bold baroun . . . ek oon the grettest of this town', whereas Criseyde is reduced to having no identity other than, 'This womman' (ll. 188–92). The fact that after the immediate threats to her survival (following Calkas' treachery) had been weathered Criseyde became 'both of younge and olde/Ful wel biloved' (I, l. 130–1), that she 'nevere dide hem scathe' (IV, l. 207), that Hector is correct in asserting she is not officially a prisoner, and that she desperately wishes to remain, all this is irrelevant before her social status as 'womman'. Parliament naming and classifying her like this signifies the exact power structure being invoked as once more the realities beneath and within the various courtly forms of love and respect for women are made plain at a key juncture in the poem. Hector is soon silent.

As the transaction takes place we are thus shown quite clearly that the ensuing disintegration of the love between Troilus and Criseyde, and the psychic disintegration they each suffer, is precisely grounded in the social structure and conventional male attitudes to women. Criseyde can be sold because she is a female without a personal male owner in Troy (husband) and belongs to a male ruling group now prepared to cash her suddenly increased value. Chaucer added Hector's intervention to the narrative he found in Boccaccio, and in doing so he drew further attention to the centrality of male attitudes and public practices to the tragic destruction of a great human achievement.[16] But he was also to focus on the complex processes by which the dominant culture is made psychologically active in even those it does not benefit.

The long discussion between the lovers, once they have gone to bed after the parliament's decision, actually exemplifies such processes, despite their great love and commitment to each other.[17] Just as Criseyde took the sexual initiative on their first night together in Book III, so she does now in offering comfort and reassurance that they will be re-united (ll. 1261 ff.). It seems like a brave attempt to make the best of a bad situation without capitulating to it, an initiative taken in the face of and against tremendous pressures. But as we scrutinize this passage more closely we find that her admirable attempt at initiating action turns into the complex submission of a victim to the dominating groups that control her world. Chaucer's own insight and art is especially subtle as he shows how her seemingly confident claims of being an initiating agent are gradually undermined within her own discourse by womanly accommodation and compliance to a specifically *social* fate. A fundamental social conservatism, the product of her whole life, traps her into total accommodation with an alien reality in which she is sacrificed to the self-interest of a male ruling group.

The overt claims of her role as agent are illustrated in sentences like the following:

> Now, that I shal wel bryngen it aboute,
> To come ayeyn, soone after that I go,
> Thereof am I no manere thyng in doute.
> (*T & C*, IV, ll. 1275–7)

This bodes well for Troilus. But having said that the urgency of the occasion means she will have to cram 'an heep of weyes' by which she will effect this 'in wordes fewe', she expends the next twelve stanzas without specifying one way in which *she* will ensure the desired outcome, let alone a heap (ll. 1279–365). What does happen is significant, for she is not only completely vague: when she does envisage some ways by which she could be with Troilus again the agents in these cases act quite independently of her:

> Men trete of pees; and it supposid is
> That men the queene Eleyne shal restore,
> And Grekis us restoren that is mys.
> (*T & C*, IV, ll. 1346–8)

From being agent in a process she initiates ('I shal wel bryngen it aboute') she has now become syntactically absolutely deleted, invisibly waiting upon events under the control of 'men' and rumours about what 'men purposen' (l. 1350). This shift characterizes these twelve stanzas. She may then sense that her promising opening has not been maintained and she says, 'Have here another wey, if it so be/That al this tyng ne may yow nat suffise' (ll. 1366–7). This involves persuading her father to send her back to Troy to collect, and intercede for, his property (ll. 1368–414). Again the original initiatory role is dissolved as she substitutes accepted male authorities for herself in effecting her deliverance from misery. Her socialization as woman has been so successful that she has internalized the values and norms of her male governors, leaving her unable to imagine any coherent opposition to their utterly selfish and cruel decrees – 'My goyng graunted is by parlement/So ferforth that it may nat be withstonde/For al this world' (ll. 1297–9). It is important to notice how in this she is quite unlike the male aristocrat Troilus, for despite his own deep vested interest in the *status quo*, his training and life has encouraged a far more active and independent role in the social world. He proposes that they defy the parliament's ruling and elope. He sees that their only way of surviving as fulfilled and happy lovers is to break out of this society, so inimical to their relationship (ll. 1501–26). Nor is this an irresponsible flight of fancy, for he is a well-proven knight who has also taken thought of their need for material subsistence and survival (ll. 1513–26). It is Criseyde who refuses to pursue this rebellious course (though she later regrets it, V, ll. 736–65), and the terms in which she does so again emphasize the manner in which the repressed and subordinate learn to internalize the values and assumptions of the repressing and dominant groups – to their own detriment and destruction.[18] It is not mere idiosyncratic timidity that guides Criseyde, but official (male) ideology about women and values. She says:

> But that ye speke, awey thus for to go
> And leten alle youre frendes, God forbede,
> For any womman, that ye sholden so!
> (*T & C*, IV, ll. 1555–7)

Here she, a woman, downgrades the full heterosexual love of a man for a woman in relation to inter-male friendship and the cohesion of the male aristocracy, and she downgrades women. Next she places a male-instigated war above their love (ll. 1558–9) and uncritically accepts crude militaristic notions of 'honour' (ll. 1561, 1575) rather than the claims of so fully humanizing a love as we saw celebrated in Book III. She moves on to consider what 'the peple ek al aboute/Wolde of its seye?' (ll. 1569–70). This is a fine representation of the uncritical nature of her ideology, for these are the very same 'peple' we listened to in the parliament, in a scene already discussed (IV, ll. 183 ff.). They showed a total contempt for Criseyde's identity as a mere woman, and no hesitation in selling her for their own (supposed) immediate advantage. Yet their obnoxious but conventional attitudes and behaviour are the norms their victim appeals to in a crisis where her own aristocratic lover advocates flight and rebellion. The power of training, habitual subordination and convention could not be more powerfully demonstrated. So profoundly has she internalized anti-feminist norms, and the downgrading of Eros, that she defends a dominant ideology in which war, male self-interest and the defence of the male ruling group are more important than human love and her own survival and happiness.[19] Chaucer rounds off this brilliant exploration by having her appeal to stoical 'reason' and 'patience' to confirm her resignation in the face of a social fate against which cogent human action was, as Troilus asserted, possible (IV, ll. 1583–9). There is not space to develop this observation here and it will have to suffice simply to note that this use of stoical and Boethian stances pervades Book IV. That is, the Book shows the narrator, Troilus, and Criseyde using Boethius to rationalize and sanctify resignation in the face of a social order willing to trade human beings and wage long and totally destructive war. As so often in the history of thought and religion we see metaphysics being used to construct defences of contemporary social organization. But the movements of the poetry subvert such strategies, as they disclose human agency, ideology and history at the core of metaphysical projections, however attractive and fascinating these projections were to Chaucer.[20]

By the opening of Book V Troilus and Criseyde have accommodated themselves to the crippling social reality against which Troilus suggested they rebel. Chaucer shows them fully controlled as Criseyde is 'muwet, milde, and mansuete' (V, l. 194) and Troilus completely involved in subduing his feelings and behaving in a supposedly manly fashion in public. To me it seems that criticism of the poem has again paid insufficient attention to Chaucer's continuing evolution of a rich social psychology in which the final disintegration of the mutual love is placed in a social situation imaginatively and aesthetically realized with precision and depth.

Chaucer stresses how Criseyde's weak and subordinate position, her social heritage as a woman (not as a morally weak or oddly timid individual), is made many times worse in the Greek camp (V, ll. 687–765). She is a prisoner of the enemy army, much more isolated than in Troy, even at the beginning of Book I, and completely lacking in that most vital of stays – warm human support. Whereas Troilus at least has Pandarus to talk with and is in his own customary milieu, a powerful figure with friends and public identity, Criseyde is frighteningly alone, 'With wommen fewe, among the Grekis stronge. . . . There was no wight to whom she dorste hire pleyne . . . she was allone and hadde nede/Of frendes help.'[21] The poet's emphasis is unmistakable, and the word 'dorste' is well chosen. When her father-ruler refuses to let her return she is frightened of attempting a clandestine escape. Her soliloquy about these fears is very moving and once more shows Chaucer imagining his way into individual consciousness and history, in a manner quite untypical of medieval characterology represented by Lydgate, Gower or saints' legends. Away from any idealizing literary conventions, Criseyde voices her real and justifiable social and sexual fears, fear of the Greek state, fear of rape.[22] Her movement away from commitment to Troilus must always be discussed in these contexts which Chaucer has created so understandingly. His approach is the absolute antithesis to the abstract inquisitorial moralism favoured by certain groups in many ages and countries.

Her total situation, with all its pressures working on an individual trained by her society to *accommodate* to an antagonistic reality rather than rebel (as Troilus recommended) now expands to include a new aristocratic lover, Diomede (V, ll. 771 ff.). In her painful isolation she is cruelly exposed to Diomede, for whom she is a (doubtlessly goddess-like) fish to be netted (ll. 775–7). So when we come to the now famous phrase describing aspects of her being as 'slydynge of corage' (l. 825), we have been given ample grounds for grasping this in the full light Chaucer has cast on the crippling social reality and ideology which constitute her circumstances. He has created a profound vision of a social individual whose bad faith was almost impossible to avoid, encouraged and prepared for by the habits and practices of the very society which would, of course, condemn such a betrayal with righteous moral indignation. (The contradiction Chaucer grasps so clearly has had a long life in western society and ethics.) The poet himself should be quoted as he realizes this theme in Criseyde's shift away from Troilus:

> Retornyng in hire soule ay up and down
> The wordes of this sodeyn Diomede,
> His grete estat, and perel of the town,
> And that she was allone and hadde nede
> Of frendes help; and thus bygan to brede

> The cause whi, the sothe for to telle,
> That she took fully purpos for to dwelle.
> (*T & C*, V. ll. 1023–9)

This explicitly encourages the reader to acknowledge the central role of social organization and individual situation in breeding the fundamental grounds of moral and spiritual failure. It is a statement which draws our attention to the poem's social psychology and rejects the simpler paths of abstract moral accusation and judgment favoured by the Parson in *The Canterbury Tales*, and those many conventional moralists like him. Furthermore, it is worth noticing how syntax is made to enhance our imaginative participation in the movements of Criseyde's consciousness, contributing to our understanding of the nature of what we would tend to describe as human choice basic to moral action. The first line in the passage just quoted begins with the word 'Retornyng', a present participle which helps convey the circular processes within the lonely woman's mind, a continuous present that seems to dissolve any possibility of an initiating, controlling act of self-determination. The next three-and-a-half lines mime the fragmented and undirected way imposed circumstances are mediated in her receptive consciousness, beautifully showing us how she experiences events in this stage of her overwhelming isolation and unhappiness. Chaucer then leaves the original present participle ('Retornyng') in a strikingly incomplete form for he does not give it the subject noun or pronoun (Criseyde, or she) we expect. Instead he begins a new sentence, 'and thus bygan . . .'. This also enacts the elimination of anything we could readily define as volitional powers at this stage of her life, as Chaucer decides not to let her feature as the direct initiating subject in a sentence involving agent, verb (describing the process), effected participants and results.

In the new sentence he strengthens this impression by presenting her 'purpos for to dwelle' in a way which again suggests that mental events now seem to happen *to* her, or *in* her, rather than to be the outcome of her mental activity: 'and thus bygan to brede/The cause whi' – by choosing the infinitive 'to brede' the poet once more removes any specific agent from the process in question (*who* is breeding . . .), if anything implying that the fragmented events breed her purpose. We are left to realize that in cases such as this one can hardly say that the person made a decision with certain specifiable motives, for we are shown, in the minutest particulars of the poet's art, how the interactions between her desolate circumstances and her subjugated consciousness breed a daily state in which a great escape, a decisively rebellious act of will, was quite unimaginable.[23]

Chaucer also reveals wonderful comprehension and sympathy in his depiction of Criseyde's real misery at betraying Troilus, during the very processes out of which that betrayal emerges, allied to a simultaneous and pathetic, but authentic wish to move from the extremely unsatisfying life in which she is now immersed to one more structured by freely chosen fidelity:

> Ther made nevere woman moore wo
> Than she, whan that she falsed Troilus. . . .
> But syn I se ther is no bettre way,
> And that to late is now for me to rewe,
> To Diomede algate I wol be trewe.
> (*T & C*, V, ll. 1052–3, 1069–71; see 1051–85)

This desperate fantasy is poignant, for the fine relationship that we have just followed is not the kind that is easily replaced, and the new man, with his 'hook and lyne' is using her for his present gratification in a context where the word 'trewe' could have little meaning. The sadness here, the power and universal relevance of this psychological realization should never be lost by attempting to collapse Chaucer's art into the conventional norms of medieval characterization and abstract moralism.

Criseyde's final appearance in the poem shows her using her genuine fears and miserable resignation in a letter designed to manipulate the sympathies of the lover she has now betrayed, perhaps even to keep him hanging on to her a little longer (V, ll. 1590–631, especially ll. 1618–20, 1627). In Troilus' response, free of all the earlier egotistical histrionics, Chaucer manifests the quality of love and commitment that this relationship has developed in his own being:

> Thorugh which I se that clene out of youre mynde
> Ye han me cast; and I ne kan nor may
> For al this world, withinne myn herte fynde
> To unloven yow a quarter of a day!

In corsed tyme I born was, weilaway,
That yow, that doon me al this wo endure,
Yet love I best of any creature!
(*T & C*, V, ll. 1695–701)

Troilus still cannot see the primary role of his own culture and social organization in creating the present tragedy, and so he perceives Criseyde's actions in a very different perspective from the one open to Chaucer's readers. But this only increases the intensity of his admirable commitment to Criseyde. This evokes the real possibilities and achievements of human relationships, even as it makes us grieve over the intolerable pressures to which they may be subjected and their frequent, painful failures. It is Pandarus who represents this society's deepest conventional wisdom in the tragedy it has prepared. Having treated Criseyde as an amiable creature whose sole object in life should be the gratification of his male friend, he now turns on her in blind outrage:[24]

What sholde I seyen? I hate, ywys, Cryseyde;
And, God woot, I wol hate hire evermore! . . .
And fro this world almyghty God I preye
Delivere hire soon! I kan namore seye.
(*T & C*, V, ll. 1732–3, 1742–3)

Chaucer's own work should have delivered us not only from any such reaction, quite lacking in reflexive imagination and psychological insight, but also from all abstract moralization which comfortably ignores social realities and cultural controls. In doing so, one of its central achievements was the poetic evocation of a social psychology which grasped complex interactions between individual consciousness, action, conflicting ideologies and social organization.

At the end of the poem Criseyde is left in the Greek camp, Chaucer's study of this stage of her development left as he sets about closing his work. The relationship between the supreme achievements we have been following and the lines following the death of Troilus is primarily one of contrast in poetic modes and styles of thought, as Elizabeth Salter and others have maintained. The very last function they can serve is to provide an authoritative and relevant lesson in how to read *Troilus and Criseyde* and extract its meaning.[25] For these lines (ll. 1807–55) are marked by a simple and unreflexive assertiveness which is the antithesis of the modes created in the treatment of Criseyde and the antithesis of the complex moral thought integral to these modes. This trait is exemplified in the conventional observations the 'goost' of Troilus allegedly makes (ll. 1807–25). From the eighth sphere he begins to 'despise' our world as 'al vanite' compared with heavenly felicity and 'dampned al oure werk that foloweth so/The blynde lust, the which that may nat laste'. The language is so generalized that within its terms one could not discriminate between Troilus and Diomede, between Criseyde and, say, Damyan in the *Merchant's Tale* – 'al' would be despicable 'vanite', all damned as 'blynde': such static generalizations are substituted for the subtle realizations of human processes we have followed through the work. There is no attempt to create any poetic specificity for the abstraction 'felicite' leaving it instead as a generalization which could be filled with Boethian, epicurean or other contents. Even the instruction to set 'al oure herte on heven' fails to become more than a conventionally pietistic gesture, since it does not begin to notice the problematic nature of this recommendation for the incarnate beings inevitably engaged in social practices which make the question asked in *The Canterbury Tales* a serious religious one: 'How shal the world be served?' (*General Prologue*, l. 187). No more than *Piers Plowman* does Chaucer's work encourage glib answers.

Similar comments are called for by the language and moral postures of the incantatory stanzas about the rather vague end of Troilus, pagan religions, 'thise werecched worldles appetites' and the homiletic address to the youth of today, instructing them to return from 'worldly vanite' to love of Christ (ll. 1828–55).[26] Even some of the same phrases used by the 'goost' of Troilus reappear and when the speaker typically insists that we should think 'al nys but a faire/This world, that passeth soone as floures faire,' he fails to notice some very relevant aspects of the image. If life is a medieval 'faire' then we are the producers, the buyers and sellers in a community without which there would be neither individuality nor human spirituality, for we are not ghosts but incarnate beings whose choices and actions are necessarily and as profoundly affected by the 'faire' as were Criseyde's.[27] Speakers who exclude this awareness from their own discourse exclude a reflexivity which proved essential to Chaucer's imagination. It is natural for a Christian to invoke Christ as the supreme model of faithful love:

> For he nyl falsen no wight, dar I seye,
> That wol his herte al holly on hym leye.
> And syn his best to love is, and most meke,
> What nedeth feynede loves for to seke?
>
> (*T & C*, V, ll. 1845–8)

Far from suggesting that we humans need and should engage with feigned and imperfect earthly versions of divine love, as some have supposed, it puts forward the incoherent idea that people who want stable, mutual and committed relationships deliberately seek 'feynede loves', asking why they do so. Yet the poem has just created an example of human and thoroughly sexual love that is not 'feyned' but so great and powerful that even when Criesyde proves unable to withstand the pressures she is subjected to, after the Trojan parliament trades her to the Greeks, Troilus' love for her never changes, becoming a memorable image of commitment and fidelity attainable in heterosexual (and non-Christian relationships). The invocation just quoted is also inadequate in religious terms. The question about why people seek 'feynede loves' when a true and faithful love that is totally satisfying awaits them, could stimulate real and troubling religious questions – ones concerning the corruption of the will, the individual's ability to commit himself 'al holly' to God, predestination, grace.[28] Of course, *Troilus and Criseyde* is not *Piers Plowman*, and this was not the place to pursue such questions, but my point is that the mode fails to present them as problematic questions, proving as superficial in its religious orientation as in its psychological, moral and literary directions. It is Chaucer's own poetic processes which teach us to see the inadequacies in style of thought and language in the closing lines, however well they may fit conventional didactic and moralistic formulations. It is not a language for serious moral, religious or psychological inquiry, not the mode in which Chaucer undertook his creative exploration of Criseyde.

In my own view there are two plausible accounts of why Chaucer composed the closing lines in the manner I have outlined. The first has been splendidly explained by Monica McAlpine:[29] the statements of the 'goost' of Troilus are partial and limited, a further example of his personal development and vision. To emphasize the lack of definitive authority here the poet refuses to speculate about God's judgment of Troilus and does not give him any clear location in the after-life to which he refers (l. 1827). The other stanzas are also treated as the utterance of a speaker other than the poet – the narrator. Chaucer uses this figure to exhibit the conventional wishes for clear-cut closures and simple and fixed judgments on the poem's characters and the issues they raise. He himself undermined these aspirations (while acknowledging their importance in his culture), and carefully established the limitations and the inevitable partiality of human knowledge and fictions. He wished to suggest that all attempts at total and impersonal judgment will, like the narrator's in the face of *Troilus and Criseyde*, prove hopelessly inadequate to the complex processes being judged. As the final stanza of the poem reminds us, there is a divine perspective on human life which is inaccessible to us and demands that our own approach be self-reflexive and open-ended.

The second plausible account has been fruitfully discussed by Elizabeth Salter and Alfred David:[30] Chaucer, the Christian poet, was deeply disturbed by the implications of his own work and felt the need to retreat into a more affirmative position with regard to conventional forms of moral judgment and didactic discourses concerning human and sexual love, even though his own poetic processes quite superseded such forms. In this account the closing lines represent understandable and powerfully felt divisions within the writer's own imagination and intellect.

The first account comes close to the comments on Chaucer's reflexive and critical treatment of the *Parson's Tale*, in the last chapter, the second to those made on the pressures and fears which divided Chaucer from his own creative achievements in his 'retractions'. I believe that both accounts of the conclusion to *Troilus and Criseyde* can be convincingly maintained through analysis of the text and attention to the writer's cultural and ideological situation. If a reader decides between them this will probably be based on his overall version of narrative voices in the poem and his views about the development of Chaucer's vision at the time he completed *Troilus and Criseyde*. What I wish to stress here is that his poetic exploration of the complex and fluid interactions between individual and circumstances, his grasp of the real contexts and processes of human choice, makes it impossible for an attentive reader to go on repeating conventional formulae about unambiguous vices and virtues propagated in the mass of contemporary homiletic work. This was inevitably disturbing to traditional and seemingly uncomplicated certainties as it works to subvert all absolutes and static finalities. Leszek Kolakowski's essay on the antagonism between what he calls 'the priest and the jester' seems relevant:[31]

> The priest is the guardian of the absolute; he sustains the cult of the final and the obvious as acknowledged by and contained in tradition. The jester is he who moves in good society without belonging to it, and treats it with impertinence; he who doubts all that appears self-evident . . . to unveil the nonobvious behind the obvious, the nonfinal behind the final.

Chaucer (unlike many of his exegetes) was, in the sense Kolakowski expounds, a jester rather than a priest or inquisitor. Nevertheless, as Kolakowski adds, 'there are more priests than jesters at a king's court, just as there are more police-men than artists in his realm,' and the poet must have realized the unsettling implications of his own profoundly social psychology and imaginative ethical thought, the disturbing implications of being a jester in a culture where priests and intellectual policemen played a major role. But as for Criseyde, woman in society and woman in love, Chaucer was neither of her party without knowing it, nor one of the conventional moralists' party against her. Instead this jester at a king's court developed a complex, profoundly dialectical grasp of the interactions between individual and society which is subversive of all priestly absolutes, and which is as meaningful today as it was in his own culture.

CHAPTER 6

Chaucer: Love, Sex and Marriage

For no effect of tyranny can sit more heavy on the Commonwealth, then this houshold unhappiness on the family. . . . Love in marriage cannot live nor subsist, unless it be mutual; and where love cannot be, there can be left of wedlock nothing, but the empty husk of an outside matrimony; as undelightfull and unpleasing to God, as any other kind of hypocrisie.

Milton, *Doctrine and Discipline of Divorce*, 2nd, 1644

Among unequals what society
Can sort, what harmony or true delight?
Milton, *Paradise Lost*, VIII, ll. 383–4

In *The Canterbury Tales* Chaucer's fascination with the interactions between individual being, predominant social practices and received ideas focussed on those living within the institution of marriage. Here I think we will respond to the poetry more fully if we recall some basic points about marriage in Chaucer's period. Marriage was primarily a transaction organized by males to serve economic and political ends, with the woman treated as a useful, child-bearing appendage to the land or goods being exchanged. As Eileen Power wrote, '"Let me not to the marriage of true fief admit impediments" may be said to have been the dominating motive of the lord with son or daughter or ward to marry. Weddings were often arranged and sometimes solemnized when children were in their cradles. . . . Grown women could also be summarily married off.' Once married, the woman lost any economic rights and possessions she had before marriage, and while there may perhaps be some signs that peasant women could have been in a slightly better position in relation to their own social groups than other women, the basic structure of the institution was the same throughout society.[1]

Conventional male attitudes to this institution, and the place of women in it, are well displayed in two works contemporary with Chaucer, the book translated by Eileen Power under the title *The Goodman of Paris*, and the *Book of the Knight of the Tower*. The former was written by a man of over sixty to his fifteen-year-old wife, and includes a host of exempla to show the woman her duties of unquestioning submission and minute attention to the husband's every need, while insisting she should love him devotedly. The following is a representative illustration:[2]

> For to show what I have said, that you ought to be very privy and loving with your husband, I set here a rustic ensample. . . . Of domestic animals you shall see how that a greyhound or mastiff or little dog, whether it be on the road, or at table, or in bed, ever keepeth him close to the person from whom he taketh his food and leaveth all the others and is distant and shy with them; and if the dog is afar off, he always has his heart and his eye upon his master; even if his master whip him and throw stones at him, the dog followeth, wagging his tail and lying down before his master to appease him, and through rivers, through woods, through thieves and through battles followeth him.

This sentiment is perfectly conventional and it is worth noting how it lacks any reflexivity, how closed it is against any critical voice. There could be no place here for suggestions that 'love' and 'maistrie' might actually be incompatible; no place for reflection on the implications of treating another human being as a dog ('in bed' too); no pause to wonder what kind of 'love' such a relationship could generate. Chaucer would subject this male voice of 'reason' to some profound poetic scrutiny, however complacently entrenched it was in his culture.

The Knight of the Tower demonstrates just how well entrenched it was, for he assumes that the best attitudes are utter subservience on the part of women and unquestioning domination on the part of men, supported by male aggression and physical violence towards women in a culture of discourse quite alien to self-criticism or reflexivity. One typical example of the work's outlook is its account of a wife who answered her husband back: in response, he 'smote her with his fyste to the erthe, and smote her with his foote on the vysage so that he brake her nose by which she was ever after al disfygured. And so by her ryotte and ennoye she gat her a croked nose, moche evyll.'[3] The celebration of male violence at the slightest challenge to the male ego permeates the work, as does a total lack of reflexivity. Here, for instance, he does not look at his own language and wonder whether *riot* is a proper description for a wife answering her husband, or whether it might not more appropriately apply to a man beating up a woman, or even to an author who lauds such an action; he never questions the morality of the husband nor does he recall texts like St Paul's, 'Husbands, love your wives even as Christ also loved the church, and gave himself for it' (Eph. 5:25). All talk about 'love' in the Knight's text actually turns out to be the male's demand for a totally unquestioning obedience from the female he owns. In return, the man would abstain from violence towards the woman.

Mention of St Paul may encourage readers to wonder whether Christian teaching about marriage significantly altered this situation. The answer is that it offered no serious challenge to the situation outlined, and did much to sanctify these attitudes. Readers concerned to follow the theologians' ideas about marriage, love and sex are fortunate in having the fine study by J. T. Noonan, *Contraception: A History of its Treatment by the Catholic Theologians and Canonists*. What this demonstrates exhaustively is that orthodox Christian tradition consistently separated love both from sexuality and the primary purposes of marriage.[4] Procreation and the avoidance of adultery were the primary purposes of marriage. Noonan observes the influence of the social structure, patriarchalism and dominant male attitudes in shaping theologians' ideas, and concludes that, 'The failure to incorporate love into the purpose of marital intercourse was largely a failure of theological analysis. The failure occurred in a society whose mating customs made procreation, not love, the most prominent value of marriage.' H. A. Kelly, examining the purposes theologians and canonists attributed to Christian marriage concludes likewise that 'mutual love between the spouses is notably absent from their lists'.[5] In attempting to understand the depth of Chaucer's exploration of love, sex and marriage we need to bear in mind the orthodox religious tradition as well as social realities he knew so well.

On top of the theological failure Noonan describes, we should also remember the very positive contribution orthodox Christian ideas made to the traditional downgrading and oppression of women celebrated by the Knight of the Tower or the Goodman of Paris. The Wife of Bath has an excellent knowledge of the anti-feminist tradition sponsored by the medieval church. St Thomas Aquinas was quite orthodox in following St Augustine's assertion that the only point God could have had in making woman was as a procreating instrument, 'since man can be more effectively helped by another man in other works':

> As regards the individual nature, woman is defective and misbegotten, for the active force in the male seed tends to the production of a perfect likeness in the masculine sex; while the production of a woman comes from defect in the active force or from some material indisposition, or even from some external influence; such as that of a south wind, which is moist . . . .

So spoke 'auctoritee'. With statements like this, backed up as objective doctrine by the church, went a web of traditional and vulgar forms of male double-think and double standards, from which we are still far from free.[6] The orthodox teaching on the sacrament of Christian marriage thus contributed to the disastrous separation of love from sex and marriage, the downgrading of women who did not choose the path of virginity, and the unreflexive male prejudices pervading the culture.

Before moving on to Chaucer's work we should acknowledge the existence of important counter-tendencies to the dominant ideologies and practices we have sketched.[7] Probably the most relevant of these were being developed in courtly literature of the high and later Middle Ages. Scholars such as J. Frappier and M. Lazar have shown how the oppositions between *fin' amors* and marriage in earlier troubadour poetry were gradually superseded in courtly literature of northern France in the later twelfth century, a process involving transformation of both *fin' amors* and images of marriage. The history is a complicated one, still being written, but it seems clear enough that Chrétien de Troyes was the outstanding artist in this development. The incorporation of passionate, non-coercive mutual and sexually vital love into marriage was a vision which obviously contradicted the power relations of the period and the dominant attitudes to marriage and women propagated by laymen and ecclesiastics alike. What Chrétien did was to give form and voice to new aspirations very much in conflict with established realities.[8] In doing this he (with those who followed him) was putting art to one of the great roles it has continually played, giving expression to wishes, experiences and beliefs which go against the predominant values and sentiments of the established culture, creating visions of alternative forms of life and relationship. Such art may even lead people to see themselves, their relationships and their culture in new ways.

Unlike Criseyde, the Wife of Bath may seem to resist the prevailing order with abundant energy and dedication. Her project for survival is to *make* spaces in the culture for her own energies to find expression. She seems to rebel against conventional controls and the attitudes we have outlined, for which she has been severely chastized by sermonizing and would-be 'historical' critics.'[9] Yet while Chaucer presents her rebellion as real, he simultaneously discloses the complexities involved in opposing dominant social and ideological forms. He dramatizes the affirmation of the established culture in her negation of it, creating an aesthetic representation of the way subordinate groups or individuals may so internalize the assumptions and practices of their oppressors that not only their daily strategies of survival but their very acts of rebellion may perpetuate the outlook against which they rebel. Their penetration of dominant ideology and practice is distorted and displaced into a significant conformity with the established values which they are opposing. In grasping and embodying this dialectical process Chaucer was meditating on his own patriarchal culture, its values, its organization of love, sexuality and marriage.

Before the publication of Alfred David's fine study of Chaucer, *The Strumpet Muse*, one would have had to argue this case about her rebellion and conformity at some length, but his chapter on the Wife makes this unnecessary. He shows how the Wife's attitudes to marriage 'are the sound economic ones of her time', and that having penetrated the connection between male domination and economic power she sets about gaining control of property in approved male fashion. She states that in her culture 'al is for to selle' (l. 418) and so, in Alfred David's words 'regards "love" like any other commodity to be bought and sold in the world's market place'. In these terms she succeeds in the conventional 'business of marriage'. The dialectic mentioned in my previous paragraph is very evident here as she succeeds by accepting the reduction of self and body to the status of a commodity to be bought by males, by accepting the reduction of female sexuality to an instrument of manipulation, control and punishment, powers partly retained even when she has been purchased. In her first four marriages she accepts that the institution cannot be the place for loving, affectionate relations. She does reject the traditional role of the passive and devotedly servile wife (her rebellion), but only to take on the traditional and culturally celebrated role of the domineering, egotistic husband (her affirmation of the culture) – 'myself have been the whippe' (l. 175). The *Wife's Prologue* provides real insight to the pervasiveness and nature of the dominant culture and male ideology, something that has been overlooked by her moralistic antagonists.[10]

The issue of procreation and marital sex is another area where the presence of rebellion and conformism is striking. The Wife's text includes some memorable celebrations of her wish for sexual fulfilment and happiness, something always condemned by authoritative Christian tradition, as the Wife knows very well (ll. 37–8, 614). She makes it clear that it is sexual pleasure she relishes as a good in itself. The delights she recounts from her fifth marriage. 'in oure bed he was so fresh and gay', have nothing to do with procreation of the official Christian duty of pleasurelessly 'paying the debt' of intercourse to deliver the incontinent spouse from adultery (ll. 508–14; see also ll. 35–46, 146–50, 469–70, 617–18). Indeed, Joseph Mogan, in an article on 'Chaucer and the *Bona Matrimonii*', observed that 'Alison is not drawn as trespassing a given theological framework but as advocating a new theology entirely, and in this she is much ahead of her time.'[11] Nevertheless, when she discusses God's purposes in making sexual organs (ll. 11–34) she begins by failing to distinguish the different potentials of sexual organs and labels them members 'of generacion' (l. 116). This classification undermines her case before her argument is even launched, revealing the power of 'auctoritee' in moulding her perceptions and reasoning about her 'experience', for there she has lived through very definite distinctions between dutiful wifely copulation and the kind of joyful love-making she describes in her fifth marriage. She is quick to mock those who claim sexual organs 'were maked for purgacioun/Of uryne' or as markers of gender, appealing to the 'experience' of sex (ll. 118–24). Yet Chaucer again shows received 'auctoritee' taking her over, and makes the very syntax enact the processes of consciousness involved:

> So that the clerkes be nat with me wrothe,
> I sey this, that they maked ben for bothe,
> This is to seye, for office, and for ese
> Of engendrure, ther we nat God displease.
> (*W of B Pr.*, ll. 125–8)

The first two lines take up her appeal to 'experience' against 'the clerkes' and promise to state her own meaning explicitly. The next line seems to fulfil this promise 'they maked ben . . . for ese'. Here, we feel, the rebellious Wife makes her stand. Despite the opening classification, she now places sheer *ese* as one of God's aims in giving humans their sexuality. The 'clerkes' are put in their place. But not for long, since the next line forces us to re-interpret and qualify 'ese' in a strictly orthodox sense – 'ese/Of engendrure'. The Wife's 'experience' of sexual pleasure as an end in itself within her fifth marriage collapses into the traditional clerkly orthodoxy regarding sexual intercourse. After this it is no surprise to see her move on to the second orthodox purpose of marriage, according to what 'men . . . in hir bookes sette': to make 'paiement' of the marital 'dette' (ll. 129–32). Nor is it a surprise that she concludes with further confirmation of the ideological orthodoxies against which she is overtly in rebellion: 'Thanne were they maad . . . To purge uryne, and eek for engendrure' (ll. 113–14). In fact, this passage witnesses to the difficulties of going beyond received paradigms and orthodoxies within received concepts and vocabulary. The result is again an affirmation of the traditional and orthodox failure to integrate love, sex and marriage.

Even her rebellious experiments with sexuality freed from the corrupting economic determinants of the medieval marital institution show the effects of orthodox ideology, for here too she perpetuates and mirrors central aspects of the tradition she opposes. As the latter separated love and sexuality, downgrading and dehumanizing sexual relations, just so the Wife presents her own sexuality in terms of an impersonal force and a sexual organ quite abstracted from the complete human being, body and soul:

> Ye shul have queynte right ynogh at eve.
> He is to greet a nygard that wolde werne

A man to lighte a candle at his lanterne;
He shal have never the lasse light, pardee. . . .
I koude noght withdrawe
My chambre of Venus from a good felawe.
(*W of B Pr.*, ll. 332–5, 617–18)

This fragmentation and depersonalization of sex separates it from any constant and total human love, and is actually the very image of orthodox ecclesiastical tradition, again something the Wife's modern antagonists have overlooked. It contrasts absolutely with the committedly personal love uniting all aspects of the individual which we saw in *Troilus and Criseyde* and which Chrétien located in marriage (*Yvain*), suggesting a real alternative to both dominant tradition and the Wife's perpetuation of it in her libertarian rebellion.

Of course, the Wife also has a complex self-awareness (as in her moving meditation of her past and present, ll. 469–79), as well as the generosity and craving for love described by Alfred David. Before leaving her, we will look at the final recorded marriage in which she attempted to continue her rebellion in a manner which could unite what medieval Christianity and society sundered – love, sexual happiness and marriage (ll. 508–14, 585–602). My fifth husband, she notes 'I took for love and no richesse' (l. 526). Through her previous marriages and her successful 'cloothe-makyng' she had accumulated enough money to exercise her free choice in a way the culture made impossible for younger women. This is a most promising though inevitably belated development. But Chaucer's imagination was so engaged with the realities of his own culture in relation to the Wife's consciousness and actions that he did not allow the fifth marriage to achieve any straightforward transcendence of these realities. First, as Alfred David noticed, she continues to envisage it in terms of the market, human relations seen as the exchange of commodities (ll. 515–24), however incompatible this is with the attempt to deliver herself and marriage from the market.[12] In this way she again perpetuates normal outlooks and practices. Second, Chaucer shows the powerful presence of the dominant culture she wishes to oppose in the way it has shaped the man's expectations and values. These, the poet conveys, are not admirable. The Wife, now accepting standard practice, hands over 'al the lond and fee' (l. 630) to the young husband, although neither she nor the reader can avoid suspecting that his motives include the mercenary ones around which medieval marriage was constructed.[13]

Furthermore, the male reacts to the Wife's love and generosity as a conventional domineering husband, the sort admired by the Knight of the Tower (ll. 632–85). He tries to enforce his rejection of mutuality by repetitive and lengthy appeals to the anti-feminist tradition (ll. 641–787), which Chaucer now satirizes and exposes as the superficial product of the unreflexive male ego. Even the form of speech embodies the tyrannical norms it assumes by precluding dialogue and any concern for anyone but the speaking self. Chaucer, a poet whose imagination was exceptionally reflexive and able to generate a multiplicity of perspectives, captures the one-dimensional folly of the highly respectable tradition Jankyn deploys.[14] The Wife now inevitably fights back using her experience to regain economic and psychological control over the man who would bully and subject her (ll. 788–822). In her rebellion Chaucer has her once more perpetuate and illustrate the male-governed norms of the culture and their structuring of marriage. So total is the continuity with the dominant culture of discourse that she refers to her marital role in the traditional imagery which presented one partner as a human rider, the other (traditionally the woman, of course) as an animal to be ridden and controlled by the bridle. The Wife merely inverts the traditional positions within the structure of domination as she gains 'bridel', 'governance of hous and lond' and 'al the soveraynetee' (ll. 811–18).[15] Too many scholars have attacked the woman here while ignoring how Chaucer has enacted a highly critical and dramatic reflection on orthodox marital ideologies and practices showing us how difficult it is to transcend them even when they are experienced as gravely inadequate.

Chaucer's critical and reflexive meditations on medieval marriage also inform the *Merchant's Tale*. Scholars have tended to treat its central relationship as a gross perversion of the admirable medieval sacrament and institution of Christian marriage, to see May and Januarie as extravagantly corrupt individuals who cast no light on the standard assumptions and practices of Chaucer's world from which they are, allegedly, gross deviants.[16]

But as Chaucer explored cultural norms through the *Wife of*

Bath's Prologue so he did in the *Merchant's Tale*, creating an imaginative vision which disclosed the structures and human consequences of the medieval institution of marriage and the ideologies which legitimated it, religious and profane.

The 'worthy knight' around whom the tale evolves is an elderly Christian gentleman whom we join as he is deciding to get married.[17] At once Chaucer evokes the economic nexus which both moulded medieval marriage and was supported by it. The old man 'lyved in greet prosperitee' and determined to use his 'tresor' to get a young and fair wife 'on' whom he might enjoyably beget an heir, ensuring his property stayed in his own family (ll. 1245–73, 1437–40). When Januarie proceeds to purchase himself a wife we must not assume he is being unusual or idiosyncratic. Chaucer images the medieval marriage market in action, displaying how old men like the Goodman of Paris could acquire brides. If readers take Januarie's conduct here as a perverse aberration from a decent norm they not only manifest unnecessary ignorance about Chaucer's society but misread the tale in a way which will consistently overlook the powerful critical dimensions of the poet's imagination engaging with his own world. Even Justinus, who has received a good press from scholars, actually shares many commonplace assumptions with the old knight. The counsel he offers is obsessed with material possession and his whole approach to marriage is centred on his acceptance that it is another business transaction. He perceives individuals in terms of land, cattle and goods, viewing personal commitment purely as a transference of property rights (ll. 1523–9). He wants a wife to be a good and safe investment for the man, telling Januarie to set up an inquiry into her wealth, attitude to property and temper. He has nothing to say about love, mutual responsibility or the self-sacrifice St Paul recommended to husbands (ll. 1530–3). The 'Justice' Justinus counsels is no more than the pragmatic wisdom of the market-place allied to warnings about Januarie's sexual decline which seem to echo his own experience (ll. 1555–65).

Chaucer then represents the processes through which the knight decided who to bid for on the marriage market, a process of 'Heigh fantasye and curious bisynesse':

> Many fair shap and many a fair visage
> Ther passeth thurgh his herte nyght by nyght,

As whoso tooke a mirour, polisshed bryght,
And sette it in a commune market-place,
Thanne sholde he se ful many a figure pace
By his mirour. . . .

(*Merchant*, ll. 1580–5)

This reveals the individual's most intimate fantasies and his very forms of perception being shaped by his milieu and the practices and outlook it encourages. The economic sphere and the sexual are brought together in the passage as we see how the market and the attitudes it sponsors can be totally internalized. Women are reduced to desirable commodities which the male can purchase and, although this is Januarie's 'fantasye and curious bisynesse', we should not miss its more than idiosyncratic nature in Chaucer's culture, as the Wife of Bath's text also reminds us.

Once he has decided on the woman he wants the old knight uses well qualified friends who understand the workings of the marriage market:

They wroghten so, by sly and wys tretee,
That she, this mayden, which that Mayus highte,
As hastily as evere that she myghte,
Shal wedded be unto this Januarie.
I trowe it were to longe yow to tarie,
If I yow tolde of every scrit and bond
By which that she was feffed in his lond.

(*Merchant*, ll. 1692–8)

This is explicitly presented as a socially accepted and perfectly normal procedure. The males organize a market transaction in which woman is a commodity and marriage the particular institution which will secure the transaction, stabilize the inheritance of property and, hopefully in the purchaser's eyes, allow the useful enjoyment of his new possession. Even the grammar of the passage mimes the woman's helpless passivity in the face of these customary negotiations – she 'shal wedded be', in the passive tense indeed. Still too many scholars vent moral indignation which only attacks individuals while remaining silent about the powerful social forces which constrained and partially limited the choices, relationships and perception of people in that culture. For instance, one scholar recently accused May of 'a willing prostitution'. Few statements about the text could be less justified, as I have noted, but it illustrates a common unwillingness to acknowledge that most (probably all) marriages in the middle and upper social groups were transactions in which human beings, their labour-power and their sexual-power were sold. In such a situation it would make more sense to call medieval parents, guardians and those holding rights over wards coercive but respectable pimps than to call May, and the women she represents 'willing' prostitutes.[18]

As if to ensure we do not miss the normality and culturally sanctioned nature of Januarie's conduct Chaucer moves us straight from the market to the church, from the social realities of marriage to the mediator of grace, doctrine and the saving sacraments, one of which is marriage:

> But finally ycomen is the day
> That to the chirche bothe be they went
> For to receyve the hooly sacrement.
> Forth comth the preest, with stole aboute his nekke,
> And bad hire be lyk Sarra and Rebekke
> In wysdom and in trouthe of mariage;
> And seyde his orisons, as is usage,
> And croucheth hem, and bad God sholde hem blesse,
> And made al siker ynogh with hoolynesse.
>
> (*Merchant*, ll. 1700–8)

This transition is most significant for it embodies the absorption of the church in the economic fabric and prevailing social practices of the world, even where these were in plain conflict with elements of its public doctrine. My impression is that the major implications of Chaucer's decision to emphasize the church giving its unqualified blessing to this marriage, 'as is usage', have been missed. The poet examines the church's use of its spiritual and material influence over individual Christians. In his text the church is clearly decisive in turning the exploitationary and loveless purchase of a young person into a more than respectable union, a sacramental one. Chaucer completes this picture by telling us that when the appalled bride is brought to bed 'as stille as stoon' (again stressing the situation is imposed on her), it is the priest who blesses the bed in which this marital union, this sacramental mystery of Christ, and his church, is to be consummated (ll. 1818–19). In the context, the assertion that the priest 'made al siker ynogh with hoolynesse' (ll. 1708) works in two directions. As most commentators state, it ironically exposes Januarie's delusions, his misunderstanding of the Christian dogma that enjoyment of marital sex is sinful, either venial or mortal, thus connecting it with his bizarre claim that a man cannot hurt himself with his own knife (an image discussed towards the end of chapter 4). But the second direction is at least as important, and it works against the priest and the church he represents. *Piers Plowman* and the *Pardoner's Prologue* showed sacraments becoming part of a chronically simoniac set of practices in which they were exchanged for money or land, their effects purchased in a market exchange. In this situation people could very easily be led to believe that the sacramental ritual did indeed make 'al siker ynogh with hoolynesse', thus having some of their most vicious propensities legitimated and encouraged by the church. We note the priest offers no challenge to Januarie whatsoever, and makes no effort to ascertain whether May, 'as stille as stoon', genuinely had the inward consent theoretically necessary for a valid sacramental marriage. In this silence Chaucer mirrors the prevailing relationships between leading secular groups and the orthodox church, as well as the latter's inability to transform practices and attitudes in which it was fully immersed.[19] Thinking about the church's role here, we may also see how it recalls what Noonan and Kelly described as its 'failure to incorporate love into the purpose of marital intercourse', the absence of 'mutual love between the spouses' in theologians' and canonists' lists of the chief ends of marital union.[20] The fragmentation of love, marriage and sexuality in dominant and traditional ideology had its counterpart in the relationships experienced by individuals, as Chaucer's poetry continues to reveal.

For Januarie, the wife he has acquired only exists to serve his ego, a totally obedient servant, housekeeper and nurse with the added ability to provide sexual gratification and heirs. His outlook is an ordinary male one, but Chaucer now looks closely at some of the forms of relationship which emerge from it and the institution of marriage, using his art to make us engage with the human consequences of the established realities. Januarie approaches sexual intercourse as a vehicle in which the male ego can confirm its own power in a self-gratifying consumption of the 'yong flessh', 'the tendre veel' recently acquired. Like the orthodox Parson,

Januarie perceives male sexuality as a 'knyf', an area of being quite separate from love and affection.[21] The poetry which makes Januarie physically present is justly famous and has often been discussed (ll. 1821–50). Kisses, which should be expressions of love and friendship become acts of male violence over the subordinate female and we are made to envisage the specific effects of his 'thikke brustles . . . Lyke to the skyn of houndfyssh, sharp as brere' on her 'tendre face'. By choosing the verb 'rubbeth' to depict Januarie's kissings Chaucer suggests a deliberate intention to hurt May with this painful sandpapering, an impression which links his action both to his feelings at the feast, when 'he gan hire to manace' (l. 1752), and to the ensuing intercourse which he sees in terms of self-gratification which she must experience as an assault, an offence (ll. 1828–30, 1840). The last thing that Januarie considers, any more than the Knight of the Tower, is the woman's separate existence as a human being with her own wishes and thoughts. Such was the sacramental union imposed on May, a woman deprived of any possibilities of self-determination before marriage in a culture where there were few forces to encourage male self-criticism and affectionate awareness of the woman's feelings. Chaucer's art was actually one of the forces that did so, and he draws attention to this aspect in passing:

> But God woot what that May thoughte in hir herte,
> Whan she hym saugh up sittynge in his sherte,
> In his nyght-cappe, and with his nekke lene;
> She preyseth nat his pleyyng worth a bene.
>
> (*Merchant*, ll. 1851–4)

As readers have often observed, the horror of the performance to which May is subjected is conveyed through the poet's particularization of the knight's physical age as he croaks out his aubade, the slack skin shaking about his lean neck. But as important is the utterly complacent and unself-conscious attitude of the old knight, a complacency that is dependent on the support received from the major cultural institutions which licensed and blessed this union. Chaucer (for it is he, not the egotistic, self-deceiving and thoroughly foolish merchant 'narrator' (ll. 1213–39)), breaks off the description of the male to remind his readers of the feminine consciousness so habitually excluded from attention in the dominant traditions controlled, as the Wife of Bath objected, by men. What the woman 'thoughte in hir herte' was hardly a habitual male concern.[22] Having made this consideration prominent, he acknowledges the inevitable limitations of the comic modes in which he was working – 'God woot' what May thought, and the reader has been invited to empathize, but Chaucer himself passes on. He is not writing in a form which allows the detailed psychological exploration we followed in *Troilus and Criseyde*, and his interest in May is, of course, quite unlike his interest in Criseyde. Nevertheless, he leaves readers with no cause to make easy moralistic judgments about May which abstract her from the system which directly engenders the situation she must suffer.[23] Chaucer, we have seen, stresses that the husband's power of command over his wife's body is culturally approved, like her initial response – 'she obeyeth, be hire lief or looth' (ll. 1957–64; also ll. 1920–8, 2008).

When May seeks to alleviate her unhappy existence it is in an alternative relationship which will not overtly challenge the accepted power relations between husband and wife. The affair between her and Damyan can only be reasonably discussed when it is taken where Chaucer placed it, within the context of the marriage and the treatment May has received. The relationship is a *product* of the legitimate marriage. We may laugh at May's 'pitee' for the randy squire (ll. 1986–2000), but we read poorly if we stop at mockery and moralism. For however perverted by the culture in which she has been sold to Januarie, her aspirations include an aspect whose significance should not be ignored. It is made clear that she aspires to a relationship with a man of her own choice, one which transcends the economic and religious nexus in which she has been sold and violated:

> whom that this thyng displese,
> I rekke noght, for heere I hym assure
> To love hym best of any creature,
> Though he namoore hadde than his sherte.
> (*Merchant*, ll. 1983–5)

Of course, Chaucer shows us that May's partial resistance to her culture's values is deeply compromised by the situation in which she has learnt to exist. So her version of 'love', while it transcends the market, not surprisingly lacks any very articulate demand for close mutual affection and commitment. As for Damyan's outlook, we have no reason to believe it is any different to that of his old master, who had 'folwed ay his bodily delyt/On wommen, ther as was his appetyte' (ll. 1249–50). That May seeks for a day and place where 'she myghte unto *his* lust suffise' (l. 1999, my italics) suggests how the structures of domination and exploitation will be perpetuated in the society's extra-marital relationships, May accommodating to '*his* lust' just as she has had to do to her husband's. She is still very closely guarded by her legal owner, hardly propitious circumstances for developing a personal and loving relationship even if the mutual wishes were there. May is compelled to read and dispose of Damyan's letter 'in the pryvee' (ll. 1946–54) and the utterly joyless affair, lacking in any sensual fulfilment whatsoever, has to be hurriedly consummated in a tree guarded by her husband embracing its trunk in a grotesquely apt masturbatory gesture (ll. 2330–53). That the alternative relationship is thus consummated within the husband's arms is a beautifully chosen symbol of both its generation and gross limitation by the official marriage and its contexts.

I will conclude this discussion of the *Merchant's Tale* by looking at Januarie's use of the Canticle, or Song of Songs, before he enters his own enclosed garden.[24]

> 'Rys up, my wyf, my love, my lady free!
> The turtles voys is herd, my dowve sweete;
> The wynter is goon with alle his reynes weete.
> Com forth now, with thyn eyen columbyn!
> How fairer been thy brestes than is wyn!
> The gardyn is enclosed al aboute;
> Com forth, my white spouse! out of doute
> Thou hast me wounded in myn herte, O wyf!
> No spot of thee ne knew I al my lyf.
> Com forth, and lat us taken oure disport;
> I chees thee for my wyf and my confort.'
> Swiche olde lewed wordes used he.
> (*Merchant*, ll. 2138–49)

The contemptuous dismissal of Januarie's poem to 'my love, my lady free' as 'olde lewed wordes' is fully justified, for the same words in different contexts can take on very different meanings. Here the words of the Canticle do become 'lewed', as their appropriation by Januarie for his own marriage enacts a destruction of a poetry which could possibly be made a fitting celebration of love. The erotic Old Testament text had, of course, been subjected to one of the classic works of sublimating allegory in the tradition of Christian exegesis – for instance, when the text reads, 'my beloved put his hand through my opening [*misit manum suam per foramen*] and my bowels were moved at his touch', exegetes claimed that it expressed, allegorically, how the mystical bride (church, Virgin Mary, soul) opened the door of the heart (*not* what the Wife of Bath celebrated as her *bele chose*) to Christ or divine illumination (*not* to the sexual touches of the male). It is hardly surprising that the erotic power of the text survived its allegorization, simultaneously enjoyed and dissolved. Indeed, Augustine himself talks about his puzzlement at finding Christian doctrine 'sweeter' when he hears what he assumes to be 'the same thought expressed in plain words' without the richly erotic similes of the Old Testament work.[25] It is this combination which makes the text especially significant here.

For the unashamed and overtly carnal love was juxtaposed with a description of the union between Christ and the church (or Virgin Mary, or soul), while in Christian marriage the carnal union was said to involve a mysterious sacrament representing the union of Christ and his church (Eph. 5:23). The Old Testament text was thus potentially one which might possibly be used to bring together a language of carnal love and the religious dimensions attributed to Christian marital union, *potentially* able to overcome what Noonan documented so clearly as 'the failure to incorporate love into the purposes of marital intercourse'. In doing so it could possibly meet aspirations, evident in the later medieval world, to unite a love which involves the complete, incarnate human being with the institution of marriage.[26]

But these aspirations, still utopian in Chaucer's society, are disastrously negated by being used in the contexts of the Christian marriage around which the present tale develops. Here we should again be careful not to let our disgust at the old knight blind us to the representative aspects of what has happened. It is the current institution of marriage, blessed by the church, which has turned the woman from a 'lady free' into an object for egotistic male use, excluded the expression of love and mutual happiness from sexual union, downgraded sexual intercourse from being an act of love to something obscene and dirty, something only tolerable as a pleasureless and instrumental act for begetting children to serve God, or for preventing adultery. Any condemnation of the knight, as of May, remains superficial unless integrated with a response to Chaucer's specific and detailed exploration of the culture's disastrous fragmentation of love, sexuality and marriage, joined with its pervasive acceptance of capricious male power over women. In my own view, these explorations would not have been possible without the utopian aspirations around marriage mentioned on more than one occasion in this chapter. In the *Merchant's Tale* the utopian images of marriage as a paradise, marriage as a union which could fuse the erotic with the spiritual dimension of human love, these are appropriated and negated by Januarie. Such, Chaucer had to acknowledge, was the likely fate of the utopian vision in his world.[27] But without the vision Chaucer could never have attained sufficient detachment from dominant practices and ideologies to penetrate their contradictions and make them highly problematic topics in a thoroughly critical and creative poetic exploration.

In the *Franklin's Tale* Chaucer continued these explorations and now concentrated on the utopian perspective so essential to his own art. There has been much lively commentary on the tale, but most of it may be placed into two basic groups. One, stimulated by G. L. Kittredge's influential article on 'Chaucer's discussion of marriage' sees the Franklin joining mutual love and marriage in an unorthodox view which Chaucer *unequivocally* approved: 'the marriage of Arveragus and Dorigen was a brilliant success. Thus the whole [marriage] debate has been brought to a satisfactory conclusion.' The second, represented by D. W. Robertson, sees the poem as an elegant but conventional homiletic text defending the traditional 'hierarchy of marriage' (the one illustrated by the Knight of the Tower and the Goodman of Paris), satirizing the wish 'to maintain the delights of the God of Love in marriage', satirizing Arveragus, Dorigen, Aurelius, the magician and the Franklin who admires all these foolish and sinful characters.[28] The reading of the poem I wish to propose draws on both these conflicting schools.

I think Chaucer puts forward certain of his own aspirations for a marital institution in which the couple engage in non-coercive personal relations founded in a mutual love incorporating sexuality. In his historical context this comprises a utopian transcendence of conventional relationships based on an economic exchange and rampant male egotism sanctioned by secular and religious traditions. This is the aspect of the tale the scholars I have grouped with Kittredge have responded to with enthusiasm, and good reason. But their response has been distorted by a failure to recognize the utopian nature of these aspirations in that culture, and a failure to register Chaucer's extraordinarily reflexive mediation on major *problems* of such utopianism. Many manifestations of such problems in the tale have been noticed by those I group with Robertson, only they have been forced into a conventional homiletic framework which is not Chaucer's. The poet's own procedure was far from simple. His work included *both* cherished utopian aspirations, which constituted a fundamental perspective from which to develop a critique of the present, impoverished reality, *and* his imaginative scrutiny of such aspirations as they might fare in the present. The interaction between utopian perspective and the present was thus central to the poem's meaning. It is in this process that we should see the teller of the tale. He does not express Chaucer's 'final' views nor is he merely exposed by Parson-Chaucer to a damning orthodox and satiric homily.[29] The Franklin both gives voice at various points to important hopes the poet shares, and yet also serves as another means for the poet to examine significant problems in their present articulation.

The poem opens with a courtship which displays some striking features. There is absolutely no mention of land and money transactions so basic to medieval marriage, and although the woman has kindred who are socially much superior to the man, a fact which exerts some psychological pressure on him, she herself is apparently not subjected to normal controls imposed by male guardians concerned with land, money and family alliances.[30] Nor is there any sign that the knight has a thought for such normal concerns (ll. 729–42). In elaborating an image of a freely-chosen marriage between people rather than between fiefs, or between purchaser and commodity, the poet has bracketed the socio-economic nexus whose crucial effect on marriage he had examined. He also bracketed the institutionalized Christianity of his culture, the most authoritative sanctification of traditional male egotism in the domination of women, a most influential ideological force in downgrading sexuality and in resisting any incorporation of mutual love and its sexual expression into the prime purposes of marriage.[31] Bracketing specifically economic, patriarchal and Christian determinations over the institution of marriage made it possible to elaborate aspirations to mutual, non-coercive and loving relations while focussing on the difficulties concerning power, mutuality and an appropriate language of love which could persist even if the most obvious adversaries of the utopian imagination had been removed.

The husband expresses the aspiration to supersede the coercive and domineering norms sanctioned by the religious and profane circumstances Chaucer had already presented. He voluntarily renounces the traditional powers of coercion and bullying, believing that this act will lead to 'moore blisse' in their lives (ll. 744–9).[32] The narrator's enthusiasm is unqualified as he offers his own thoughts on this marriage (ll. 761–98). Appropriately, he draws heavily on explicitly utopian passages in the *Romance of the Rose*. There the Friend describes the Golden Age when there was no domination and private ownership of property and all 'know well the saying, neither lying nor foolish, that love and lordship never kept each other company'. Contrasting present marital relations he finds that now a husband habitually assumes a violent 'control over the body and possessions of his wife', treating her 'just as if she were his slave'. He comments: 'love must die when lovers want lordship. Love cannot endure or live if it is not free and active in the heart.'[33] Chaucer's narrator, rightly impressed by the lucid comments on 'love' and 'maistrie' in this section of the *Romance of the Rose* now wants the attitudes of the Golden Age to transform the present, inviting males to overcome the customary double-standards in their relations with women and to see that if someone is 'constreyned as a thral' the inevitable destruction of even the possibility of love is a loss for both the female-slave and the male-master (ll. 761–70). The passage is the result of Chaucer's own analysis of contemporary marriage and an expression, as Kittredge and others have maintained, of his own desires for higher forms of married relationships than those currently available. But, as Jean de Meun's poem observed, these are utopian desires. And here the poet begins to examine the problematic nature of such aspirations.

The narrator's language itself shows the depth of the difficulties faced as his statement unfolds:

freendes everych oother moot obeye. . . .
Thus hath she take hir servant and hir lord, –
Servant in love, and lord in mariage.
Thanne was he bothe in lordshipe and servage.
Servage? nay, but in lordshipe above,
Sith he hath bothe his lady and his love;
His lady, certes, and his wyf also,
The which that lawe of love acordeth to.
(*Franklin*, ll. 762, 792–8)

It seems the poet is revealing the absence of a common language for reciprocal and free relations. The idea of obedience, in the first line quoted, entails disparities of power in which one party has the position of giving commands, the other of obeying, something quite incompatible with the mutuality which the narrator is striving to define. Utopia has to be expressed in current language and concepts and these, we see, inevitably carry many elements of the conventional practice and assumptions the utopia must negate. In the remaining lines quoted, the narrator tries to graft the language of courtly male service of women on to the conventional language of male domination in marriage.[34] Trying to do so, he falsifies Arveragus' promise since this was to renounce 'maistrie' and the reality of lordship in marriage (ll. 745–52). He had *not* demanded to keep 'lordshipe', resting content with the mere 'name of soveraynetee' in deference to a non-utopian public's expectations. The narrator's language creates real confusion. The juxtaposition of 'servant' and 'lord', of 'love' and 'mariage' in these lines actually maintains the conventional splits so trenchantly criticized in the *Romance of the Rose* and the narrator's own use of that work (ll. 761–70). He seems to sense that his lines are becoming incoherent, for having asserted that the knight's status was both lordship and servitude, he corrects himself most revealingly: 'Servage? nay, but in lordshipe above.' But what 'lordshipe' is above remains obscure. Above 'servage'? Would this mean the male is more like a lord than a servant, more a traditional husband than Troilus? Or, and this reading seems to me definitely one of those required by the text, simply 'above' the woman? The narrator thus emerges with conventional norms against which Arveragus pledged himself, to the speaker's delight. On top of this, the lines collapse into a totally male-oriented utterance (he . . . his . . . his . . . His . . . his), while the last line displays a marked confusion. For which 'lawe of love' he now refers to, and which part of his statement he is now crediting, cannot be determined.

The narrator then moves into his story, leaving the difficulties to the readers. We should not miss their relevance to the poem and their significance in Chaucer's own continuous meditations on love, marriage and sexuality. The very confusions of the narrator exhibit fundamental problems in utopian thought in these areas, and are a dramatic product of Chaucer's reflexive attention to these aspects of his own imagination. The confusions stem from the narrator's perpetuation of received categories and the attitudes they bear while wishing to transcend them. But there may be no alternatives; utopian and critical thought may just have to accept the inevitability of some confusions and work through them as reflexively as possible. This is what the poet was doing in the *Franklin's Tale*.

In pursuing these difficulties he decided to focus on the consciousness of the couple trying to initiate this new, utopian marital union. Just as Criseyde internalized norms created by males and serving peculiarly male interests, so we find Dorigen explicitly offering to accept Arveragus as a traditionally dominant husband, even though in her case the coercive external forces have been expelled in the writer's utopian experiment (ll. 742–3). She then replies to the knight's alternative proposals in a similarly revealing way:

> Sire, sith of youre gentillesse
> Ye profre me to have so large a reyne, . . .
> Sire, I wol be youre humble trewe wyf;
> *(Franklin,* 11. 754–5, 758)

She uses the very image we found at the conclusion of the *Wife of Bath's Prologue*, when the Wife reported how she took 'al the bridel in myn hond', inverting traditional roles of husband and wife and keeping the structure of domination the traditional image mirrors so well.

Dorigen has the chance of a marriage in which both members regard each other as full human beings, yet she accepts it in an image which declares the thorough internalization of traditional marital outlooks and ideology. Her reply shows how females' self-images, their perception of their own identity, are profoundly determined by male ideas and myths concerning women. She sees herself as the animal, Arveragus as the human controller, albeit an unusually generous one. This traditional outlook emerges in her utterly dependent behaviour in the crisis she faces towards the end of the poem (ll. 1339–465), and it offers a fine insight into dangerous distortions of the utopian imagination which tends to underestimate the power of traditional ideologies and practices over human consciousness. The power persists even in changed circumstances when received patterns are neither imposed by an irresistible superior force nor in the interests of the group or individual in question. Chaucer built his awareness of this into his own poetic expression of utopian ideas he valued.

Chaucer's treatment of Arveragus manifests similar preoccupations, as we can see from his response when his weeping wife tells him her tale (ll. 1459–92). These responses have sharply divided scholars, those in the line of Kittredge offering fulsome praise: 'an extraordinarily wise and idealistic man' who shows his 'respect for his wife as an independent human being', one who is '"trouthe" incarnate'. Those who have opposed this reading, by no means only followers of Robertson, have assessed the knight's action in very different terms: 'Arveragus has no right to put Dorigen's "word" to Aurelius above their mutual love', while he is 'only enough of a husband to threaten his lady to be quiet about what she does "up peyne of deeth"'.[35] On this scene, A. T. Gaylord pointed out that Arveragus fails to utter a word about his wife's woe and that threatening someone 'up peyne of deeth' (l. 1481) is hardly surrendering lordship.[36] When we look closely at what Arveragus actually says I think we must agree that the criticisms of the knight are well-founded in Chaucer's text, although there is a need to offer a rather different explanation of the husband's behaviour:

> Ye shul youre trouthe holden, by my fay!
> For God so wisly have mercy upon me,
> I hadde wel levere ystiked for to be
> For verray love which that I to yow have,
> But if ye sholde youre trouthe kepe and save.
> Trouthe is the hyeste thyng that man may kepe' –
> But with that word he brast anon to wepe,
> And seyde, 'I yow forbede, up peyne of deeth,

That never, whil thee lastesth lyf ne breeth,
To no wight telle thou of this aventure, –
As I may best, I wol my wo endure –
Ne make no contenance of hevynesse,
That folk of yow may demen harm or gesse.'
(*Franklin*, ll. 1474–86)

What starts out most sharply from our present perspective is the emergence of a familiar male egotism and violence sanctified by traditional attitudes. Now it is exalted under the name of the 'verray love' supposedly fostered by the admirable utopian proposals Arveragus made to Dorigen, and allied to a thoroughly confused version of truth, but it is recognizable enough. The husband claims to be so full of love that he is capable of absolute self-sacrifice for her, and this would certainly be a utopian transformation of the attitudes of men in marriage. But the claim is rather hollow, for Arveragus is not even able to bear the thought that his public reputation as a husband might be tarnished by gossip. He finds this affront to his ego (and in the fear of being known as a cuckold, to his virility) so unbearable that he warns Dorigen he will kill her if she ever breathes a word to anyone about the event he is organizing. This is marital language in accord with that relished by the Knight of the Tower, but hardly an example of the devoted self-sacrifice he announces or of the promised renunciation of coercion. Given his earlier aspirations, his speech is astonishingly lacking in affection and care for *her* misery, as A. T. Gaylord observed. When the knight bursts into tears it is out of self-pity and his language to her is self-righteous and utterly self-centred – 'As *I* may best, *I* wol *my* wo endure.'

One would hardly gather that it is not he who is unwillingly being sent off to be screwed by someone for whom he has no affection whatsoever, a male May.[37] Chaucer's dramatization of the knight's admirable utopian aspirations thus culminates in a strange but most coherent manner. The husband who has attempted to initiate mutual and non-coercive love, orders his obedient but unwilling wife to subject herself to another male while he himself displays the unreflexive masculine egotism habitual in the traditional culture.

Here Chaucer's poetry does not stop at the individual's errors, as critics of Arveragus have done. Instead it shows us that the generous attempt to create a higher form of marital union has collapsed under pressures from without which revealed how the individuals concerned had internalized traditional assumptions more deeply than they, or the Franklin, had acknowledged. Furthermore, the collapse is not just a decisive negation of the utopian aspirations. In fact, it comprises a subtle affirmation of them, for it is in the light of utopian perspectives evoked by Arveragus and the narrator that we see the knight's behaviour at the end as an unacceptable egotism and the wife's unquestioning obedience of her husband's command (based on a complete failure to distinguish levels of obligation) as a wretched collapse. This encourages us to take such behaviour as a distortion of love and marriage rather than accept it as a 'natural' reassertion of the male domination and self-centredness of the kind celebrated by the Knight of the Tower, and to continue meditating on the difficulties presented to any attempt at critical transcendence of the present reality, stimulated by the utopian imagination.

In the poem's conclusion the narrator proves most unwilling to accept the dialectical movement we have just followed. As Dorigen leaves her husband he tries to avoid all ambivalence in his ending and intervenes directly to assure the audience that the tale may now give Dorigen 'bettre fortune' than the situation seems to allow (ll. 1496–8). The narrator draws back from the problems the poem has raised and tries to terminate its delicate movements of thought in a cosy but alien ending.

Suddenly the squire abandons his lust and becomes full of 'greet compassioun . . . franchise . . . gentillesse', admiration for the husband we have been scrutinizing and respect for Dorigen's married love. It is true that his performance in the courtly garden, and when he made his later outrageous demands on the woman, had been in terms of his devoted 'servyce' to her. But as in *Troilus and Criseyde* Chaucer had made plain the realities underlying the courtly forms of male worship and service of the female, so here he had provided excellent evidence for J. Huizinga's contention that in the Middle Ages 'all the conventions of love are the work of men: even when it dons an idealistic guise, erotic culture is altogether saturated by male egotism'.[38] Aurelius renounces his fraudulent claim to the wife, and the narrator applauds the timely conversion so implausibly effected, and praises both squire and husband for 'a gentil dede' (ll. 1514–44, 1593–7). No criticism of either male is offered by the Franklin, emphasizing his distortions of the poetry to fit the comforting ending he wishes to impose. He concludes with a question which fits the imposed ending but remains a bizarre and superficial evasion of the poem's preoccupation and significance: 'Which was the mooste fre, as thynketh yow?' (l. 1622). After the behaviour of Arveragus in the crisis, the paralysed dependence of Dorigen, the dramatization of problems intrinsic to utopian thought (itself an integral element in Chaucer's critical imagination), including the exhibition of difficulties in finding an appropriate language, the Franklin's final question is a misleading and comic trivialization which abandons the poem. It is this cosy and evasive imposition which justifies the criticism of the narrator, perhaps most cogently made by Alfred David.[39]

Yet handing the poem's conclusion to the Franklin was more than a clever way for the poet to avoid tragedy while keeping his own thumb out of the balance and his aesthetic conscience clear. It is an integral part of the poem's movement sketched at the opening of my own analysis. Chaucer has used this pilgrim, with his blend of insight, enthusiasm, confusion and superficiality, to suggest the temptation of the utopian imagination to substitute what Alfred David calls 'wish fulfilment' for the creative encounter of utopia and established reality. His own profoundly reflexive art thus characteristically builds into its organization a perspective from which certain of its own basic tendencies can be viewed with a critical detachment which does not entail their rejection. We come to see that the narrator's error is not his enthusiasm for the utopian perspective on marriage, nor his generous faith that people may experience conversions which break the bonds of selfhood, allowing them to perceive and appreciate other people in their own being. Rather his mistake is in his refusal to concentrate on the power of dominant tradition and attitudes to resist and pervert utopian alternatives, his refusal to accept the poem's disclosure of this power and its human consequences. In a way, the failure involves a *lack* of faith; faith pays scrupulous attention to the present, the weight of the past on the minds of the living who wish to change it, and yet can construct a vision on glimpses and pre-semblances of a more fulfilling human future which is perceived as latent but emerging as possibility. The utopian perspective and the role of fantasy and dream is an essential component of much great art for it allows the writer to posit and explore alternative values to those prescribed in the dominant codes. It allows him to generate images for aspirations he knows are part of his world, but as yet lack material realization or ideological elaboration. The poet can free these aspirations, repressed in conventional and orthodox discourse, to challenge the established realities, to question and criticize dominant values and prevalent relationships. It is this interaction between the present and utopian perspective that the poem embodies and if, as Donald Howard claims, the *Franklin's Tale* 'is not the final word on marriage',[40] this is ultimately because the form of poetry Chaucer created here is dialectical and open, responding to a historical movement in which more and more people would come to share the 'utopian perspective' described, until it ceased to be a 'utopian' project.

I shall complete this chapter with some comments on the *Clerk's Tale*. A great many scholars read it as a poem in which Chaucer teaches what they assume to be unquestioned medieval doctrine about the individual's duty to absolute and unquestioning obedience to superiors, whatever they command or do; they seem to view the poet as an authoritarian writer propagating the absolutism allegedly conventional in his day, another Knight of the Tower.[41] On both scores I believe such scholars are mistaken, and there has certainly been dissent from their approach. The line of dissent I wish to single out as most in accord with my own understanding of the *Clerk's Tale* is lucidly expressed by Donald Reiman. He focusses on the way Chaucer's text carefully brings out Walter's 'recalcitrant self-will' and its 'unambiguous censure' of his decision to afflict Griselda. In the light of this he argues that Griselda's patience becomes 'as much a source of evil as was Walter's arbitrary wilfulness', for her decision to be 'an accomplice to the murder of her own children without so much as a frown of protest' shows a disastrous failure to distinguish between her husband, explicitly presented as a selfishly cruel, mortal man, and God, the sovereign to whom both she and Walter owe allegiance and whom they both ignore.[42]

The *Clerk's Tale*, as Reiman's study suggests, exhibits the kind of critical thought and reflexivity about authority which I have traced in this and the preceding two chapters. It involves an exploration of irresponsible absolutism which brings together domestic, psychological and political dimensions. In the *domestic* sphere Walter's marriage is founded on a determination to ensure that whatever he claimed about the loss of liberty in marriage (ll. 143–71) he should be able to continue a life in which 'on his lust present was al his thoght' (l. 80). With this end, he tells the young peasant girl, 'be ye redy with good herte/To al my lust' (see ll. 351–3). He assumes the woman only has identity as an instrument for his 'lust', an assumption he shares with men like the Knight of the Tower and Chaucer's own Januarie. Chaucer reminds us of Walter's representative nature by stating that although his tyranny over his wife is evil there are undoubtedly men who will admire it (ll. 455–62, 622–3) – such men, it should be clear by now, are far removed from the poem's maker.

Griselda assents, like her father, 'quakynge for drede' (ll. 358, 317) and this scene sums up the marital union well. On the man's part, a capricious imperialism, on the woman's part, such an obedience that she surrenders her moral and religious responsibility and assents to the murder of her children by a man whose arbitrary 'lust', 'crueel purpos' and 'wikked usage' is recurrent and explicitly presented as such.[43]

It is in Walter's 'lust' that a most important psychological dimension of the text resides, for the poet continually presents him as a man who is overwhelmed by a desire he cannot control. He so longs to afflict his wife in his exercise of absolute and irresponsible sovereignty,[44]

> That he myghte out of his herte throwe
> This merveillous desir his wyf t'assaye;
> Nedeless, God woot, he thoughte hire for t'affraye.
>   He hadde assayed hire ynogh bifore,
> And foond hire evere good; what neded it
> Hire for to tempte, and alwey moore and moore
> (*Clerk*, ll. 453–8)

He seems to feel guilty enough to make some attempt at checking his 'merveillous desir', but fails and renounces any effort at resistance. To emphasize this the poet adds an image to his sources, likening Walter to people who become fixated on one course of action, 'right as they were bounden to a stake' (ll. 701–7). The all-powerful husband and ruler whose free will is unchecked is thus perceived as a powerless prisoner. Chaucer presents him as an authoritarian personality who fulfils his egotistic lust for dominion under the tyranny of his own sick will. Interestingly this combination was analysed by St Augustine himself with considerable acumen. With the reflexivity so abundant in the *Confessions*, he writes of himself: 'From a perverted act of will, desire had grown, and when desire is given satisfaction, habit is formed; and when habit passes unresisted, a compulsive urge sets in: by these knit links I was held.'[45] One of the most prevalent and vicious imprisonments the will suffered, in his opinion, was the 'lust of rule', in which the ruler was 'ruled by the love of ruling', a lust which 'lays waste men's hearts with the most ruthless dominion'.[46] These are appropriate psychological and moral concepts for discussing the condition of Walter as Chaucer creates it, and they lead us to the tale's *political* dimensions.

The way Chaucer illustrates the mentality which absolute rule thrives on and produces can be exemplified by his treatment of the sergeant. The poet stresses that this man's unquestioned obedience, his 'feithful' service to his ruler makes him peculiarly prone to do evil 'thynges badde'. Chaucer changes and considerably expands his sources to bring this out in his description of the obnoxious nature of the loyal and obedient man, and he has the sergeant himself remind Griselda that 'men moote nede until hire [lordes] lust obeye' (ll. 519–32).[47] The poet's critique of 'swich folk' as the sergeant implies a far more individualistic ethical outlook than any attributed to him by scholars who try to assimilate his art to some untroubled medieval totalitarianism in which hierarchy, authority and social obligation were fixed, unproblematic and never subject for critical reflection. The individual, we are shown, needs to assess the moral and religious grounds of the superior's commands for himself rather than just obeying because the command comes from someone of higher position in the social and political hierarchy. The consequences of this view are subversive of any hierarchy where social place and inherited allegiance, rather than articulate moral reasons and the assent of independent individual conscience, are the justification and explanation of authority and obedience.[48]

The political dimensions of the *Clerk's Tale* are lost on those who assume late medieval political thought provided a *carte blanche* for absolutism and therefore assume that Chaucer's text must simply fit this universal situation in his day. Such assumptions are mistaken and recent work on fourteenth-century political theory, and practice, makes this very plain.[49] For an intellectual writing in the reign of Richard II the distinction between legitimate rule and arbitrary absolutism was very much a live issue, of especial interest to a poet who attended as a member of parliament when the magnates threatened to depose the King, and who later accepted Henry IV, a magnate who overthrew a ruler judged to be tyrannous and wilful.[50]

And in this connection it is worth recalling that in his own work, as Margaret Schlauch documented many years ago, Chaucer constantly depicted tyranny as arbitrary acts of will. She also noted that accusations of arbitrary will were a major theme in the 1399 Articles of Deposition, while the new king, whom Chaucer addressed in his 'Complaint of Chaucer to his purse', pledged himself to pursue the 'commune profyt' and to preserve the laws above his self-will. In this, significantly enough, he was promising to rule as Griselda did in Walter's absence, not like Walter.[51]

I believe that major historical studies of recent years have reconstructed the political and intellectual contexts in which we can situate Chaucer's own critical examination of Walter's arbitrary will and absolutism, for they document the emergence of fully articulate theories of *limited* monarchy in the later Middle Ages in which the ruler was viewed as the servant of a community where individuals rather than corporate wholes were to be the prime beneficiaries of government. They trace the *desacralization* of secular power together with the supersession of the hierocratic thesis of sovereignty in which all secular authority, law and government derived its legitimation from God through the ruler rather than through the community.[52] Here it may not be far-fetched to wonder whether the long-lived metaphor in which the marriage of man and woman is used to examine political questions concerning sovereignty and responsibility could have been an element in Chaucer's treatment of the ruler and his wife in the *Clerk's Tale*. It is particularly interesting that according to M. Wilks's investigations this metaphor had acquired an anti-absolutist meaning by Chaucer's day in which the ruler's authority ceases at the point it becomes harmful to the community of individuals symbolized by his wife.[53] And certainly the traffic between the two areas of discourse being metaphorically related was two-way, so that domestic relations could be seen in terms of political ones. In this perspective a husband's tyranny would be judged in very different terms than those of the Knight of the Tower. It is in these ways that the metaphor may have contributed to the resonance of Chaucer's treatment of Walter and Griselda. It may have been a minor, but significant element in the poem's fusion of the domestic, psychological and political spheres I have outlined, pointing towards the intellectual and political contexts which would have encouraged Chaucer's own critical imagination in its magnificent explorations of love, sex and marriage.

CHAPTER 7

Imagination, Order and Ideology: *The Knight's Tale*

Till one shall rise
Of proud ambitious heart, who not content
With fair equality, fraternal state,
Will arrogate dominion undeserved
Over his brethren, and quite dispossess
Concord and law of nature from the earth,
Hunting (and men not beasts shall be his game)
With war and hostile snare such as refuse
Subjection to his empire tyrannous:
A mighty hunter thence he shall be styled
Before the Lord, as in despite of heaven,
Or from heaven claiming second sovereignty;
And from rebellion shall derive his name,
Though of rebellion others he accuse.

Milton, *Paradise Lost*, Bk XII, ll. 24–37

When Charles Muscatine argued that the heart of the *Knight's Tale* was an assertion of aesthetic, cosmic and metaphysical order, and that Theseus represents the underlying 'principle of order' to which Chaucer was committed, he offered what has proved to be an extremely influential interpretation. Theseus has been represented time and again as the figure who understands 'man's proper life in submission to the perfect harmony of the universe', the authoritative bearer of Chaucer's own 'philosophical insight'.[1] Against what has become an orthodox position some alternative readings have been developed, most outstandingly by Elizabeth Salter and R. Neuse, the scholars on whose very different work this chapter builds. I wish to argue that the *Knight's Tale* involves a most illuminating scrutiny of the versions of order, styles of thought and life embodied in Theseus, rulers like him and their culture.[2] No more than in the *Clerk's Tale* did Chaucer confine his imagination to fit some simple and absolutist norms attributed to the 'medieval mind' by many who write on his poetry.

When we first meet Theseus in the *Knight's Tale* he is depicted, 'In al his wele and in his mooste pride' (l. 895). There is an obvious ambiguity here which plays round the word 'pride'. Chaucer, as Jill Mann's study of the *General Prologue* demonstrated, was sharply aware of conflicting grounds of evaluation in his own culture, with their linguistic manifestations, and here he makes use of one such conflict over 'pride' – traditional moral and religious teaching attacked pride, recommending humility and abasement of self within a social structure where pride and self-display was an intrinsic part of aristocratic status, power and daily life.[3] This ambivalence introduces us to the problems Chaucer will raise around Theseus, as does the ruler's own response to the widowed ladies whose lamentations welcome him home (ll. 896 ff.). Henry Webb rightly noted the 'hints of selfish motives' and thoughts of 'his own honour and popularity' and Chaucer makes the duke's self-centredness rather pronounced ('myn', 'my', 'myn honour' (ll. 905–8)), while his motives in attacking Creon are inextricably bound up with his public military fame (ll. 960–6) – hardly unusual traits in rulers.[4]

But it is the next image associated with Theseus which will prove particularly important as the poem unfolds its full range of significance. As he rides off, he displays his banner:

> The rede statue of Mars, with spere and targe,
> So shyneth in his white baner large,
> That alle the feeldes glyteren up and doun;
> And by his baner born is his penoun
> Of gold ful riche, in which ther was ybete
> The Mynotaur, which that he slough in Crete.
> Thus rit this duc, thus rit this conquerour,
> And in his hoost of chivalrie the flour. . . .
>
> (*Knight*, ll. 975–82)

Chaucer thus joins Theseus and Mars emblematically at the poem's opening. The language in which he does this represents heraldic and emblematic modes, so appropriate to unexamined assertions of power in the way they preclude attention to the real human motives and consequences of the activity celebrated, offering a glamour which, as Elizabeth Salter observed, is a comfort and a protection.[5] Whereas some readers have succumbed to this form, Chaucer did not. He chose to de-sublimate this emblem by drawing out its human implications in very different literary modes. These disclose the meaning of commitment to Mars and encourage reflection on the kind of order which legitimates and glorifies such commitment. The process can be seen in Chaucer's description of the conqueror's actions after his victory over Thebes, and, most decisively, in 'the temple of myghty Mars the rede', the figure whom Theseus elected to follow and celebrated on his banner.

The 'order' Theseus imposes on Thebes has no constructive elements at all, for he 'rente adoun bothe wall and sparre and rafter', and whereas in his source the duke has the plain searched so that the wounded could be given medical help and all the dead properly buried, Chaucer eliminated this action from Theseus' conduct. Instead, he introduced an entirely new passage:

> And dide with al the contree as hym lest.
> To ransake in the taas of bodyes dede,
> Hem for to strepe of harneys and of wede,
> The pilours diden bisynesse and cure
> After the bataille and disconfiture.
>
> (*Knight*, ll. 1004–8)

The reality of militarism and the attitudes it sponsors among human beings is concisely evoked. People are reduced to dead bodies, piled up and ransacked for profit, in a passage where Chaucer may well have been putting his own direct experience of war and its motives to use. The impression I get from this addition to Boccaccio is that Chaucer's imagination had great sympathy with the growing criticism of war (the lust for conquest and its economic foundations) among late medieval writers, an impression the poem's evolution confirms.[6] In the present episode the 'pilours' tear two royal Thebans from the heap of bodies and take them to Theseus (ll. 1009 ff.). The 'worthy' duke's reaction to the gravely wounded men is revealing, for he 'ful soone' sent them to prison in Athens, refusing to accept any ransom for these two prisoners (ll. 1022–4). Webb's assertion that the conqueror was denying his prisoners a customary right is correct, and it was one Chaucer himself had cause to thank when he recalled his own capture and ransom in 1359–60). We have no reason to believe that the poet would have disagreed with Honoré Bonet when he stated that a victor who refused reasonable ransom is a 'tyrant', as Palamon judges Theseus to be (l. 1111).[7] Webb also noted that Chaucer altered Boccaccio's description of the imprisonment imposed on the young men. Whereas his source has the duke keep them at ease in his palace, Chaucer has them confined in a 'grete tour, that was so thikke and stroong', in fact 'the chief dongeoun' where they even have 'fettres' placed on their legs (ll. 1030–2, 1056–8, 1279). If Theseus represents 'the principle of order' in this culture, then Chaucer is leading us to see that we should never celebrate abstractions such as 'order' but inquire about the kind of order and its specific human content.[8]

The poet's own inquiry into the order of those who celebrate Mars is perhaps most concentrated as he takes us into the temple of Mars.[9] The imagery introducing the passage conveys the utter sterility of the way of life chosen by whose who admire the god (ll. 1975–94), and this moves into one of the poem's central disclosures about the commitments of those whose order is founded in the pursuit of Mars, a pursuit shared by Theseus, Arcite and many in Chaucer's own world:

> The smylere with the knyf under the cloke;
> The shepne brennynge with the blake smoke;
> The tresoun of the mordrynge in the bedde;
> The open werre, with woundes al bibledde;
> Contek, with blody knyf and sharp menace. . . .
> The colde deeth, with mouth gapyng upright. . . .
> The careyne in the busk, with throte ycorve;
> A thousand slayn, and nat of qualm ystorve;
> The tiraunt with the pray by force yraft;
> The toun destroyed, ther was no thyng laft,
> (ll. 1999–2003, 2008, 2013–6)

In Theseus' war, his destruction of Thebes, his pillagers rummaging through heaps of dead and dying people, or in Arcite and Palamon trying to resolve their frustrations by violence, we have already encountered the effects of devotion to 'force'. As Chaucer now evoked some details of human misery and loss produced by militarism and violence, so he negated the aestheticization of legalized and organized violence, whether in courtly literature, aristocratic banners, emblems, pageants, or the ceremonies where the glorified soldier displays himself 'in his mooste pride'. While the passage points towards the ghastly physical consequences of 'force', it yokes together sorts of violence habitually separated. This stresses the connections between those valued or glorified in aristocratic culture and those officially condemned. Even the most obviously purposeless and meaningless horror is connected with the followers of Mars:

> The hunte strangled with the wilde beres;
> The sowe freten the children right in the cradel;
> (ll. 2018–19)

We are made aware of the links between the predatory 'tiraunt' and the 'pykepurs' or 'smylere with the knyf under the cloke'; between the towns and livelihood destroyed with thousands killed on glorified battlefields and the secret murders, the sow eating the child in the cradle. Chaucer's 'insistent probing of misery' is a probing of abstractions such as 'law' and 'order' to reveal the continuities between official, legal violence and illegal, between the celebration of Mars and the most grisly particulars of human destructiveness.[10] The poet's imagination suggests that certain traditional distinctions concerning modes of violence are the product of the highly partial official ideology sponsored by militaristic conquerors and their followers, and his own poetry undermines them. Our interest in Theseus, the great conqueror, makes us appreciate the relevance of another image in the temple:

> Saugh I Conquest sittynge in greet honour,
> With the sharpe swerd over his heed. . . .
> (*Knight*, ll. 2028–9)

We should remember this when later Theseus presents himself, 'Arrayed right as he were a god in trone' (l. 2529).

The final passage in the temple alludes to Theseus' banner. There the 'rede statue of Mars' shone in glory, and here we see it in a fuller perspective which is undoubtedly disturbing:

> A wolfe ther stood biforn hym at his feet
> With eyen rede, and of a man he eet. . . .
> (*Knight*, ll. 2047–8)

The dispassionate manner of the description is part of the meaning. It captures the contempt of humanity central to those committed to the values of Mars and 'his glorie' (l. 2050). Chaucer makes it clear that in a culture where Mars is valued, as he is by Theseus, there will not be much encouragement of creative human love, let alone a 'faire cheyne of love' binding all elements and events (cf. ll. 2987–93). We must emphasize that this is not to say such cultures lack 'order' or that Theseus is not the 'principle' of that order: only, that what matters is the nature of the order in question. And Chaucer's poetry has become rather specific about the one realized in the *Knight's Tale*.

It is typical of this order that the deity who provides the solution to the celestial conflicts is Saturn, Chaucer expanding the slightest hint in Boccaccio who has no wish to dwell on discord among the gods and nothing to say about how it was solved.[11] The new material Chaucer introduced is an essential component in our understanding of his own assessment of Theseus' final speech as well as of the values held by those at the commanding heights of this universe (ll. 2438–78). We must note the absolute impotence of Jupiter in the dispute, his anxious ineffectuality lacking in vision, providential foreknowledge or power (l. 2442). The 'principle of order', to use Muscatine's phrase again, is Saturn, quite unmentioned by Boccaccio. It is Saturn's intervention which brings 'order' out of strife and is thus vital in illuminating the specific order created and scrutinized in the poem. Chaucer shows that Saturn's knowledge is based on 'olde experience', the 'wysdom and usage' of the old pragmatist quite uncritical of the Martian world, celebrating violence and human wretchedness which he has 'power' to manipulate into one version of order:

> Myn is the drenchyng in the see so wan;
> Myn is the prison in the derke cote;
> Myn is the stranglyng and hangyng by the throte,
> The murmure and the cherles rebellyng,
> The groynynge, and the pryvee empoysonyng;
> I do vengeance and pleyn correccioun,
> Whil I dwelle in the signe of the leoun.
> Myn is the ruyne of the hye halles,
> The fallynge of the toures and of the walles
> Upon the mynour or the carpenter. . . .

> The derke tresons, and the castes olde;
> My lookyng is the fader of pestilence.
> Now weep namoore. . . .
>
> (*Knight*, ll. 2456–70)

This order is reflected in a poetic mode Chaucer used for the followers of Mars. The fragmentized details of violence are accumulated in a way which thoroughly undermines any claims about benign harmonies and unity favoured by all theodicies, whether traditional religious ones or their secularized development. The version of order is as alien to any creative love as to the higher forms of reason and reflexivity. Elizabeth Salter, commenting on the decisive positioning of this addition to Boccaccio, writes that it 'sums up, in relentless detail, what we may have long suspected – that the "remedie" for strife will not depend upon any weighing of just dispensation, but only upon the supreme craft and executive power of one god over another'.[12] Saturn's repeated 'weep namoore' after his recitation and the description of himself as 'the fader of pestilence' drives home the absence of love and care towards humans in this world-order. Only participants with a comfortingly dishonest refusal to contemplate the revealed powers and practices, or those with ulterior and pragmatic motives, could talk about the fair chain of love shining through the mere appearances of disharmony, evil and suffering in this order. Chaucer follows Saturn's crucial intervention with Theseus arraying himself publicly 'as he were a god in trone' (l. 2529), thus inviting us to acknowledge continuities between this earthly ruler and Saturn, between this godly conqueror and the temple of Mars with 'Conquest sittynge in greet honour'.

Even an apparently un-Martian act of Theseus from his godly throne turns out to be thoroughly contradictory and finally ambivalent. He suddenly decides to modify 'his firste purpos' and that the tournament should be limited to the lance, sword and mace (ll. 2537–60). This modification cannot be taken as a rejection of his former life since he determines to continue with the tournament he has planned and the decision to settle the question of whom Emily should marry by sheer violence – rather than by consulting the oracles, drawing lots, detailed inquiry into the knights, or by letting Emily do what she wants and reject them both, preventing the violence altogether. Furthermore, he rules that each knight should ride a course 'with a sharpe ygrounde spere', then fight on foot, exhorting them, 'gooth forth, and ley on faste!/With long swerd and with maces fightethe youre fille' (ll. 2549, 2558–9). This they do and Chaucer describes the fighting at length and in detail: the helmets are hacked to pieces, blood flows in red streams, bones are smashed by the maces Theseus allowed, men fight like 'crueel' tigers, lions mad with hunger for blood (ll. 2601–35). It would be quite implausible to claim that Chaucer's imagination and moral intelligence were unable to grasp the double-think involved in Theseus' organization of such violence (when originally the matter had been a conflict between two young knights for a woman who wanted neither of them), and his public protestation that he did not wish to shed upper-class blood (l. 2539). The fact that the moral status of tournaments was at least a controversial topic in the period offers further support for the conviction that Chaucer wished to exhibit the contradiction between gestures of compassion and militaristic commitments in knights and rulers like Theseus, showing how these very gestures are embedded in a form of life which undermines and inverts them, a contradiction plainly visible in our world.[13]

Before going on to analyse the poem's conclusion we need to look briefly at the ruler's attitudes to love, for these could possibly reveal alternative orientations to those observed so far, more fitting prefaces to his final talk about 'the faire chene of love'.[14] It is not chance that, alongside his Martian banner, Chaucer gave the duke a pennon recalling his heroic adventure in Crete (ll. 978–80). From the poet's treatment of Theseus when he separates Palamon and Arcite it seems we should recall the past he himself alludes to. After stating that he need not torture the knights to extract information but can kill them directly, 'by myghty Mars the rede' of course (ll. 1746–7), he is placated by the weeping ladies trying to kiss his feet (an incident Chaucer invented for his own Theseus, not one found in Boccaccio) and his gradual exercise of a 'resoun' which has often been admired by modern scholars.[15] Yet it is a version of reason and love that merits closer scrutiny than it usually receives. First of all it sanctions the kind of anarchic egotism in love which Arcite had expressed earlier in his argument with Palamon over who should have Emily: 'in his resoun . . . he thoghte wel that every man/Wol helpe hymself in love' (ll. 1766–8). Arcite had seen 'love' as an irresistible and impersonal urge which took precedence over all, appealing to 'olde clerkes' to support the proverb 'who shal yeve a lovere any lawe?' (ll. 1163–86). But he uses this old saying in exactly the way Pandarus does, not in the way the 'olde clerkes' like Boethius had done. Whereas the latter had expounded the supersession of what is taken as lawless love in a neoplatonic framework exhorting the ascent of the soul to some heavenly fatherland, Arcite does nothing of the sort any more than does Palamon or their new lord, Theseus.[16] Far from encouraging the young knights to reflect on the different forms of love, and to imagine different forms of life to their present one, his mockery of their 'hoote fare' never posits alternatives to their outlook and concludes with some impenitent reminiscing on his own past which he sees mirrored in the young knights (ll. 1785–818). He recalls that he too was once 'a servant' in love, like them, and 'syn I knowe of loves peyne/ . . . As he that hath ben caught ofte in his laas', he will forgive them (ll. 1813–18). This allusion links with his pennon celebrating the adventure in Crete, and judging from Chaucer's own accounts of it he would have been most sharply aware of the self-indulgent and comically uncritical attitude of Theseus. For in both the *House of Fame* and the *Legend of Good Women* (*LGW*) Chaucer presents Theseus as a man who exhibits 'the grete untrouthe of love' (*LGW*, l. 1890), making the expedition to Crete a story of the duke's callous egotism, faithless manipulation and abandonment of a woman (his wife) on an island inhabited only by wild beasts.[17] The sympathy Theseus displays to the young knights is thus understandable – as Arcite said, 'at the kynges court, my brother,/Ech man for hymself' (ll. 1181–2). Similarly he delights the young men by deciding to escalate the violence and treat Emily purely as an object deserved by the strongest in the sports of Mars.[18] Here it is clear that his versions of 'resoun' and 'love' lack any concern with moral or metaphysical issues. This lack is part of the order he represents and Chaucer's exposure of it is an important contribution in establishing the contexts in which we are to understand the final moments of the poem and the duke's closing speech.

The tournament ordained by Theseus culminates in the grisly 'myracle' performed by the poem's gods, an eloquent image of the divine and earthly order informing this world. Saturn organizes 'a furie infernal' to inflict a fatal injury on Arcite in an episode central to the total meaning of the poem (ll. 2684 ff.). Anyone who compares Chaucer's source will be struck by his introduction of 'clinical detail' and a sharply particularized focus on the body, quite alien to the Italian text (ll. 2743–56).[19] As in the temple of Mars, or Saturn's self-revelation, Chaucer uses art against the traditional aestheticization of violence, challenging literary traditions which celebrate aggression and militarism (a task Milton still found relevant in the seventeenth century – *Paradise Lost*, Bk IX, ll. 5–47). The poet attends to Arcite's painfully swelling body, the clotted blood, the collapse of essential muscles, along with the medical attempts to counteract the 'venym and corrupcioun' from blood-letting and vomiting to 'downward laxatif'. In doing so, he makes us concentrate on experience readily dissolved into comforting generalities about the benevolent order of the whole; his text resists the absorption of individual identity and the particulars of misery into those grandly abstract patterns of consolation favoured by many Christian versions of theodicy as well as in certain of their secular successors.[20] This resistance will be remembered when we find the tournament's organizer asserting his own brand of theodicy at the poem's close, for Chaucer has made the idea and function of theodicy a topic for reflection.[21]

Arcite's response is far less elaborate and ritualized than in Boccaccio's poem. He expresses his misery and the failure of his projects without any concern for his past military and knightly values, and without any comforting thoughts about an after life in Elysium:[22]

> What is this world? what asketh men to have?
> Now with his love, now in his colde grave
> Allone, withouen any compaignye.
> Fare wel, my sweete foo, myn Emelye!
> And softe taak me in youre armes tweye
> (*Knight's Tale*, ll. 2777–81)

This is a most admirably honest response to his discovery that the whole framework provided for his life by his aristocratic culture and its order, guided by Theseus, is groundless. The dying knight acknowledges that the patterns of chivalry and the culture's deities have failed to offer any account of human existence and its possibilities which even begin to seem adequate. Worse still, we realize that the knight's pursuits, encouraged and later reaffirmed by Theseus, have actually diverted him from grappling with the key questions he now asks.

It is worth remembering that earlier Chaucer had in fact shown both Arcite and Palamon attempting to reflect on their adverse experience and what it might convey about the grounds of their world. Arcite, for instance, had meditated on the 'purveiaunce of God', the ignorance of the human will, including his own, and like many thinkers in Chaucer's own century (if not like Boethius and neoplatonic cum stoic metaphysicians) had stressed the contingency of the created world (ll. 1251–74).[23] Similarly, despite his confusions and rage, Palamon had shown some desire for philosophical reflection which his culture and the plans of the duke had not nurtured. His earlier complaint in prison had made theodicy a topic for scrutiny;

> O crueel goddes that governe
> This world with byndyng of youre word eterne, . . .
> What is mankynde moore unto you holde
> Than is the sheep that rouketh in the folde?
> For slayn is man right as another beest, . . .
> What governance is in this prescience,
> That gilteless tormenteth innocence?
> (*Knight's Tale*, ll. 1303–4, 1307–9, 1313–14)

Chaucer does not give Palamon the responses to these probings which Boethius received from his philosophy, but this is certainly not to encourage readers' unexamined assumption that Boethius' philosophy gave satisfactory answers to all the controversial issues raised in the *Consolation of Philosophy*. As Elizabeth Salter showed, the narrative actually validates Palamon's ideas about the 'crueel goddes' and their order. Nevertheless, he does modestly confess his perplexity with theological and metaphysical problems that troubled Langland, Chaucer and many others in the fourteenth century, and suspends judgment: 'The answere of this lete I to dyvynys' (l. 1323). Metaphysicians, divines of any kind or creed, seem conspicuously absent in Theseus' culture and we hear no more of their existence.[24]

Instead, the young knights become re-integrated in the active aristocratic and courtly life guided by Theseus, that very earthly god (l. 2529). Not surprisingly they stop all philosophical reflection and settle for the unexamined worship of the culture's gods. It is only at his death that Arcite re-opens the major questions – 'What is this world? what asketh man to have?' As I pointed out, he then rejects the framework given him by his culture, but he goes further than this to ignore the problems about the gods and their order which had puzzled him and Palamon. Quite unlike Boccaccio's knight, Arcite now feels no need for metaphysical construction or the comforts of theodicy. His attention is on our world and human relationships. He affirms incarnate human love and friendship even as he fully experiences and acknowledges the miserable precariousness of individual life. Against the 'colde grave' he sets 'love', a thoroughly embodied one, asking Emily, 'softe taak me in youre armes tweye'.[25] From this moving and self-consciously fragile affirmation, the dying man makes a request to Emily which is astonishingly magnanimous. Having confessed his 'strif and rancour' with Palamon, he praises his kinsman and begs her, 'if that evere ye shul ben a wyf,/Forget nat Palamon, the gentil man' (ll. 2783–98). The selfless generosity transcends the values we have seen him and others pursuing. It is an impressive manifestation of human love, a glimmer of the human potential distorted and perverted by the culture over which Theseus presides, one where the appropriate metaphysical beings are the vicious deities ordered by Saturn. This glimmer is one of the lights Chaucer asks us to use in furthering our scrutiny of Theseus and his order.

When Arcite dies, Chaucer makes one of his most famous changes to the *Teseida*. The opening three stanzas of Boccaccio's eleventh book describe the ascent of Arcita's soul, his vision of cosmic order and the delightful music of the spheres, together with his new contempt for all human beings. The very idea of such a vision in the universe of Theseus and Saturn is bizarre, and Chaucer decided to delete it and substitute the following lines:

> His spirit chaunged hous and wente ther,
> As I cam nevere, I kan nat tellen wher.
> Therfore I stynte, I nam no divinistre;
> Of soules fynde I nat in this registre,
> Ne me ne list thilke opinions to telle
> Of hem, though that they writen wher they dwelle.
> Arcite is coold, ther Mars his soule gye!
>
> (*Knight's Tale*, ll. 2809–15)

This constitutes a refusal to offer any consoling theodicy or comforting metaphysical sentiments which would have lacked foundation within the poem. Because of its integrity to the poem's movements we should respect this judgment and ensure we do not impose religious consolations which the text has pushed aside.[26] Chaucer completes the passage by referring us back to the emphasis of his own work, commending the knight's soul to Mars, rather than the Mercury of the *Teseida*. He plainly has no wish for us to evade the centrality of Mars and his order in the *Knight's Tale*.

In this he is unlike Theseus and the retired ruler, Egeus. Whereas in death Arcite had uttered questions the poem takes seriously, and revealed human potentials all too rare in the universe he inhabited, the old man now indulges in a series of generalizations designed to remove any discomfort spectators may feel at what has happened (ll. 2837–52). He observes that men are mortal:

> 'Right as ther dyed nevere man,' quod he,
> 'That he ne lyvede in erthe in some degree,
> Right so there lyvede never man,' he seyde,
> 'In al this world, that some tyme he ne deyde.
> (*Knight's Tale*, ll. 2843–6)

To utter such platitudes so portentously, especially in the present context, exemplifies marked intellectual and emotional debility. Everything in the poem invites us to reflect critically on a wide range of substantial issues (including Theseus's version of order, and problems concerning theodicies) and to test out generalizations against particulars. The poet is the last person to have missed how Egeus evades the topics and the experiences realized for imaginative exploration in the tale. All distinctions about the different forms of life and death are dissolved into the old man's commonplace abstractions. Nor are the next lines more impressive, for all their plangent solemnity:

> This world nys but a thurghfare ful of wo,
> And we been pilgrymes, passynge to and fro
> Deeth is an ende of every worldly soore.
> (*Knight's Tale*, ll. 2847–9)

In the claim that our world is *nothing but* a thoroughfare full of woe for everyone passing through it, Chaucer nicely displays a conventional piece of pseudo-religious cant. For Egeus is a privileged, comfortably-placed old man, with a long life behind him as a ruler, and he inhabits a court in which we see the traditional courtly enjoyments of hunting, feasting, singing, love-talk, jousting, dancing and 'blisful', 'rich' and 'healthy' marriage, not to speak of the pursuit of fame and profits through war. The speaker evaporates the vital and massive differences between lives such as those led by Theseus and those subjected to the miseries the poem has also represented.[27] His statement is also, ironically, thoroughly imprecise in the religious dimension at which it gestures: pilgrims passing 'to and fro' actually conveys nothing about the kind of pilgrimage (something readers of the *Canterbury Tales* and *Piers Plowman* will be especially aware of), nor the crucial issue of its direction and final cause. Nothing in Chaucer's poem encourages us to settle for such language and the complacent superficiality it bears. Even the final line of the old man's oration is an unnecessarily inadequate response to the contexts, 'Deeth is an ende of every worldly soore'. Showing us Arcite calling for Emily, generous towards Palamon, and thinking about the marriage of his kinsman, duly to take place in courtly festivities, the poet makes it obvious that Egeus conveniently forgets how death is as much the end of every worldly joy as of worldly 'soore'. It is also clear that the line begs all the metaphysical problems raised by other figures, the poem's deities and the death of Arcite. Chaucer wryly observes that Egeus said, 'muchel moore/To this effect', and leaves us grateful that he chose not to report any more of this 'wise' discourse (ll. 2850–2). In the face of the issues the poem has raised, the experiences it has mediated, only the least reflective of people would be consoled by such trite and imprecise comments. That Theseus is consoled by his father's words is significant, but can hardly be a surprise at this stage of the poem.

The final movement in the *Knight's Tale* includes the long speech Theseus makes in parliament concerning order, love, wisdom and the perfect joy he intends to create by marrying Emily to Palamon (ll. 2967–3093). This speech has been much admired as a piece of profound Boethian wisdom which Chaucer himself presented uncritically to clarify the 'principle of order' informing poem, society and cosmos.[28] It is not impossible that the Theseus we have followed could have undergone a philosophic and religious conversion at the conclusion of the narrative, but if we pay close attention to both the context and the particulars of his speech, I believe we will have to concede that no such event occurred. The first point to make about the speech is that it takes place in parliament as a move in a pragmatic political plan. R. Neuse depicted the situation well when he wrote of Theseus' organization that 'his watchword is: politics as usual. Hence his philosophical reflections are enlisted rhetorically in the service of his marriage plans for Palamon and Emily.'[29] The cause of parliament is, 'To have with certein countrees alliaunce,/And have fully of Thebans obeisaunce' and it is explicitly in the service of this political, dominating and self-centred order that Theseus sent for Palamon and Emily (ll. 2970–80). This is Chaucer's special emphasis for it has no basis in his source and demanded preparatory changes earlier in the narrative – in Boccaccio the duke promised the dying Arcita to let Palemone have Emilia, and there is no political or imperialistic motivation whatsoever (*Teseida*, X, ll. 16–35; XII, 3–19). Chaucer's Theseus, however, is now in one of those public situations he dominates with such conviction (ll. 2981–6; compare ll. 2528–32).

Like other rulers through the ages, Theseus sets about presenting his order in a solemn setting and with a language which exalts, sanctifies and seemingly depersonalizes his thoroughly material and partial ambitions. He now eschews those indulgent reminiscences about his service of what he called 'love', and with a 'sad visage' and a carefully weighted sigh he begins to deliver his 'wille'. Chaucer selected the word 'wille' (l. 2986) carefully for, instead of suggesting that the ensuing utterance will be a philosophic meditation or dialogue, it carries the sense of a predetermined decision, the expression of a ruler's personal command. The setting is part of a brilliant dramatization of the possible connections between political rule and metaphysical ideas in orders such as that of Theseus.

The first half of the duke's address involves a patchwork of abstractions from different parts of the *Consolation of Philosophy*.[30] He starts with the assertion that his world is bound together by 'the faire cheyne of love' in an order which unambiguously and unproblematically demonstrates the existence of a stable and eternal 'Firste Moevere' (ll. 2987 ff.). The 'experience' he asserts, is enough to prove such assertions:

Thanne may men by this ordre wel discerne
That thilke Moevere stable is and eterne.
(*Knight's Tale,* ll. 3003–4)

Rather than trying to maintain the existence of a real but hidden structure to the phenomenal world, one which may be grasped by philosophic and religious reflection, he claims that the metaphysical order he gestures towards can be proved by immediate and unstructured experience (ll. 3000–4). There is certainly no reason to attribute such a naive view to Chaucer and, as Elizabeth Salter has noted, the poem itself has foregrounded the empirical difficulties that would have to be met in constructing any metaphysical claims about a benevolently ordered world:[31]

> It gradually emerges that the speech will be in the nature of a substitution, a statement which will attempt to transcend the difficulties, rather than analyse and solve them. . . . Why speak of the exercise of divine love in the design of this drama, when the narrative has so openly exposed no more than the exercise of divine power and resourcefulness?

Before answering this question through analysis of the function such claims serve, we need to be clear that the 'difficulties' Elizabeth Salter points out are by no means the only ones undermining the duke's new-found role as thinker.

When we look at the 'experience' the duke now feels is proof of the presence of divine love and its benevolent ordering of our world, the result is to strengthen our sense that he is not given to examining such matters with any scrupulousness. Theseus offers the inevitable death of all generated things 'in this wrecched world' as the experiential proof of a stable and eternal first mover who binds all in a chain of love (ll. 2994–3004). He finds this argument so impressive that he later spends more lines stressing the same commonplaces, still assuming that this picture is unambiguous evidence of the first mover's 'wise purveiaunce' (ll. 3011–40). One hardly needs to be familiar with fourteenth-century criticism of traditional metaphysical proofs of God's existence to notice the incoherence of this particular version of the argument from design, vulnerable enough in any form and place let alone in the contexts established by the *Knight's Tale*.[32] From a 'wrecched world' in which all is subject to decay and death the last thing one can simply read off is the existence of a loving, omnipotent and eternal first mover. A more plausible speculation about the design and designing agency might go along lines such as the following: the order revealed by 'experience' mediated through the text, suggests a world made by a crippled or apprentice deity whose work has always been the scorn of more competent ones; or, perhaps, it was made by conflicting and competing deities of limited but often malevolent powers, deities such as those in the heavenly dispute (ll. 2438–78); or, joining some manichean and gnostic traditions, the world we experience was the product of a fallen and evil principle; or, if there was a superior deity, who was not malevolent, then he was quite unconcerned with this 'wrecched' order that had evolved among lesser gods and humans. Yet, although Theseus has no equivalent to the Christian doctrine of the Fall, to square the existence of an omnipotent and loving God with the evils of 'this wrecched world', he does not even consider such possible lines of speculation. Instead he asserts an argument from design which is not only inept in itself but made obviously so by the contexts in which Chaucer has placed it.

The speech reveals further inadequacies in areas important to the poem. The treatment of love is one of these. Theseus assumes that an act which consists solely of binding down natural elements in fixed places and establishing a maximum to the length of life, deserves to be called 'love' (ll. 2987–93). This is a reductive and thoroughly negative handling of the notion which, in Neuse's words, 'assumes the scientific neutrality of gravitational force'.[33] This is not the product of chance, for in reducing 'love' to an impersonal controlling force exercised over subordinate elements, Theseus displays a most appropriate image of the way he regards both love and order in all spheres of existence. Its reductive dehumanization is a travesty of the poem in the *Consolation of Philosophy* used in the passage, and Chaucer shows how the ruler's metaphysics illustrates far more about himself and his own version of order than about the hidden structures of the world metaphysics had traditionally sought to disclose.[34] As a ruler who likes to pose as 'a god in trone', Theseus doubtless has an especially high valuation of fixed and certain boundaries in the social world he rules (unless it is in his interest to change them), and he projects this valuation into his impoverished picture of love and order. Its negativity reflects the idealization of sheer power over others in some vaguely apprehended design where the act of control is spiritualized with the name 'love'. It may also be relevant to wonder whether the perverse but revealing version of love encountered here may not also be partly due to Theseus' own thoroughly ungenerous experience of 'love' in the past he alluded to earlier in the poem. This would be quite in keeping with Chaucer's sharp awareness of how personal prejudices and stances are often projected into a metaphysical plane and reified as objective and autonomous entities.

The grounds of his outlook emerge plainly as his parliamentary address moves to its practical end:

> Thanne is it wysdom, as it thynketh me,
> To maken vertu of necessitee,
> And take it weel that we may nat eschue,
> And namely that to us alle is due.
> And whoso grucceth ought, he dooth folye,
> And rebel is to hym that al may gye.
>
> (*Knight's Tale*, ll. 3041–6)

Here R. Neuse commented that the speech has not led 'to a spiritual vision, but merely to the tyrant's plea, "To maken vertu of necessitee"'.[35] This is a sound observation, and I think we should also draw particular attention to the allusion Theseus makes to rebellion against the first mover. The duke simply assumes that the existing social order and its practices, under his governance, are fully sanctioned by a transcendent God who seems to be envisaged as other than the gods the poem has exhibited. Any protest about anything is branded as folly and any attempt to challenge this order presented as rebellion, not just against Theseus but against the supreme deity.[36] Although much of the misery the poet has displayed is based in specific human practices and choices encouraged by the culture over which Theseus presides, the duke never thinks of differentiating between 'that we may nat eschue' and what we *could* eschew with a change in outlook and practice. In his lack of reflexivity about his own discourse and order he never wonders whether a supreme deity might not share all his own values, and might not admire the forms of love and worship of Mars he and his followers relish. These are traits characteristic of rulers who wish to sacralize their own government, imagining themselves as gods on thrones (l. 2529) and their order as beyond discussion or criticism. The sacralization is unequivocally this-worldly and it is part of the ruler's contempt for genuine metaphysical inquiry and reflexivity. He will use any portion of any system of ideas which seem to bolster up his own exercise of power, an eclecticism hardly unknown in our own day.

This enables him to move easily to a set of values which have much to do with aristocratic culture but little to do with the Boethian language he has just been applying:

> And certeinly a man hath moost honour
> To dyen in his excellence and flour,
> When he is siker of his goode name;
> Thanne hath he doon his freend, ne hym no shame.
> And gladder oghte his freend been of his deeth,
> Whan with honour up yolden is his breeth, . . .
> Thanne is it best, as for a worthy fame,
> To dyen whan that he is best of name.
>
> (*Knight's Tale*, ll. 3047–52; ll. 3055–6)

The criteria here are the antithesis of those cultivated by neoplatonizing metaphysicians such as the author of the *Consolation of Philosophy*,[37] and although it may be unprincipled opportunism it does exhibit the real values he lives by and represents significant ideology in the culture of the court. The key terms are 'worthy fame', 'good name' and 'honour' all taken in the senses determined by very earthly aristocratic groups. He applies them to Arcite and in their light unequivocally calls him good – 'good Arcite, of chivalrie the flour' (l. 3059), recognizing him as a fellow-worshipper of Mars. Nothing could be further from the duke's imagination than that there may be other forms of worth, honour and human 'excellence' than these. He has never begun to think seriously about the questions raised by Arcite, and he transforms the knight's miserable death into a glorious fulfilment of the best possibilities of human existence, even asserting that his friends should celebrate the 'duetee and honour' of such an ending. Theseus' criteria of worth, with his total lack of reflexivity, were not Chaucer's although they do represent major tendencies in western civilization.

Theseus moves towards the festivities of the state-marriage he has planned and with a comically opportunistic eclecticism he brings together aristocratic 'chivalrie', a neoplatonic cliché about our life being nothing but a 'foule prisoun', more emphasis on Arcite's welfare' in death, courtly merriment and talk about the 'parfait joye lastynge evermo' which will now be produced by the marriage he has decreed (ll. 3057–72). Those who have followed the poet's depiction of Arcite's painful and questioning death without any other-worldly consolation, or even the sense of a meaningful pattern to his life and projects, will recognize the duke's talk about his 'welfare' (and about Jupiter's benevolent 'grace' in this case) as nonsense. But Chaucer shows just what kind of significant nonsense it is. He places Theseus' statement in contexts which bring out its dismissal of the particulars of suffering and perplexity, and in doing this he exemplifies the desensitizing of individual conscience and imaginative sympathy which can be so marked an aspect of theodicies in both their religious and secular forms. His own art encourages us to see just what is involved in Theseus' style of thought and arouses us to a critical response to his language, his ideas and the order he governs.

The final part of the ruler's speech is addressed to Emily:

> 'Suster,' quod he, 'this is my fulle assent,
> With al th'avys heere of my parlement,
> That gentil Palamon, youre owene knyght,
> That serveth yow with wille herte, and myght,
> And ever hath doon syn ye first hym knewe,
> That ye shul of youre grace upon hym rewe,
> And taken hym for housbonde and for lord.
> Lene me youre hond, for this is oure accord.
> Lat se now of youre wommanly pitee.
> He is a kynges brother sone, pardee;
> (*Knight's Tale*, ll. 3075–84)

Part of the comedy here comes from issues Chaucer also raised in his treatment of love, sex and marriage in works discussed earlier (chapters 5 and 6) – the woman, honoured with male service, from her own knight, is *commanded* to give her grace (a free gift!) and womanly pity which will result in Palamon taking her, as her lord. Theseus utters these conventional phrases without allowing Emily to discuss the matter or even break into his monologue. His values, underpinning the courtly language of service and grace, come across clearly in the last line quoted, where the grounds of 'grace' in this culture seem to be social status. This recalls his initial assessment of 'worth' in terms of 'roial lynage and richesse' (ll. 1829–32), and while this is a realistic enough example of aristocratic motives it again hardly has much to do with neoplatonic and Boethian ideas about love he had tried to exploit in his parliamentary address. His attitudes to 'the bond/That highte matrimoigne or mariage' are plainly part of the same culture as his discourse about the 'cheyne of love' we have just examined, discourse grounded in the service of an order he himself, unlike his creator, would never bring into reflexive attention. Our response to the very brief statement that Palamon and Emily lived happily ever after (ll. 3097–107) is deeply affected by these considerations and the total context in which it occurs. Its cursoriness and conventionality point towards its evasion of the wide range of problems evoked by a poem which is anything but a romance centred on 'Palamon and Emelye'. Quite as much as the *Franklin's Tale* (discussed in chapter 6) this text resists any conventional closure. True, the poet gives it one, and thus allows an audience steeped in romance to feel relieved and consoled, latching on to the few brief assertions about the future of Palamon and Emily, feeling reassured at the role of official secular authority in the marital union, and abandoning the disturbing meditations stimulated by the complete work. But there is no cause for readers more deeply concerned with the particulars of Chaucer's art and imagination to respond in this way. Quite the opposite in fact, for their attention to the poem will rather make them suspect that Chaucer was also thinking about the implications of traditionally consoling closures in romances, that while writing one down, to satisfy conventional expectations, he simultaneously invited the reader to grasp its distorting limitations and move beyond this particular form of closure. Having done so, he exposes the poem to the reactions of both 'gentils' and class-conscious miller within his fiction, developing a literary form which will constantly resist attempts at closure of any kind.[38]

Far from being a text which exalts Theseus, his practices or his ideas, Chaucer's poem encourages our imagination and intellect to penetrate and supersede the forms of language and life represented by the duke and his order, one which has many continuities with major tendencies in the culture Chaucer inhabited and of which we are heirs. He inserted abstractions which had become reified (like 'order', 'necessitee', 'love') in poetic processes which persuade us to explore their particular roles in actual human relations, desublimating them in ways which encourage critical discriminations unknown to Theseus. Chaucer's work is an outstanding poetic inquiry into problems of order in cultural and metaphysical dimensions, one which includes especial attention to the uses of metaphysical language by those in power, the transformations of metaphysics into an ideology of unreflexive secular domination.

Notes

Chapter 1 Imagination and Traditional Ideologies in *Piers Plowman*

1 Criticism has characteristically maintained that Langland was quite straightforwardly 'a traditionalist if not a reactionary', E. T. Donaldson, *Piers Plowman: The C-text and its poet* (1949), Cass, London, 1966, p. 108. In chapter 3 of his book *Poetry and Crisis in the Age of Chaucer*, University of Notre Dame Press, Notre Dame Ind., 1972, Charles Muscatine suggests that the poem's 'form and style are symptomatic of some sort of breakdown'. His work points in fruitful directions, seeing art as a 'response to a cultural situation', but the task needs specific analysis of the areas which prove problematic for Langland and this Muscatine does not attempt. His own sketch of both age and poem seem to me misleadingly negative and one-dimensional, for he sees poet and text as 'victims' of an 'age of decline', and of 'economic depression' (p. 16). My differences with his own stimulating work will be clear enough. In thinking about ideologies and their changes I have found the following works equally helpful: T. S. Kuhn, *The Structure of Scientific Revolutions*, University of Chicago Press, 1970, 2nd edn., and Kuhn's essays in *Criticism and the Growth of Knowledge*, ed. I. Lakatos and A. Musgrave, Cambridge University Press, 1970, pp. 1–23, 231–78; A. W. Gouldner, *The Dialectic of Ideology and Technology*, Macmillan, London, 1976.

2 Thomas Wimbledon's sermon is edited by N. H. Owen in *Medieval Studies*, 28, 1966, pp. 176–97, here quoting from p. 179.

3 *Seriatim* see Wimbledon in Owen, *Medieval Studies*, p. 179; Gower, *Mirour de l'omme*, ll. 27229–30, quoted in J. H. Fisher, *John Gower*, Methuen, London, 1965, p. 170; *Middle English Sermons*, ed. W. O. Ross, *EETS*, O.S., 209, 1940, pp. 224, 237.

4 On 'estates satire', see R. Mohl, *The Three Estates in Medieval and Renaissance Satire* (1933), Ungar, New York, 1962 and J. Mann, *Chaucer and Medieval Estates Satire*, Cambridge University Press, 1973. For examples of criticism which does not question the paradigm, see Ross, *Middle English Sermons*, pp. 124, 201–3, 237–9, 255–6, 266, 310–11. For examples in Lollard texts, see *The Lanterne of Li3t*, ed. L. M. Swinburn, *EETS*, O.S., 151, 1917, pp.

33–4, 117–21; *Select English Works of John Wyclif*, ed. T. Arnold, 3 vols, Oxford University Press, 1869, 1871, II, p. 246. For Wyclif on the theme, see *Dialogus*, ed. A. W. Pollard, Wyclif Society, 1876, pp. 2–5.

5 For a classic example of the 'monstrous' in the perception of Rebellion see John Gower, *Vox Clamantis*, I, chapters 2–8, trans. E. W. Stockton, *The Major Latin Works of John Gower*, University of Washington Press, 1962.

6 See R. Hilton, *Bond Men Made Free, Medieval Peasant Movements and the English Uprising of 1381*, Temple Smith, London, 1973, p. 229; pp. 221–32 relevant.

7 Hilton, *Bond Men*, p. 233: see too 16 below.

8 Donaldson, *Piers Plowman*, p. 106 (and chapter 4 *passim*); G. R. Owst, *Literature and Pulpit in Medieval England* 2nd edn, Blackwell, Oxford, 1966, chapter 9; P. Gradon, *Form and Style in Early English Literature*, Methuen, London, 1971, p. 102.

9 All quotation of *Piers Plowman* is from the B version eds. G. Kane and E. T. Donaldson, Athlone Press, London, 1975, unless otherwise stated. (References in the text are to passus and line numbers.)

10 The religious whom Langland thinks likely to escape the pervasive practices are those who become genuine 'Ancres and heremites þat holden hem in hire selles' (Pr 28–30), itself an indication of how alien the emerging world is from the one projected in the traditional ideology he accepts.

11 On the fable see discussion and references in J. A. W. Bennett, *Piers Plowman: The Prologue and Passus I–VII*, Oxford University Press, 1972, pp. 100–1.

12 See, for example, X. 29; XIII. 391–8 and XIX. 396–401, discussed later in the chapter; the whole issue is placed in a *theological* context in Passus XVII and XVIII (eg. XVII. 233–80 and XVIII. 396–9).

13 The problems here are also theological – those concerning grace, predestination and free will. Holy Church evades them, but the dreamer and the poet will doggedly confront them.

14 See II. 53–73, 158–88, 211–37.

15 The passage on Covetise is relevant here, V. 188–295 (also XIII. 355–98), as is that concerning Haukyn, XIII. 238–70, discussed in slightly different contexts later in the chapter. Brewing and baking were characteristic of traditional rural economies, but the point here is the role they serve in Langland's poem and in his changing world. In his *English Peasantry*, Oxford University Press, 1975, Rodney Hilton documents relevant developments in commodity production of the kind Langland had in mind (eg. pp. 43–57, 82–94, 152–3, 167–70, 196–208, 213–14). In a letter replying to my questions on this topic Rodney Hilton comments:

It is true of course that there were bakers and brewers in the

> peasant economy before. The assize of bread and ale which attempted to control them goes back (from Langland's day) more than a century and a half. All the same I think there *was* something new which gave life to Langland's bakers and brewers, and to Haukyn. What I think was new was the relaxation of seigneurial pressure not simply on the peasants and agricultural producers but on the retail trade in the villages. . . . In the fourteenth century brewing is . . . a trade which attracts the capital of entrepreneurs.

He also mentions his own recent work on some small town records of the period (Thornbury, South Gloucestershire) where he has apparently found a ruling élite largely composed of traders – bakers, brewers, grain and stock dealers, and retail traders. This seems to me the kind of situation Langland had in mind, but there is certainly room in this area for collaborative work between literary critics and historians.

16 For an introduction to this important subject see the following: S. L. Thrupp, *The Merchant Class of Medieval London* (1948), University of Michigan Press, Ann Arbor, 1962, pp. 288–99, and *passim*; *Economic Organization and Policies in the Middle Ages*, eds M. M. Postan *et al.*, *Cambridge Economic History of Europe*, Cambridge University Press, 1963, chapter 4 and pp. 287–90, 570; B. Geremek, *Le salariat dans l'artisanat parisien du XIIIe s. au XVe s.*, Mouton, The Hague, 1968; J. Le Goff, 'Le temps du travail dans la "crise" du XIVe s.', *Le Moyen Age*, 69, 1963, pp. 597–613; H. A. Miskimin, *The Economy of Early Renaissance Europe, 1300–1460*, Prentice-Hall, Englewood Cliffs, NJ, 1969, chapters 2 and 3; F. R. H. Du Boulay, *An Age of Ambition*, Nelson, London, 1970, chapter 3; F. Rorig, *The Medieval Town*, University of California Press, 1969; G. A. Williams, *Medieval London*, Athlone Press, London, 1963; R. Bird, *The Turbulent London of Richard II*, Longmans, London, 1949; E. M. Veale, *The English Fur Trade in the Later Middle Ages*, Oxford University Press, 1966, chapters 3 and 6; E. Power, *Medieval English Wool Trade* (1941), Oxford University Press, 1969, pp. 46–51, 104–23; M. Mollat and P. Wolff, *The Popular Revolutions of the Late Middle Ages*, Allen & Unwin, London, 1973.

17 Here I summarize the findings of G. Le Bras, 'Conceptions of Economy and Society', chapter 8 in Postan *et al.*, *Economic Organization and Policies in the Middle Ages*, especially pp. 560–1, 564–70; see too Thrupp, *Merchant Class*, pp. 174–80 and R. de Roover, *San Bernardino of Siena and Sant 'Antonio of Florence*, Baker Library, Harvard, 1967.

18 R. E. Lerner, *The Age of Adversity*, Cornell University Press, Ithaca NY, 1968, p. 17, and G. Leff, in *The Medieval World*, ed. D. Daiches and A. Thorlby, Aldus, London, 1973, p. 260. For introduction to this topic, another major one in studying the period,

see the following: Mollat and Wolff, *The Popular Revolutions of the Late Middle Ages*; F. R. H. Du Boulay, *An Age of Ambition*, Nelson, London, 1970, pp. 64 ff.; Miskimin, *The Economy of Early Renaissance Europe*, pp. 30–51; Hilton, *Bond Men* and 'Feudalism and the origins of Capitalism', *History Workshop*, 1, 1976, pp. 9–25; G. Duby, *Rural Economy and Country Life in the Medieval West*, Arnold, London, 1968, pp. 277–8, 283–6, 329–36; D. Nicholas, *Town and Countryside*, De Tempel, Bruges, 1971, pp. 63, 77 ff., 333–40.

19 This commons' petition of 1376 is translated in *The Peasants' Revolt of 1381*, ed. R. B. Dobson, Macmillan, London, 1970, p. 73. The Statute of Labourers: see B. H. Putnam, *The Enforcement of the Statute of Labourers*, Columbia University Press, New York, 1908.

20 Compare the attacks on law and lawyers in the uprising of 1381: Hilton, *Bond Men*, pp. 226–7; and for links with *Piers Plowman* see R. B. Dobson, *The Peasants' Revolt of 1381*, Macmillan, London, 1970, p. 380.

21 Wimbledon in Owen, *Medieval Studies*.

22 This topic is developed in chapter 3.

23 For examples of the endemic violence so easily solved by Langland at this point see Hilton, *English Peasantry*, pp. 240–3; J. Barnie, *War in Medieval Society*, Weidenfeld & Nicolson, London, 1974, chapters 1–3; H. J. Hewitt, *The Organization of War under Edward II*, Manchester University Press, 1966, chapters 2, 5, 7.

24 When Langland came to revise the B version he may have acknowledged this in this addition of a passage claiming that 'Love' will give the king more silver than merchants, ecclesiastics, Lombards and Jews, thus thrusting the difficulties he was tempted to evade into the forefront of the work, re-directing attention to the world where spiritual struggles are waged by economic man. See C. version, ed. W. W. Skeat, *Piers the Plowman in Three Parallel Texts* Oxford University Press, 1968; V. 191–4, (pp. 115, 117), and the edition by D. A. Pearsall, *Piers Plowman*, Arnold, London, 1978; IV. 191–4 (p. 96).

25 It is worth recalling that M. W. Bloomfield found later medieval moralists judging covetousness rather than pride as the worst and most prevalent sin: *Seven Deadly Sins*, Michigan State College Press, 1952, pp. 90–1.

26 In the light of the whole poem the 'grace of gyle' so essential to market practices has especially tragic irony, for Langland is actually writing after the victory of Christ over the prince of guile in Passus XVIII: see XVIII. 333–72 and contrast XVI. 154 ff. and II. 214 ff.

27 Explicitly involved are the landed classes, merchants retailers, financiers and the poor. The religious pilgrimage, product of confession itself has an economic motive – V. 228–9.

28 I have written about this, from a different perspective, in *Piers Plowman and Christian Allegory*, Arnold, London, 1975, chapter 5.

29 On the image here also see XV. 161 ff., and Elizabeth Salter [Zeeman], 'Piers Plowman and the pilgrimage to truth', *ES*, 2, 1958, pp. 1–16.
30 The relevant literature here is immense, but I have found the following particularly illuminating in relation to the period's literature: Hilton's *Bond Men* and *English Peasantry*, together with his *Decline of Serfdom in Medieval England*, Macmillan, London 1969; Miskimin, *The Economy of Early Renaissance Europe*, chapter 2; R. Brenner, 'Agrarian class structure and economic development in pre-industrial Europe', *P and P*, 70, 1976, pp. 30–75; C. Howell, 'Stability and change 1300–1700', *Journal of Peasant Studies*, 2, 1975, pp. 468–82; E. Miller's chapter 6 in *Economic Organization and Policies of the Middle Ages*, ed. Postan *et al.*; G. A. Holmes, *The Estates of the Higher Nobility in Fourteenth Century England*, Cambridge University Press, 1957, pp. 114–20; Duby, *Rural Economy*. The picture emerging from these works seems common among historians who differ considerably in accounting for the causes and in emphasis on different factors in describing the situation.
31 *Bond Men*, pp. 221–2, and see role of knights in I. 94–104, VIII. 100–6; and E. T. Donaldson quoted at opening of n. 1.
32 In quoting lines 38–40 I have rejected two conjectural emendations of their base MS made by Kane and Donaldson: they insert 'þee' in place of 'yow' and 'ye', to accord with their own view of Piers's status, views they do not explicate or defend, understandably enough given their monumental editorial task (p. 170 and critical apparatus, p. 350). I have written at some length on Piers's status here and given my ground for denying a clerical and allegorical role here, *Piers Plowman*, pp. 77–81, 113–24, and a reader could also cast his eyes over the following lines to see how Piers is *not* presented as an image of the clerical estate here: 27, 92–5, 101 ff., 152 ff., 159, 169 ff., 202 ff., 253 ff., 280 ff. See too A. V. C. Schmidt's judicious comments in his edition of *The Vision of Piers Plowman*, from the same MS, Dent, London, 1978, p. 272. Also Pearsall, *Piers Plowman*, pp. 147–8.
33 Hilton's *English Peasantry*, pp. 21–7.
34 The tone of the knight's reply (VI. 164–6) probably itself is a small example of Langland's orthodox ideology imposing itself: his non-coercive courtesy to anarchic peasants and ineffectual ploughman comprises a brief assertion that the upper and lower estates can still be fixed in a mutually beneficial and respectful order, despite the present events.
35 A shrewd assessment of the uprising in terms of increased aspirations was made by Froissart – text in Dobson, *The Peasants' Revolt*, p. 370. On literary complaint about the peasantry, B. White 'Poet and peasant', in *The Reign of Richard II*, ed. F. R. H. Du Boulay and C. M. Barron, Athlone Press, London, 1971, pp. 59–63, 65–7, 73.

36 See texts in Dobson, *The Peasants' Revolt* pp. 136–7, 371–83: see especially the egalitarian communism attributed to him by Froissart in Dobson, p. 371, and Hilton, *Bond Men*, chapter 9.
37 In this paragraph I am paraphrasing and quoting Hilton, 'Feudalism and the origins of Capitalism', pp. 20–2; see too references in n. 30 above. Some aspects of the argument here coincide with some views of J. H. Fischer, 'Wyclif, Langland, Gower and the Pearl poet on the subject of aristocracy', *Studies in Medieval Literature*, ed. M. Leach, University of Pennsylvania Press, Philadelphia, 1961, pp. 139–57.
38 Ed. W. N. Francis, *EETS*, O.S., 217, 1942, p. 34.
39 See earlier discussion and n. 12 above.
40 On the tradition, n. 36; also, for example, *English Works of Wyclif*, ed. F. D. Matthew, *EETS*, O.S., 74, (revised 1902), pp. 227–8, 233–4.
41 The passage attacking ideas of communal ownership (XX. 273–9) could be taken as Langland's wish to ensure his views are not merged with those of contemporary radical Christians, but it must also be read in its context where it is primarily part of a polemical attack on friars and their concepts of ownership and use.
42 For introduction to the Pardon scene, its problems and the literature on it, J. Lawlor, *Piers Plowman*, Arnold, London, 1962, pp. 71–84; E. Kirk, *The Dream Thought of Piers Plowman*, Yale University Press, 1972, pp. 80–100; Aers, *Piers Plowman*, pp. 121–3; R. W. Frank, *Piers Plowman* Yale University Press, 1957, chapter 3.
43 See works cited in no. 16 above on relevant developments in the period.
44 Thrupp, *Merchant Class*, chapter 7; quoting here from pp. 290, 311.
45 Thrupp, *Merchant Class*, p. 174.
46 On the difficulties of distinguishing usury see the statement at XIX. 348–50; here the quote is from Thrupp, *Merchant Class*, p. 177.
47 Thrupp, *Merchant Class*, 15, pp. 177–80, 313–15. Thrupp sees foreshadowing of 'Puritan culture' in these developments. To her comments should be added the fascinating studies on changing attitudes to poverty during this period collected by M. Mollat, *Études sur l'histoire de la pauvreté jusqu'au XVI*[e] *s.*, 2 vols, Sorbonne, Paris, 1974. I believe Langland's own text illustrates a shifting and uncertain attitude to poverty which is related to developments outlined in this collection, but this is another area where collaborative work between literary critics and historians could be most fruitful.
48 Doubtless his own social position, as he experienced and represented it, encouraged such critical integrity: a de-classed, wandering intellectual, one of the vagrant types he attacked, he had no place in the social and religious ideology he affirmed. See, eg. C version, ed. D. A. Pearsall, V. 1–101 (Skeat's VI. 1–101).

49 In my *Piers Plowman*, chapter 5, I tried to show how Piers functions as a lens mediating the fullest spiritual perception available at particular stages of vision in the poem, and here he mediates what the author takes to be the best available social ideas.

50 In the lines referred to I see no reason for rejecting MSS reading 'bely ioye' for Kane and Donaldson's emendation to 'bilye', although the latter too keeps the sense of livelihood (cf. XIX. 235). Langland's own resistance to this split is described in the present and following two chapters.

51 I say Trajan's speech but it is actually often impossible to tell whether it is Trajan or Will or the poet himself to whom the poetry is attributed: eg. for lines 171–319, 171 says, 'quod Troianus', but for how much further is he the speaker, and how appropriate are lines like 317–18 to him rather than Langland *in propria persona*? The statements, whoever their formal speaker, are very dear and central to Langland's own hopes.

52 See earlier discussions of this and n. 12 above. On Trajan, see J. S. Wittig's comments in *Traditio*, 28, 1972, pp. 249–63.

53 For a good summary of readings emerging from such approaches, and references, see Schmidt, *Piers Plowman*, p. 346.

54 On exegesis and picture models, see Aers, *Piers Plowman*, chapters 2–3.

55 Patience's statement at XIII. 164–71; Conscience's enthusiasm here recalling his own earlier messianic vision (III. 284–330) where the period leading to the conversion of the Jews was to be introduced by an apocalyptic king, a very different path to the one envisaged here. Conscience seems rather unstable in the ways he envisages, and he should never be simply identified with a final authoritative-authorial viewpoint (even if there was one final one, which there is not).

56 Besides the earlier discussions referred to here, see n. 12 above.

57 On the dissolution of historical existence in 'picture model' allegory, Aers, *Piers Plowman*, chapters 2–3.

58 *City of God*, XIX. 5, tr. M. Dods, Random House, New York, 1950, p. 680.

59 From XIV. 104–273 the speaker is formally Patience: he now speaks with one of the characteristic voices of the poet in his own person – see for example the immensely powerful addition in the C version on the lives of poor people, Skeat's C text, X. 71–97, Pearsall's IX. 71–97.

60 Aers, *Piers Plowman*, chapter 5, *passim*.

61 Respectively see: XVI. 100–7; XVI. 215; XVIII. 212–15 and 222–5: of the many examples of brotherhood in Christ see XI. 199–212; XVIII. 393–9; and V. 384–90, 503: on Christ as one of the contemporary poor, see especially XI. 185–96 (and Luke 14); XI. 232–7; X. 460–81. On Piers teaching Christ, and the powerful dramatization of the Christian version of history in Passus

XVI–XX, see Aers, *Piers Plowman*, respectively pp. 107–9, 79–130 *passim*.

62 For some of the major imagistic connections between XIX–XX and VI see M. W. Bloomfield, *Piers Plowman as a Fourteenth Century Apocalypse*, Rutgers University Press, New Brunswick NJ, 1961, pp. 130, 115, and Aers, *Piers Plowman*, pp. 109–31.

63 For the Holy Spirit as released by Christ's acts, XIX. 199 ff., XVI. 46–52, and John 16:7, Acts 2:1–8.

64 See XIX. 225 ff.: at line 228 he quotes 1 Cor. 12:4. On the changing concepts of the *corpus mysticum* in medieval ideology, the major study is by H. de Lubac, *Corpus Mysticum* (2nd edn.), Aubier-Montaigne, Paris, 1949.

65 Kane and Donaldson read 'coke' at line 238 meaning 'to make hay cocks', and they give their reasons for preferring this to 'dyke' or 'dyche' on pp. 174–5.

66 So total is Holy Spirit's evasion here that he does not even attempt to repeat the ideas: compare the earlier discussion of the treatment of merchants in the gloss to the pardon in Passus VII.

67 Some might feel the vagueness of the generalizations about brotherly love is explained by their reference to a remote past. But in fact the occupations Spirit refers to are not remote from Langland's day and, as we have seen, are essential to the poem's preoccupations and movement. Here Langland wants to fit them into the orthodox ideological framework and stress its divine authority. But what actually happens is that the cherished scheme is exposed as contingent and superseded, as I argue in the following paragraphs. In connection with crafts, love and unity it is worth reminding oneself of the fiercely self-regarding and bitter craft conflicts (see for example the works by Bird, Williams, and Geremek, n. 16 above, and Sylvia Thrupp's chapter on the gilds in Postan *et al.*, *Economic Organization and Policies in the Middle Ages*.

68 Discussed on a number of occasions through the chapter, see references in n. 12.

69 This topic deserves more attention than I can give it here. Conscience does resist Meed earlier in the poem, but his proneness to error is clear enough in the apocalyptic vision (discussed earlier, and at greater length in chapter 3) and in Passus XIII (see n. 55); in Passus XX the physical terrors he invokes seem totally misguided in the task of encouraging real spiritual regeneration, and his acceptance of the glib and typically inadequate friar-confessor is plainly a capitulation to present pressures, which is seen by Langland as a disaster. Aquinas himself emphasizes that Conscience may be erroneous, either through our own fault or through causes for which we are responsible, yet even when it is *wrong* we are morally obliged to follow it: see *Quodlibetum*, 3.27 and *Summa Theologica*, I. 79. 12 and 13. In my view, Langland's attitude to Conscience runs on lines such as these, with particular, and

discomforting emphasis on its proneness to err. This itself is an example of his own splendid self-reflexivity, allied to spiritual and intellectual modesty. It is interesting that he has *Jesus* himself acknowledge the potential errancy of Conscience at XVII. 138 ff.

70 XIX. 213–335, fulfilling the images of cultivation and Christian history in XVI. 1–166: Aers, *Piers Plowman*, pp. 79–109, 128–31.

71 At line 379 Kane and Donaldson revise MSS of B version in accord with C version: contrast Schmidt's edition, p. 304. On the friars' 'fynding' see X. 322–30 and XX. 228–35; Langland's rejection of the friar's fiction of collective poverty and freedom from ownership occurs throughout the poem, together with the moral and economic practices he believed the fiction encouraged. On the fierce controversies over theories of ownership and poverty as they concerned the friars, see M. D. Lambert, *Franciscan Poverty*, SPCK, London, 1961; G. Leff, *Heresy in the Later Middle Ages*, 2 vols, Manchester University Press, 1967, I, pp. 51–255.

Chapter 2 Langland and the Church: Affirmation and Negation

1 Commonplace, but see G. Leff, *Heresy in the Later Middle Ages*, 2 vols, Manchester University Press, 1967, I, prologue; *Documents of the Christian Church*, ed. H. Bettenson, 2nd ed., Oxford University Press, 1977, pp. 72–74, 115 ('Unam sanctam' (1302), 'outside this Church there is neither salvation nor remission of sins', pp. 133–5 (justification of Inquisition by St Thomas Aquinas), pp. 179–82 ('De haeretico comburendo', 1401); R. W. Southern, *Western Society and the Church in the Middle Ages*, Penguin, Harmondsworth, 1970, pp. 20–2.

2 Commonplace, but for examples see *Middle English Sermons*, ed. W. O. Ross, *EETS*, O.S., 209, 1940, pp. 183–4, 205–6, 216–17, 241, 276–82, 285–8. Here quotations from pp. 241 and 282–3. One of the preachers in this collection even gives 300 days' pardon to all who hear his sermon and say the *pater noster* five times and hear the *ave* with a good heart and name Jesus at the end (pp. 58–9). See too B. L. Manning, *The People's Faith in the Time of Wyclif*, Cambridge University Press, 1917, and W. A. Pantin, *The English Church in the Fourteenth Century*, Cambridge University Press, 1955, part 3, chapters 9–10. There is an extremely important study of the sociology and politics of the confessional apparatus by T. N. Tentler, 'The Summa for Confessors as an instrument of social control', pp. 103–37 in *The Pursuit of Holiness*, ed. C. Trinkaus and H. A. Oberman, E. J. Brill, Leiden, 1974, and the development, *Sin and Confession on the Eve of the Reformation*, Princeton University Press, 1977.

3 XX. 228–99: for examples of the special importance of the confessional apparatus through *Piers Plowman* see III. 34–75; V. 595–600; XIV. 16–28; XIX. 182 ff.; XX. 213 ff., 300 ff.; and

M. W. Bloomfield, *Piers Plowman as a Fourteenth Century Apocalypse*, Rutgers University Press, 1961, pp. 130 ff.

4 On the Latin text see Skeat, *Piers the Plowman in Three Parallel Texts* (1886), Oxford University Press, 1968, vol. 2, pp. 217–18; Isaiah 24:2 and Matthew 21:12–20.

5 The image of course connects with the tree of Charity – Aers, *Piers Plowman and Christian Allegory*, Arnold, London, 1975, pp. 79–107.

6 *Middle English Sermons*, ed. Ross, pp. 117–18; see G. R. Owst, *Literature and the Pulpit in Medieval England,* 2nd edn. reprinted, Blackwell, Oxford, 1966, p. 268, n.3.

7 X. 480–1; see XII. 105–27, 155–88 and the overlap between clerks, priests and religious.

8 Aers, *Piers Plowman*, pp. 77–131, especially pp. 77–9, 128–31.

9 See, for this power, XIX. 258–334; also Aers, *Piers Plowman*, pp. 128–31, and Bloomfield, *Piers Plowman*, pp. 133–49. On the reading 'garland' (XIX. 321) see Kane and Donaldson (eds), *Piers Plowman: The B Version*, Athlone Press, London, 1975, p. 118: contrast A. V. Schmidt (ed.), *The Vision of Piers Plowman* B Text, Dent, London, 1978, p. 300.

10 A. C. Spearing, *Criticism and Medieval Poetry*, Arnold, London, 1964, pp. 71–3, using the 1933 edition of Owst's *Literature and Pulpit*, pp. 548–9; for comparable views, T. P. Dunning, *Piers Plowman* (1937) Greenwood, Westport, 1971, pp. 7–11, 14–15, Bloomfield, *Piers Plowman*, pp. 46–7, 153.

11 The literature on the church's economic and political incorporation and power in medieval society is immense, but I have found the following especially relevant in my own studies of Langland and Chaucer: both volumes of Leff, *Heresy*; R. W. Southern, *Western Society and the Church in the Middle Ages*, Penguin, Harmondsworth, 1970; F. Rapp, *L'Église et la vie religieuse en occident à la fin du moyen âge*, Presses Universitaires de France, Paris, 1971; R. E. Lerner, *The Heresy of the Free Spirit in the Later Middle Ages,* University of California, 1972; G. Leff, *The Dissolution of the Medieval Outlook*, Harper & Row, New York, 1976, chapter 4; R. H. Tawney, *Religion and the Rise of Capitalism,* (1926) Penguin, Harmondsworth, 1964; I think it also helpful for those studying the literature of the period to consult works describing the daily concerns of church officers involved in organizing its material foundations, for example, E. Searle, *Lordship and Community: Battle Abbey and its banlieu,* Pontifical Institute of Medieval Studies, 1974; F. R. H. Du Boulay, *The Lordship of Canterbury*, Nelson, London, 1966.

12 See discussion of Chaucer's pardoner in chapter 4, and nn. 16 and 23. The next line after the quotation states, 'It is noȝt by þe bisshop þat þe boy precheþ': this line is obscure, as Schmidt rightly notes. It either means the poet has had second thoughts and wishes to preserve the bishop from complicity, implying the pardoner got the

seal without his knowledge, or, the sense Schmidt prefers, it 'allows the bishop responsibility for granting the pardoner the seal, but *not* any authority to preach in his diocese'. Schmidt translates the line: 'It is not in accordance with (the intentions of) the bishop that the rogue preaches', pp. 304, 305).

13 Here I draw especially on: H. G. Richardson, 'The parish clergy in the thirteenth and fourteenth century', *Transactions of the Royal Historical Society*, 6, 1912, pp. 89–128; A. H. Thompson, *The English Clergy and their Organization in the Later Middle Ages*, Oxford University Press, 1947, chapter 4; J. A. W. Bennett (ed.), *Piers Plowman*, Oxford University Press, 1972, pp. 91–2; Rapp, *L'Église*, chapter 9; there is a revealing example of a vicar being charged under the Statute of Labourers in B. H. Putnam, *The Enforcement of the Statute of Labourers*, Columbia University Press, 1908, p. 91.

14 Of the references in note 11, especially relevant here are Rapp, *L'Église*, pp. 212–15 and Southern, *Western Society*, pp. 125–69, 215–16, 272–99.

15 Rapp, *L'Église*, pp. 272–3:

> The Church is immersed in the world. The latter only has to stir and immediately Christian life will feel the effects of this movement. Now it is indeed change which characterizes the epoch with which we are concerned. To begin with, the sphere of production and exchange: whether we assume, with the majority of historians, that the West entered a long period of stagnation, or whether, with the marxists, we emphasize the emergence of new structures, those of incipient capitalism, the essential fact for our subject remains. After 1300, the European economy assumed a quite different appearance. . . . In the fourteenth century, ushered in with famine, war and plague, the demographic collapse, the fall in agricultural prices and the rise in wages shook the foundations of society, and more especially of lordship. . . . These diverse waves flowed right through the sacred world as they did through the profane. The church was a financial power, a social force, a political apparatus at the same time as the dispenser of knowledge and wisdom. All its functions were affected by the change which western civilization endured.

16 Southern, *Western Society*, 158–9, here I quote from pp. 160 and 164. See n. 11 above, and also J. A. Yunck, *The Lineage of Lady Meed*, Notre Dame University Press, Notre Dame, Ind., 1963; J. H. Lynch, *Simoniacal Entry into Religious Life*, Ohio State University Press, 1976. On the passage's place in literary traditions, see A. L. Kellogg, *Chaucer, Langland and Arthur*, Rutgers University Press, New Brunswick, 1972, pp. 32–50, and Elizabeth Salter, '*Piers Plowman* and *The Simonie*', *Archiv*, 203, 1966–7, pp. 241–54.

17 See J. Mann's excellent discussion of Chaucer's transformations of tradition in *Chaucer and Medieval Estates Satire*, Cambridge

University Press, 1973, pp. 17–37.

18 On the fish-out-of-water tradition, Mann, *Chaucer*, pp. 29–31.

19 Mann, *Chaucer*, 54.

20 Southern, *Western Society*, pp. 214–72; Rapp, *L'Église*, pp. 216–20.

21 In the next chapter we will consider how he moved beyond conventional moral criticism in another way – to think about the need for a revolution in the property relations of the religious orders.

22 For Langland and the friars see Bloomfield, *Piers Plowman*, pp. 45–6, 71–2, 148–9, 198 n. 16, 200–1 n. 36; R. W. Frank, *Piers Plowman* (1957), Archon, 1969, pp. 106–7 n. 2, 112–16, and above, n. 71 chapter 1. For traditional criticism, Mann, *Chaucer*, pp. 37–54.

23 Southern, *Western Society*, pp. 247, 272–99: here quotes from pp. 288–9, 291–2; see Rapp, *L'Église*, pp. 220–2.

24 II. 213, 233 ff.; III. 35–72. On the 'coueitise of copes', the choice of the word 'maistres' and the confessional, see Mann, *Chaucer*, pp. 43–4, 39, 47–9.

25 For a different slant, Bloomfield, *Piers Plowman*, p. 146.

26 On Piers in Passus V–VII, Aers, *Piers Plowman*, pp. 77–9, 109–23; Reason is distinct from ecclesiastics, eg. V. 41–7; on Conscience, see chapter 1, n. 69 above and text.

27 This alone seems quite incompatible with P. Gradon's suggestion that Piers is some kind of Wyclifite layman (*Form and Style in Early English Literature*, Methuen, London, 1971, p. 107): see too VI. 76 and 149 likewise.

28 For interpretations of the Pardon scene see chapter 1, n. 42 above.

29 This central aspect of the poem (and its historical contexts) has been quite missed by the badly misnamed 'historical critics', D. W. Robertson and B. F. Huppé, *Piers Plowman and Scriptural Tradition*, Princeton University Press, 1951, but not by Charles Muscatine, *Poetry and Crisis*, University of Notre Dame Press, Notre Dame, Ind., 1972, pp. 78–9, 107, nor by Bloomfield, *Piers Plowman*, pp. 20–1. See the important statement on conventional didactic handbooks and *Piers Plowman* at XII. 10–28.

30 See similarly Holy Church, I. 85–93, 128–35, and the Athanasian Creed, VII. 113–18, and on continuities in XIX, Bloomfield, *Piers Plowman*, p. 130. A host of theological problems of burning importance to Langland are pertinent to such statements and treated in Passus IX–XII, problems concerning grace, justification and predestination, free will. With Elizabeth Kirk, I believe H. A. Oberman's study, *The Harvest of Medieval Theology*, Harvard University Press, 1963, is especially relevant to students of Langland's theological concerns and their contexts, here particularly in relation to the concepts of '*facere quod in se est*' and *justification* (pp. 120–85, 191–3, 207–11, 218–20): E. Kirk, *The Dream Thought of Piers Plowman*, Yale University Press, 1972, pp. 97–8 and notes.

31 There is a fine account of St Augustine's development of the psychological aspects of these issues in Peter Brown, *Augstine of Hippo*, Faber, London, 1967, pp. 149–57, 173–4, 178–9, 372–4 and chapters 16, 29–31. For indications of inadequacies in the friars' response from a different aspect, see Schmidt, *Piers Plowman*, p. 326.

32 Their later claim that if the individual wills to do deadly sin then God allows such 'sleuþe' is again hopelessly superficial for it begs all kinds of questions about the necessity of grace to do well at all and ignores the effects of the fall on the human will (see n. 31 above).

33 See the concluding pages of chapter 1 and on Piers and Christ in XVI–XX, Aers, *Piers Plowman*, pp. 71–131 *passim*.

34 Bloomfield, *Piers Plowman*, pp. 20–1, and see p. 149; also Muscatine, *Poetry and Crisis*, pp. 78–80, 107.

35 One could return to the treatment of Patient Poverty and Conscience (XIII–XIV) in these terms too, looking at them from a perspective not present in the first chapter. There we focussed on the evasory, false forms of transcendence they offered, revealed as such by the poem's own imaginative particulars and movement. Here we could concentrate on the *extra-institutional* nature of their path, taking the emphasis on the sacrament of confession at XIV. 85–97 as a sign of the poet's conscious commitment to the orthodox institution and traditional ideology, something we have seen often enough, and recalling how the poem continually shows the inadequacy of such inherited schemes in the present situation, pushing dreamer and reader *outside* the institution in the poet's quest. The judgments made and the mode of life pursued are thus seen as extra-institutional, however much such a vision distresses the poet.

36 See XIX. 182–90, 258–335; and Jesus's statements at XVII. 93–100, 120–1.

37 XIX. 396–402, 451–76.

38 See II. 169 ff., discussed earlier in chapter 2, and Southern, *Western Society*, p. 133.

39 Referring here to XX. 126–30, 217–27, 253–61.

40 This was becoming a common attack among radical reformers and would become a marked feature in Protestant ideology – Leff, *Dissolution*, pp. 128–9.

41 Langland should have felt sympathy for claims by Wyclif and Lollards that if Christ lived then he would be crucified by the church as a heretic – Wyclif, *De blasphemia*, quoted in Leff, *Heresy*, II.558, and *Ploughman's Complaint* in T. Wright (ed.), *Political Poems and Songs*, Longman, London, 1859, vol. 1, p. 322.

42 See chapter 3, n. 34, on this. For typical examples of heretics seeing the Papacy and established church as Antichrist, see *Heresies of the High Middle Ages*, ed. W. L. Wakefield and A. P. Evans, Columbia University Press, 1969, pp. 173, 424–7, 431–4.

43 For example see: M. D. Lambert, *Medieval Heresy*, Arnold, London, 1977, pp. 174–81, 205–6, 211–15, 240–6, 287–9; Leff, *Heresy*, vol. 2, pp. 523–4, 577–8 *et passim*; Southern, *Western Society*, chapter 7; Rapp, *L'Église*, pp. 328–30; R. E. Lerner, *Heresy of the Free Spirit,* University of California Press, 1972; A. S. McGrade, *The Political Thought of William of Ockham*, Cambridge University Press, 1974, pp. 53–77, 113 ff., 134 ff., 142 ff., 185 ff.; M. J. Wilks, *The Problem of Sovereignty in the Later Middle Ages*, Cambridge University Press, 1964.

44 Leff, *Dissolution*, pp. 120–1, and chapter 4 *passim*.

Chapter 3 Langland, Apocalypse and the *Saeculum*

1 M. W. Bloomfield, *Piers Plowman as a Fourteenth-Century Apocalypse*, Rutgers University Press, New Brunswick NJ, 1961; see P. M. Kean in *Piers Plowman. Critical Approaches*, ed. S. S. Hussey, Methuen, London, 1969, p. 333.

2 Bloomfield, *Piers Plowman*, pp. 99, 105, 112, 114; the penultimate phrase quoted is repeated on p. 116. On the writers Bloomfield aligns with Langland see the indispensable study by Marjorie Reeves, *The Influence of Prophecy in the Later Middle Ages*, Oxford University Press, 1969; also G. Leff, *Heresy in the Later Middle Ages*, 2 vols, Manchester University Press, 1967; vol. 1, part 1.

3 Bloomfield, *Piers Plowman*, chapters 4 and 5 *passim*, especially pp. 98–9, 118–23.

4 For example contrast discussions of the tree of Charity in Passus XVI by Bloomfield in '*Piers Plowman* and the Three Grades of Chastity', *Anglia*, 76, 1958, pp. 227–53 (also Bloomfield, *Piers Plowman*, pp. 122–3), with the one in D. Aers, *Piers Plowman and Christian Allegory*, Arnold, London, 1975, chapter 5; trying to make the poem fit his alien scheme he turns the Harrowing of Hell into 'the true end of the poem' (p. 125) whereas Langland, as our study makes clear, wrote a poem whose movement, power and honesty could never have reached a 'true end' where Bloomfield claims; his treatment of Dowel, Dobet and Dobest is another example of the imposition of his scheme on material that is strikingly resistant to it. It may also be suggested that Bloomfield seems to underestimate the significance of *non*-Joachite apocalypticism, a common enough phenomenon in the late Middle Ages, as Gordon Leff observes, *The Dissolution of the Medieval Outlook*, Harper & Row, New York, pp. 133–4.

5 Bloomfield, *Piers Plowman*, pp. 102–3; E. T. Donaldson, *Piers Plowman*, Cass, London, reprinted 1966, pp. 109–10; and chapter 1 above.

6 See chapter 1 *passim*, and the references in note 16 to that chapter.

7 See discussion of this area of the poem in chapter 1.

8 *Piers Plowman*, ed. J. A. W. Bennett, Oxford University Press, 1972, p. 141. The comments on language I make here merely tap the surface of the major study on language, ideology and culture by R. I. V. Hodge and G. R. Kress which I was able to read in MS form: it is of great relevance to anyone interested in literature, history and cultural analysis: *Language as Ideology*, Routledge & Kegan Paul, London, 1979.

9 I offer some comments on Langland's use of Wycliffite ideas later in this chapter, but his relationship to this aspect of his milieu needs sustained investigation. This would perhaps also cast light on pre-Wycliffite criticism and ideas of reform directed at the church, especially in plebeian circles. (On the class structure of Lollardy see the judicious summary in M. Lambert, *Medieval Heresy*, Arnold, London, 1977, pp. 259–65, 270–1). There is a useful select bibliography of original and secondary writing printed on pp. 231–34 of *Selections from English Wycliffite Writings*, ed. Anne Hudson, Cambridge University Press, 1978. The grammar of apocalypse is another subject that needs sustained study, using both the socio-linguistic methods of Hodge and Kress (see n. 8 above) and the more habitual methods of social and religious history.

10 At line 294 Conscience asserted 'Leaute shal don hym lawe and no lif ellis', but we commented on this above: in such contexts the abstractionism in the use of personifications like this begs the very problems that are troubling Langland, and many of his contemporaries. Who could credibly represent 'Leaute' in the contemporary society with which Langland was so engaged? It is worth noting one point about Kane and Donaldson's text here: they print 'burn' at line 321 for MSS 'baron'. This coheres well with the basic movements of Conscience's vision as I am describing it, and the reading of 'baron' in this context would seem most improbable – the appearance of an apocalyptic king here would be quite another matter of course, as would be the appearance of 'barons and erles' in an appeal to the present lay power (see discussion of Passus X and XV later in this chapter).

11 M. Mollat and P. Wolff, *The Popular Revolutions of the Late Middle Ages*, Allen & Unwin, London, 1973, p. 11; this whole study is relevant, as is R. Hilton, *Bond Men Made Free. Medieval Peasant Movements and the English Uprising of 1381*, Temple Smith, London, 1973.

12 Mollat and Wolff, *The Popular Revolutions*, p. 270; on the Hussite Revolution the splendid study by H. Kaminsky is indispensable, *A History of the Hussite Revolution*, University of California Press, 1968; see too his 'Hussite Radicalism and the Origins of Tabor', *Medievalia et Humanistica*, 10, 1956, pp. 102–30; and Leff, *Heresy*, vol. 2, chapter 9, Lambert, *Medieval Heresy*, chapters 16 and 17.

13 On the programmes recorded from the Peasants' Uprising see R. B. Dobson (ed.), *The Peasants' Revolt of 1381*, Macmillan, London, 1970, and Hilton, *Bond Men* chapter 9. On the date of the B

version see J. A. W. Bennett, in *MAEV*, 12 (1943), pp. 55–64, and B. F. Huppé in *Speculum*, 22 (1942), pp. 578–620.

14 This could mean that every current practitioner of law will be turned into a 'labourer', and/or that law will become a labourer, in the sense that law will be turned to serve the needs and justice of labourers rather than of present dominant and controlling groups.

15 There is an interesting view about the ruling landed classes in the works of Peter Chelcicky; born in about 1390 and emerging from the Taborite Movement he apparently maintained that since Christians should not make war there can be no justification for the estate of nobles. Nobility, he said, was based solely on violence, robbery and now money, while its existence was based solely on the exploitation of the peasantry. He denounced aristocrats as 'useless drones', and found the serfdom they perpetuated a sin against God and man. For Chelcicky's view, P. Brock, *The Political and Social Doctrines of the Unity of Czech Brethren in the Fifteenth and Early Sixteenth Century*, Mouton, The Hague, 1957, chapter 1.

16 Bloomfield, *Piers Plowman*, p. 112 (and pp. 4, 17, 173 *et passim*).

17 In the theological terms Bloomfield uses it substitutes a thoroughly *secularized* history of salvation for the more detached and Christocentric attitude to *saeculum* cultivated by St Augustine in his later works. In the first chapter of this book I noted some examples of the way Conscience voices aspirations or reactions Langland may share but towards which he is being critical, just as happens here. I hope to develop this reading of Conscience which, as far as I am aware, scholars have not suggested, and it would certainly have significant consequences for our reading of Conscience in *Piers Plowman*.

18 On the Middle Ages, see R. E. Lerner, 'Medieval prophecy and religious dissent', *P and P*, 72, 1976, pp. 3–24; Leff, *Heresy*, part 1; P. J. Alexander, 'Medieval Apocalypses as Historical Sources', *American Historical Review*, 73, 1968, pp. 997–1018; Sylvia L. Thrupp (ed.), *Millennial Dreams in Action*, Mouton, The Hague, 1962; E. Hobsbawm, *Primitive Rebels*, Manchester University Press, 1959, chapters 1, 4, 5. N. Cohn's well-known study, *The Pursuit of the Millennium*, Secker & Warburg, London, 1957, has grave defects of both ideological and empirical kinds – see particularly the comments in chapter 21 of Alasdair MacIntyre's *Against the Self-Images of the Age*, Duckworth, London, 1971, in Lambert, *Medieval Heresy*, pp. 47–8 and the reviews Lambert cites in n. 11, p. 42.

19 On Passus VI see chapter 1.

20 See, for example, texts in Dobson, *Peasants' Revolt*, pp. 164–5, 177, 370–1, 380–3.

21 On 'picture models' and interpretation see Aers, *Piers Plowman*, chapters 2–5. Precisely the same point applies to the riddle in Passus XIII discussed in chapter 1.

22 See especially X. 120–256, XV. 90–135, and chapter 2 above, and

the secondary materials referred to in the notes, especially useful here are F. Rapp, *L'Église et la vie religieuse en occident à la fin du moyen âge*, Presses Universitaires de France, Paris, 1971, and Southern, *Western Society*; also Lambert, *Medieval Heresy*, part 4.

23 Bloomfield, *Piers Plowman*, p. 121.

24 Ibid., pp. 72, 121, 52.

25 See *De Ecclesia*, ed. I. Loserth (1886), reprinted Johnson, New York, 1966, eg. chapters 9 and 15, the ideas about temporal lords in *Dialogus*, ed. A. W. Pollard, Wyclif Society, London, 1876, pp. 3–5, and the lucid account in Leff, *Heresy*, chapter 7. On the question of dominion and grace Leff makes a comment most relevant to the present context:

> from *De Ecclesia* onwards the disqualification of those in mortal sin from lordship was confined almost exclusively to the church hierarchy . . . [and] in *De Officio Regis* after Wyclif expressly exempted the king, and by implication the lay lords, from any challenge to their authority: they were needed to disendow and reform the church (vol. 2, p. 560).

26 Leff, *Heresy*, vol. 2, p. 543.

27 See ibid., pp. 543–4, 560.

28 Lambert, *Medieval Heresy*, pp. 228–9.

29 On Wyclif's political realism see M. Wilks, '*Reformatio Regni*: Wyclif and Hus as leaders of religious protest movements', in *Schism, Heresy and Religious Protest*, ed. D. Baker, Cambridge University Press, 1972, pp. 109–30; for a contrasting approach see H. Kaminsky, 'Wyclifism as ideology of revolution', *Church History*, 32, 1963, pp. 57–74. See below in text the comments on XIX. 466–76.

30 With chapters 1 and 2 above, see also Bloomfield, *Piers Plowman*, pp. 4, 16, 105.

31 On ideologies of poverty in the later Middle Ages see: Leff, *Heresy*, part 1; M. D. Lambert, *Franciscan Poverty*, SPCK, London, 1961; M. Mollat, 'La notion de pauvreté au moyen âge', *Revue d'histoire de l'Église de France*, 1966, pp. 6–23; F. Rapp, 'L'Eglise et les pauvres', *Revue d'histoire de l'Église de France*, 52, 1966, pp. 39–46; Rapp, *L'Église*, pp. 282–4; and see the discussion of Patient Poverty in chapter 1, above, and in n. 47 there.

32 Bloomfield, *Piers Plowman*, p. 121.

33 See n. 29 above, and Leff, *Heresy*, vol. 2, pp. 542–3, and his references. (For example of Constantine in Wyclif, see *De Ecclesia*, chapter 16.) W. W. Skeat (ed.), *Piers Plowman in Three Parallel Texts* (1886), Oxford University Press, 1968, gives analogues in Lollard works, vol. 2, p. 233. It could be instructive to consider the economic and symbolic significances of arguments about tithes (for example, see C. Hill, *Economic Problems of the Church*, Oxford University Press, 1956, chapter 5). For examples of Lollard attitudes to tithes see *English Works of Wyclif*, ed. F. D. Matthew

EETS, O.S., 74, 1880, pp. 132, 414–18, 430–3; and *Select English Works of John Wyclif*, 3 vols, ed. T. Arnold, Oxford University Press, 1871, vol. 3, pp. 309, 320, 359–60. The emphasis is on the right of individuals and particular congregations to decide who is worthy to receive tithes. This goes beyond what Langland suggests. Nevertheless, the radical nature of Langland's proposals in terms of the existing socio-economic and religious institutions should not be overlooked. The church would certainly have been transformed in significant ways by his proposals and this would in turn have had real effects on the period's structures of ideology and social order.

34 I believe that P. M. Kean's unequivocal assertion that, unlike Wyclif, Langland never identified the church with Antichrist is too confidently made and probably unwarranted (in *Piers Plowman*, ed. S. S. Hussey, Methuen, London, 1969, p. 334, n. 36). The issue is complex. Langland certainly does not wish to be or see himself as a heresiarch – quite the contrary, as we have seen. Nevertheless, his insights have pushed him to develop images and poetic actions where the visible church may indeed be identified with Antichrist, in Passus XX. All that is *not* identified with Antichrist here is a small remnant holding out against Antichrist (see the attacks at XX. 213 ff., and 294 ff.). However much small groups protest that they represent the true church, they have normally been seen by the official church as sectarian and heretical – and persecuted as such. After all, the basic defining fact of medieval heresy was persevering opposition to the established, official church. (On this, Leff, *Heresy*, Lambert, *Medieval Heresy*, and Lerner, *The Heresy of the Free Spirit*, provide countless examples.) The use of Antichrist here is to see the *official* church as under his control. On Wyclif's use of Antichrist, see Leff, *Heresy*, vol. 2, pp. 520, 528, 530, 531, 532, 535, 536–41, 546; on Lollards and Antichrist, Leff, *Heresy*, vol. 2, pp. 576, 577, 580–1, 600, 602. For examples of commonplace identifications of Antichrist see Matthew, *English Works of Wyclif*, pp. 108–13, 181–3, and *Lanterne of Liȝt*, ed. L. M. Swinburn, *EETS*, O.S., 151, 1917, chapters 3–5. Also see Hus, *Magistra Johannis Hus Tractatus de Ecclesia*, ed. S. H. Thomson, University of Colorado Press, 1956, pp. 30, 70, 226.

35 Bloomfield, *Piers Plowman*, pp. 143, 123, 153.

36 Fifteenth-century Lollardy had to learn to accept that the Wycliffite role given to lay lords was not the one they were ready to fulfil, but the *Lanterne of Liȝt* represents a not unusual mixture of acknowledgment of this fact with a continuing appeal to lay leaders (compare there pp. 16–17 and 114–15; see too the criticism of the traditional possessing classes, pp. 69–71, 117–19, 120–1).

37 On individualistic developments characteristic of late medieval religion there is much in the works by Southern, Rapp, Lambert and Lerner (cited in n. 22) and Leff, *Heresy*, vol. 2; see chapter 2 n. 43 above. See also A. Macfarlane, *The Origins of English Individualism*, Blackwell, Oxford, 1978, which came to my notice after this was written.

38 *Saeculum: History and Society in the Theology of St Augustine*, Cambridge University Press, 1970, p. 83.

Chapter 4 Chaucer: Reflexive Imagination, Knowledge and Authority

1 The most influential proponent of this view has been D. W. Robertson, in a host of publications (most systematically in *Preface to Chaucer*, Princeton University Press, 1963) and many of its assumptions about the period have permeated the work of those who would not accept Robertson's moralizing and allegorizing commentaries on Chaucer.
2 Here I quote from the following: D. R. Howard, *The Idea of the Canterbury Tales*, University of California Press, 1976, pp. 103, 106, 51 (see chapters 2 and 3); J. Mann, *Chaucer and Medieval Estates Satire*, Cambridge University Press, 1973, p. 190 (this is a most important study of Chaucer); Charles Muscatine, *Poetry and Crisis in the Age of Chaucer*, University of Notre Dame Press, Notre Dame, Ind., p. 32; S. Delany, *Chaucer's House of Fame*, Chicago University Press, 1972.
3 A. W. Gouldner, *The Dialectic of Ideology and Technology*, Macmillan, London, 1976, pp. XV, 45; see pp. 44–60, 215–16, 281–2.
4 This could have important affinities with fourteenth-century philosophy: compare, G. Leff, *Dissolution of the Medieval Outlook*, Harper & Row, New York, 1976, p. 11 and chapter 2 *passim*; G. Leff, *William of Ockham*, Manchester University Press, 1975, part 1; H. A. Oberman, 'Some notes on the theology of nominalism', *HTR*, 53, 1960, pp. 47–76.
5 For indications on this line, D. Aers, 'Chaucer's *Book of the Duchess*', *Durham University Journal*, 69, 1977, pp. 201–5; A. C. Spearing, *Medieval Dream Poetry*, Cambridge University Press, chapter 2; R. O. Payne, *The Key of Remembrance,* Yale University Press, 1963, pp. 128–39; Delany, *Chaucer's HF*.
6 All quotations of Chaucer are from *The Works of Geoffrey Chaucer*, ed. F. N. Robinson, 2nd edn., 1957, Oxford University Press, reprint 1968, by permission of Oxford University Press. References are to line numbers in this edition.
7 *W of B Pr.*, 9 ff.; for Jerome's *Epistola adversus Jovinianum* see *Sources and Analogues of Chaucer's Canterbury Tales*, ed. W. F. Bryan and G. Dempster, Routledge & Kegan Paul, London, 1958, pp. 208–12.
8 *Piers Plowman*, chapter 2; see *W of B Pr.*, 165.
9 For an introduction to the medieval Inquisition, see: Bernard Gui, *Practica inquisitionis heretice pravitatis*, translation of part 5 in *Heresies of the High Middle Ages*, ed. W. L. Wakefield and A. P. Evans, Columbia University Press, 1969, pp. 373–447; A. P. Evans, 'Hunting subversion in the Middle Ages', *Speculum*, 33, 1958, pp.

1–22; M. D. Lambert, *Medieval Heresy*, Arnold, London, 1977, pp. 103–7, 174–8, 135–7, 151–2, 162, 168–181, 194, 201–3, 266–8, 300–1; G. Leff, *Heresy in the Later Middle Ages*, 2 vols, Manchester University Press, 1967, vol. 1, pp. 34–47, and both volumes, *passim*; R. E. Lerner, *Heresy of the Free Spirit*, University of California Press, 1972.

10 The complex controversy is traced by Leff, *Heresy* especially vol. 1, pp. 164–6, 238–55 (I quote from p. 248 here). The argument that Christ and his apostles had a bag of money and therefore owned property, illustrates relevant kinds of exegetical practices and prejudices – see Leff, *Heresy*, vol. 1, p. 243.

11 For representative texts, see *Not in God's Image*, ed. J. O'Faolain and L. Martines, Fontana, London, 1974, pp. 149–52.

12 See too ll. 1919–20.

13 Prologue, ll. 58–65 and IV. 149–53.

14 For similar procedures in the *General Prologue*, see Mann, *Chaucer, passim*.

15 For the use of Jean de Meun here, see Bryan and Dempster, *Sources and Analogues*, pp. 409–11; on the pardoner see J. Halverson, 'Chaucer's Pardoner and the progress of criticism', *Ch Rev*, 4, 1970, pp. 184–202; P. Elbow, *Oppositions in Chaucer*, Wesleyan State University Press, 1975, chapter 6; Howard, *Idea*, pp. 338–76; Mann, *Chaucer*, pp. 145–52; A. David, *The Strumpet Muse: Art and Morals in Chaucer's Poetry*, Indiana University Press, 1976, chapter 13.

16 See opening of chapter 2 and its n. 1.

17 *Treatise on Preaching*, ed. W. M. Conlow, Aquin Press, 1951, pp. 1, 4, 5, 22–3, 25–9, 43, 50; for the 'mouth of the Lord', referred to in the next paragraph, p. 49; for illustration of manuals, Th.-M. Charland (ed.), *Artes Praedicandi*, Publications de l'Institution d'Études Médiévales d'Ottawa, Paris and Ottawa, 1936.

18 *Lives*, Oxford University Press, 1927: on Walton's knowledge of Donne, see R. C. Bald, *John Donne. A Life*, Oxford University Press, 1970, p. 12.

19 Howard, *Idea*, p. 376; similarly, Elbow, *Oppositions in Chaucer*, pp. 135–6.

20 It is worth recalling that radical anti-clerical lines of thought also refused to accept clear-cut traditional distinctions between individual and office – for this commonplace, see Leff, *Heresy*, vol. 2, pp. 579–81.

21 Howard, *Idea*, p. 350.

22 Conlow (ed.), *Treatise on Preaching*, pp. 51–2.

23 A. L. Kellogg and L. A. Haselmayer, 'Chaucer's Satire and the Pardoner', *PMLA*, 66, 1951, pp. 251–77; also A. Williams, 'Some documents on English Pardoners, 1350–1400', *Medieval Studies in Honour of U.T. Holmes*, ed. J. Mahoney and J. E. Keller, University of North Carolina Press, 1965, pp. 197–207; R. W. Southern, *Western Society and the Church in the Middle Ages*,

Penguin, Harmondsworth, 1970, pp. 136–43; and chapter 2 above.

24 In *Speculum*, 30, 1955, pp. 180–99, here quoted from reprint *The Pardoner's Tale*, ed. D. R. Faulkner, Prentice-Hall, Englewood Cliffs, NJ, 1973, pp. 43–69, here p. 60.

25 Gui, *Practica inquisitionis heretice pravitatis*, pp. 377, 411, 437: see n. 9 above on Inquisition. From Langland on the issues connected with Paul's passage in Ephesians 4:28, see XV. 92 ff., 290–1, and VI. 247 ff.

26 See Lambert, *Medieval Heresy*, chapters 14 and 15; Leff, *Heresy*, vol. 2, pp. 511–16, 593–8; H. A. Oberman, *The Harvest of Medieval Theology*, Harvard University Press, 1963, chapter 11 (on scripture and tradition).

27 Howard, *Idea*, pp. 374, 375.

28 There are relevant information and ideas in K. Thomas, *Religion and the Decline of Magic*, (1971), Penguin, Harmondsworth, 1973.

29 The passage is from his *Lectures on Galatians* quoted in an article I have drawn on heavily here: T. Tentler, 'The Summa for Confessors as an instrument of social control', in *The Pursuit of Holiness*, ed. C. Trinkaus and H. A. Oberman, E. J. Brill, Leiden, 1974, pp. 101–37, here pp. 124–5; see too his later book, *Sin and Confession*, Princeton University Press, 1977, and Southern, *Western Society*, pp. 133–43.

30 *Aquinas: Selected Political Writings*, ed. A. P. D'Entreves, Blackwell, Oxford, 1965, pp. 3, 5; Donne, *Devotions*, Michigan University Press, Ann Arbor, 1959, pp. 30, 108.

31 Howard, *Idea*, p. 366.

32 *Seriatim, G. Pr.*, l. 756; Fragment VII. 1943–62 and 340–60 (though this is apparently only in 6 manuscripts); Fragment II. 1173, 75; *Parson's Tale*, l. 38. For his kind of piety, *Physician's Tale*, ll. 287–302, 312. On the Host see A. T. Gaylord, *PMLA*, 82, 1967, pp. 226–35.

33 For the Lollards see Leff, *Heresy*, vol. 2, chapter 8; Lambert, *Medieval Heresy*, chapter 15; J. Fines, *Studies in the Lollard heresy*, unpublished PhD dissertation, Sheffield University, 1964; J. Crompton, 'Leicestershire lollards', *Transactions of the Leicestershire Archaeological Society*, 44, 1968–9, pp. 11–14; A. Hudson, ed., *English Wycliffite Writings,* Cambridge University Press, 1978.

34 See *G. Pr.* ll. 688–91, 669–79; excellent discussion in Howard, *Idea*, pp. 343–5, 364–7.

35 I hope the preceding discussion has made it clear that the Pardoner too exhibits bad faith: in his contradictory demands for fellowship and his total contempt for fellow humans, in his critical unmasking of the religious institution *and* his continuing service of it at the community's expense of spirit and cash.

36 See Howard, *Idea*, p. 368.

37 Ibid., p. 342.

38 Especially J. B. Allen, 'The old way and the Parson's way', *Journal*

of Medieval and Renaissance Studies, 3, 1973, pp. 255–71; J. Finlayson, 'The Satiric Mode and the *Parson's Tale*', *Ch Rev*, 6, 1971, pp. 94–116; Howard, *Idea*, pp. 379, 385–6 (though contrast pp. 380–1); C. V. Kaske, 'Getting around the *Parson's Tale*', in *Chaucer at Albany*, ed. R. H. Robbins, Franklin, New York, 1975, pp. 147–77; C. A. Owen, *Pilgrimage and Story Telling in the Canterbury Tales*, University of Oklahoma Press, 1977, p. 210. Finlayson's article includes references to the modern treatment of the *Parson's Tale* as the key to Chaucer's meaning in all his work (pp. 94–6, 105–6).

39 He does not even have an elementary theory of the accommodation of divine truth to human capacities, let alone any explorations of the implications such a theory could hold – cf. Aers, *Piers Plowman*, chapter 4.

40 For the attacks on entertainment, see *Parson's Tale*, ll. 532, 650.

41 Howard, *Idea*, p. 385.

42 The recent studies of source by S. Wenzel are important: 'The source of the "*Remedia*" of the *Parson's Tale*', *Traditio*, 27, 1971, pp. 433–54, and 'The source of Chaucer's seven deadly sins', *Traditio*, 30, 1974, pp. 351–78.

43 On use of Wenzel and this detachment see the works by Kaske and Allen cited in n. 38 above.

44 *Parson's Tale*, ll. 75 ff. (on confession, see Robinson's edition, pp. 236 ff.); Allen, *Old way*, pp. 256–60, 267–70.

45 *The House of Fame* is preoccupied with such issues – see Delany, *Chaucer's HF*.

46 Chaucer could also have been critical of the Parson's failure to take up a major nexus of questions relating to his assertions: namely, those about 'grace' (1.90), free will, predestination, and justification which recurred again and again in fourteenth-century theology as genuine problems and, *Piers Plowman* itself illustrates, in no way merely 'academic'.

47 Reference in n. 38 above.

48 See Kaske, 'Around the Parson's Tale', pp. 166–9; J. T. Noonan also comments on the *Parson's Tale, Contraception. A History of its Treatment by the Catholic Theologians and Canonists*, Harvard University Press, 1966, pp. 250–2; H. A. Kelly, *Love and Marriage in the Age of Chaucer*, Cornell University Press, Ithaca NY, 1975, pp. 262–7.

49 *Parson's Tale*, ll. 420 ff. (Robinson's edition, p. 240; metaphor also used at 1.343): Paul's text reads: 'Infelix ego homo quis me liberabit de corpore mortis huius?'; mistranslated as, 'I caytyf man: who shal delivere me fro the prisoun of my caytyf body?' Of course, questions about the readings of the actual manuscripts Chaucer used would need answering before one could be certain Chaucer had deliberately given the Parson not just an appropriately revealing selection but an appropriate mistranslation. Either way, the officially excluded subject, with all the unexamined idiosyncrasies,

is made visible as the one who constructs the discourse. The editions of Robinson and Fisher do not note the mistranslation.

50 *Parson's Tale*, ll. 431–8; Finlayson, 'Satiric Mode', pp. 114–15.

51 *G Pr*, ll. 515–18; likewise, Howard, *Idea*, pp. 378–9.

52 There is of course a grisly official Christian tradition involved here (eg. 1.840), most easily identified in the visual and verbal descriptions of the torments of the damned, but explicit enough in dogmatic theology too: see *City of God*, XXI. 12 (many more damned than saved, and approved as a good example to all) likewise XIII. 23; vivid examples of the blessed actually rejoicing in the sight of the damned given by G. G. Coulton, *Five Centuries of Religion*, vol. 5, Cambridge University Press, 1929, pp. 441–2; though he does not print the following, from the famous fourteenth-century theologian and archbishop Bradwardine:

> great profit, both in the present and in the future accrues to the elect from the reprobate, indeed the whole purpose of being for the reprobate is that they have been created for the sake of the elect . . . for the service of another creature and . . . for His [God's] own service, praise, glory and honour . . . (tr. H. A. Oberman, *Forerunners of the Reformation*, Lutterworth Press, Guildford, 1967, p. 161).

The distance of such texts from the mentality of certain modern scholars presenting their views as 'Augustinian' is very small, but the distance from Chaucer or Langland is immeasurable.

53 *Parson's Tale*, l. 888 (see too l. 923); see similarly, *Merchant's Tale*, ll. 1272, 1437–40.

54 On the manuscripts, Robinson's edition, p. 772; for text, ibid., p. 265.

55 David, *Strumpet Muse*, p. 239.

Chapter 5 Chaucer's Criseyde: Woman in Society, Woman in Love

1 An earlier version of this chapter was written and submitted to *Ch Rev* in summer 1977, published vol. 13, winter, 1979. It is deeply indebted to the generous help of Yvonne McGregor, and I am also very grateful to the commentaries on the earlier version of this chapter offered by Elizabeth Salter and Derek Pearsall. I have also been influenced by an essay I greatly admire, Elizabeth Salter's '*Troilus and Criseyde:* a reconsideration', in *Patterns of Love and Courtesy*, ed. J. Lawlor, Arnold, London, 1966, pp. 86–106.

2 R. O. Payne, *The Key of Remembrance*, Yale University Press, 1963, pp. 81, 181–3, 221, 222, 226, 223. He particularly praises A. Mizener, 'Character and action in the case of Criseyde', *PMLA,* 54 1939, pp. 65–79; similarly R. M. Jordan, *Chaucer and the Shape of Creation*, Harvard University Press, 1967, pp. 99–100; for D. W. Robertson see *Preface to Chaucer*, Princeton University Press, 1963

and 'Chaucerian tragedy', *ELH*, 19, 1952, pp. 1–37. For like-minded comments to the ones offered here, M. E. McAlpine, *The Genre of Troilus and Criseyde* Cornell University Press, 1978, pp. 193 n. 11, 208–13, 230–3. (This interesting book was published after my own essay had been submitted to *Ch Rev* but I have now added reference to her arguments where relevant, especially to chapter 6, 'The Boethian tragedy of Criseyde'.)

3 See K. Young, 'Chaucer's *Troilus and Criseyde* as romance', *PMLA*, 53, 1938, pp. 38–63.

4 He shifted Boccaccio's setting to a courtly one, and concentrated on developing the subtle ambivalences of feeling which emerge as Criseyde encounters and absorbs social and ideological pressures in determinate circumstances whose relevance Chaucer articulates in a way quite unknown to Boccaccio. Italian text in *Opere minori in volgare*, Rizzoli, Milan, 1970, English translation R. K. Gordon, *The Story of Troilus*, Dutton, New York, 1964, pp. 25–127. On the different treatment of desire and sensuality in the two poets, and on the role of circumstance in Chaucer's treatment of Criseyde, see two essays by R. P. ap Roberts, 'Love in the *Filostrato*', *Ch Rev*, 7, 1972, pp. 1–26, and 'Criseyde's infidelity', *Speculum*, 44, 1969, pp. 383–402. On political dimensions, J. P. McCall, 'The Trojan scene in Chaucer's *Troilus*', *ELH*, 29, 1962, pp. 263–75.

5 I take up the issues of medieval marriage, religious dimensions and utopian elements in Chaucer's own imagination in chapter 6. For conventional romances referred to here, E. Power, *Medieval Women*, Cambridge University Press, 1975, pp. 16–28; A. David, *The Strumpet Muse: Art and Morals in Chaucer's Poetry*, Indiana University Press, 1976, pp. 17, 55–6; P. Gradon, *Form and Style in Early English Literature*, Methuen, London, 1971, p. 220; M. A. Gist, *Love and War in the Medieval Romances*, University of Pennsylvania Press, Philadelphia, 1947. For the positive role of dream and reverie in opposition to social norms, see the outstanding essay by J. Frappier, 'Sur un procès fait à l'amour courtois', *Romania*, 93, 1972, pp. 145–93.

6 See Monica McAlpine's excellent comments on the way Criseyde 'suffers under all the disabilities of being a woman, the king's subject, Calkas' daughter, and her husband's widow', *Genre of Troilus and Criseyde*, pp. 191–2, 199–200.

7 Yvonne McGregor points out to me that in choosing not to channel her request through her uncle (transformed by Chaucer into an older man), apparently the only male relative left to her in Troy, Criseyde could be showing a measure of strong-willed independence. Her later comments on marriage (II, ll. 750–6) confirm the plausibility of this suggestion; but it is also true that she will get a better deal by prostrating her own body before that of the most powerful male in Troy.

8 Contrast *Filostrato* II, st. 68–72 with Chaucer's expansion, *T & C*, II, ll. 596–749.

9 See Power, *Medieval Women*, p. 38; F. R. H. Du Boulay, *Age of Ambition*, Nelson, London, 1970, p. 95; and Christine de Pisan's views as recounted by C. C. Willard, 'A fifteenth century view of women's role in medieval society: Christine de Pisan's *Livre des trois vertus*', pp. 90–120 in *The Role of Women in the Middle Ages*, ed. R. T. Morewedge, Hodder & Stoughton, London, 1975, here pp. 105–6 on the privileges *and* added vulnerability of widows. H. A. Kelly's thesis on the clandestine marriage of Troilus and Criseyde is strangely forgetful of these issues and the force of II, ll. 750 ff., an oversight which gravely distorts his approach to the poem – *Love and Marriage in the Age of Chaucer*, Cornell University Press, 1975, pp. 217–42.

10 See too the resistance to making 'hirselven bonde/In love' (II, ll. 1197–225) and in III, ll. 169–72 she still reminds him of this in a brilliantly equivocal passage. On the 'risks of intimacy', see also McAlpine, *Genre of Troilus and Criseyde*, pp. 199–200.

11 For example, P. Elbow, *Oppositions in Chaucer*, Wesleyan State University Press, pp. 55–8.

12 See *Filostrato*, III, st. ll. 21 ff.; for the need of Pandarus in Chaucer's poem, eg. III, ll. 274–7, 785–98, 855–980 *passim* and his reappearance at Criseyde's bed, ll. 1555–82.

13 See III, ll. 939–45 and the use of broken syntax to enact the confused movements of Criseyde's consciousness at III, ll. 918 ff.

14 See III, ll. 1116–34: Boccaccio's Criseida is little else but 'sexual initiative' in *Filostrato*, III, and Chaucer's subtle explorations of movements of consciousness and sexual desire are quite foreign to the Italian text.

15 IV, ll. 1471–5: here again Chaucer mediates medieval patriarchal realities (see chapter 6 n. 1 and discussion at opening of that chapter: I am grateful for conversations about the role of Calkas with Yvonne McGregor). For an interesting example of Chaucer's critical stance towards patriarchal powers see the *Physician's Tale,* where a 'fadres pity' is exposed in all its cruel and self-righteous egotism (although the physician himself cannot see this) – see especially ll. 218–26.

16 On these issues see too McCall, *The Trojan Scene*, and McAlpine, *Genre of Troilus and Criseyde*, pp. 198–9, 201.

17 IV, ll. 1242 ff.; the poet makes Criseyde's commitment clear: IV, ll. 699–700, 708–14, 731–945, 1128–69. It is noticeable that whereas Troilus thinks only of himself and consoles himself with metaphysics, Criseyde actually thinks about her own grief *and* about how her lover will fare – IV, ll. 794–5, 890–903, 942. Here I think Monica McAlpine (*Genre of Troilus and Criseyde*, p. 166) wrong to deny Troilus' 'self-absorption' at this stage.

18 Here I disagree with Monica McAlpine's reading of this episode: she constantly insists that what is at issue is a 'rape' of Criseyde analogous to the rape of Helen, and she simply admires Criseyde *and* Troilus for not carrying it out (*Genre of Troilus and Criseyde*,

pp. 160–2, 188–90). But what is discussed in the interview is voluntary and mutual secession from a society bent on destroying the greatest human achievement we are shown, and itself to boot! The major aspects I am discussing are quite ignored by J. Bayley's bizarre diagnosis that Criseyde's 'trouble' is her 'absence of passion' (*The Characters of Love*, (1960), Chatto & Windus, London, 1968, p. 107). The dialectic Chaucer develops here is a universal one in our civilization, though medievalists have been largely closed to it: cf. D. Aers, 'Blake and the dialectics of sex', *ELH*, 44, 1977, pp. 500–14.

19 These considerations are, once more, quite alien to his source, here being followed fairly closely by Chaucer (*Filostrato*, IV). It is characteristic that Boccaccio should climax the arguments of his Criseida by having her claim that things are not so bad really since their love can give pleasure only because they have to act furtively and see each other rarely, whereas if they were together often their love and desire would soon vanish (IV. st. 153). Nothing could be further removed from Chaucer's Criseyde or his overall approach and he does not translate this passage.

20 On this both Elizabeth Salter ('Troilus and Criseyde') and David, *Strumpet Muse*, chapter 2, have pertinent comments.

21 See V, ll. 688, 728, 1026–7. Monica McAlpine's *Genre of Troilus and Criseyde* provides similar emphasis in some excellent comments on pp. 200–4.

22 Here see V, ll. 701–6, 712–14, On the real threat of rape to medieval women and awareness of this in literature, see Gist, *Love and War*, pp. 75 ff., and the emphasis on real 'insecurity' even in peace and supposed 'hospitality' (pp. 82–3); in war, the situation was even worse, for women were part of the spoils of war (pp. 83 ff.); similarly McAlpine, *Genre of Troilus and Criseyde*, p. 204.

23 I am grateful for Derek Pearsall's suggestion that I expand the commentary offered in my earlier version of this chapter to take the syntax into closer account.

24 One could also recall the first advice offered Troilus, that if Criseyde had to leave Troy he should simply take another woman, since 'newe love out chaceth ofte the olde', and all 'is but casuel plesaunce' anyway. This is a good example of exploitative norms in much traditional male sexuality, combined with characteristic double standards of morality, although the narrator (Chaucer?) steps in to say that 'douteles' Pandarus did not really mean it, only saying it to 'help his freend' (V, ll. 400–31). Still, he *did* say it, at length too, and in what sense could something one believed was false and evil be said to 'help'?

25 Salter, *Troilus and Criseyde*, pp. 103–6, and for reference to some of the many studies on the 'Epilogue' see McAlpine, *Genre of Troilus and Criseyde*, pp. 177 n. 17, and 237 n. 19.

26 See Salter, *Troilus and Criseyde*, p. 106.

27 This theme has been discussed in relation to both the poetry of

Langland and Chaucer in the previous four chapters.

28 See reference to P. Brown's explication of Augustine's psychological analysis of these issues, chapter 2, n. 31.

29 McAlpine, *Genre of Troilus and Criseyde*, pp. 177–81, 235–46.

30 See Salter, *Troilus and Criseyde*, pp. 103–6.

31 L. Kolakowski, *Marxism and Beyond*, Pall Mall Press, London, 1969, especially 'The Priest and the Jester', pp. 29–57.

Chapter 6 Chaucer: Love, Sex and Marriage

1 See the following, E. Power, *Medieval Women*, Cambridge University Press, 1975, quoting here from pp. 38–40, the whole study is invaluable: F. R. H. Du Boulay, *Age of Ambition*, Nelson, London, 1970, pp. 92–102; *Not in God's Image*, ed. J. O'Faolain and L. Martines, Harper & Row, New York, 1973, pp. 157–9, 163–4, 182–3, 185–7; on peasant women, R. Hilton, *The English Peasantry in the Later Middle Ages*, Oxford University Press, 1975, pp. 97–108. Study of ideology concerning divorce is always revealing about attitudes to marriage, and in this period questions about love and mutual affection never entered into orthodox and official consideration, the same being true of the dominant traditions in the Reformation, opposed by John Milton (eg. *Complete Prose Works*, Yale University Press, vol. 2, pp. 256, 243–69 *passim*, 595–601): on the Middle Ages here, see R. H. Helmholz, *Marriage Litigation in Medieval England*, Harvard University Press, 1974. For some of Langland's observations on marriage, *Piers Plowman*, IX. 116–19, 159 ff., XV. 241–3. On completion of this book two advertised works were still not available: G. Duby, *Medieval Marriage*, Johns Hopkins University Press, Baltimore, Md, and J. Atkins, *Sex in Literature: the medieval experience*, Calder, London.

2 *The Goodman of Paris*, tr. E. Power, Routledge, London, 1928, pp. 107–8: see too examples at pp. 110–12, 138, 140, 149.

3 *The Book of the Knight of the Tower*, tr. W. Caxton, ed. M. Y. Offerd, *EETS*, ss, 2, (1971), p. 197, punctuation and lettering modernized: here quote from p. 35; see similar examples and statements about ideal wives at pp. 37, 90–3, 103, 129, 149–50; it should be emphasized that the knight displays conventional Christian piety in abundance, eg. chapters 1, 2, 4, 5, 9, 26, 31, 35, 75, 97, 99, 101, 102, 105.

4 J. T. Noonan, *Contraception. A History of its Treatment by the Catholic Theologians and Canonists*, Harvard University Press, 1966, see especially pp. 36–49, 126, 129, 151, 193–9, 248–54; it is hardly surprising that this outlook combined with orthodox fear and hatred of sex to make enjoyment of marital sex sinful. See too J. J. Mogan, 'Chaucer and the *Bona Matrimonii*', *Ch Rev*, 4, 1970, pp. 123–41, and H. A. Kelly, *Love and Marriage in the Age of*

Chaucer, Cornell University Press, 1975.

5 Noonan, *Contraception*, 256–7; Kelly, *Love and Marriage*, p. 247, and on the antithesis of love and sex, pp. 247–61, 316, 322–3, 325 n. 63.

6 *Summa Theologica* 1.92.1 (tr. Fathers of the English Dominican Province, Burns Oates and Washbourne, 22 vols, 1921–32); see also I.99.2, II–1. 102.3. Good discussion and illustration in Joan Ferrante, *Women as Image in Medieval Literature*, Columbia University Press, 1975, pp. 101–5.

7 Noonan, *Contraception*, pp. 286–92, 295, discusses some signs of a minority opinion emerging as an alternative to traditional theory on the purposes of marriage, but they are neither developed nor espoused by theologians and at most they seem to be reflections in theology of the strains under which the dominant paradigm had come, signs that its inadequacies were at least troublesome to some theologians.

8 See especially, J. Frappier, 'Sur un procès fait à l'amour courtois', *Romania*, 93, 1972, pp. 145–93; M. Lazar, *Amour courtois et fin'amors dans la littérature du XII*e *s.*, Klincksieck, Paris, 1964; L. T. Topsfield, *Troubadours and Love,* Cambridge University Press, 1975; R. Boase, *The Origin and Meaning of Courtly Love*, Manchester University Press, 1977, a useful and sensible survey. For relevant examples of Chrétien here, see *Arthurian Romances*, Dent, London, reprinted 1968, pp. 120–1, 178–9, 213–14 and *Yvain, passim*. For English developments, G. Mathew, 'Marriage and *amour courtois* in late fourteenth-century England', pp. 128–35 in *Essays presented to Charles Williams*, ed. D. Sayers *et al.*, Oxford University Press, 1947.

9 For a convenient bibliography of the writing on this figure, J. H. Fisher, *The Complete Poetry and Prose of Chaucer*, Holt, Rinehart & Winston, New York, 1977, pp. 999–1000.

10 A. David, *The Strumpet Muse: Art and Morals in Chaucer's Poetry*, Indiana University Press, 1976, chapter 9, here especially pp. 143–7, 153; on the market aspects in the tale originally intended for the Wife, see A. H. Silverman, 'Sex and money in Chaucer's *Shipman's Tale*', *PQ*, 32, 1953, pp. 329–36.

11 Mogan, *Ch Rev*, 4, 1970, p. 139.

12 David, *Strumpet Muse*, pp. 150–1; on her generosity and vitality, pp. 142, 147–50.

13 See l. 801 and David, *Strumpet Muse*, p. 151.

14 David, *Strumpet Muse*, pp. 138–9, 146–7, 151, and see my discussion on the Wife of Bath in chapter 4. Here compare ll. 724–6 on Hercules with *House of Fame*, ll. 402–4!

15 On this tradition see D. W. Robertson, *Preface to Chaucer*, Princeton University Press, 1963, pp. 253–4 and Figure 6; interesting illustrations in L. M. C. Randall, *Images in the Margins of Gothic Manuscripts*, University of California Press, 1966, Figures 554, 555, 557; for women beating men see Figure 394

and Power, *Medieval Women*, Figure 7, and Du Boulay, *Age of Ambition*, p. 82; for commonplace of wife-beating, Power, p. 16. For a splendid and relevant commentary on the dialectic here see S. de Beauvoir, *The Second Sex*, Penguin, Harmondsworth, p. 726. On the Wife's Tale, and its utopianism, David, *Strumpet Muse*, pp. 153–7.

16 For commentary on the *Merchant's Tale*, see J. H. Fisher, *Complete Chaucer*, pp. 1002–3. There seems no good reason for assuming a close and dramatically personal relationship between the merchant of the tale's prologue (ll. 1213–38) and the subtle tale which follows; the self-indulgent and foolish merchant who so grossly misrepresents the force of the *Clerk's Tale* could hardly be taken as the author of the tale whose imaginative and intellectual power I attempt to describe.

17 Scholars do not agree about who speaks ll. 1267–392: I take the passage as Chaucer's highly critical mediation of Januarie's consciousness revealed in all its folly and self-deception but also as representative of dominant features in male images of woman and marriage. My own view about the speaker is shared by many, eg. G. Sedgewick, *UTQ*, 17, 1948, p. 341.

18 P. M. Kean, *Chaucer and the Making of English Poetry*, 2 vols, Routledge & Kegan Paul, London, 1972; 2, p. 160; see too R. B. Burlin, *Chaucerian Fiction*, Princeton University Press, 1977, p. 212.

19 On consent, see Aquinas, *ST* III (Suppl) 45.4 and 47.1: see also *Handlynge Synne*, ll. 11, 165–70, 11, 204–14 *EETS*, O.S., 119; and J. T. Noonan, 'Power to choose', *Viator*, 4, 1973, pp. 419–34. On the constraining realities see above, n. 1.

20 Noonan, *Contraception*, pp. 256–7; Kelly, *Love and Marriage*, p. 245.

21 For Januarie's views about an ideal wife, ll. 1291–4, 1311–55, 1375–88, 1414–40. For his perception of married sex in terms of a 'knyf', see ll. 1839–40, discussed in connection with the Parson's similar outlook at close of chapter 4.

22 *W of B Pr*, ll. 688–96, 707–10.

23 See, for example, Jordan, *Chaucer and the Shape of Creation*, p. 146, and Kean, *Chaucer and English Poetry*, vol. 2, pp. 160–1, 163.

24 Much written on this topic, see especially J. Wimsatt, 'Chaucer and the Canticles', in *Chaucer the Love Poet*, ed. J. Mitchell and W. Provost, University of Georgia, Athens Ga., 1973, pp. 66–90 and R. E. Kaske, pp. 55–6 in same collection.

25 See Kelly, *Love and Marriage*, p. 311 and his examples on pp. 303–6, 310; for Augustine, *On Christian Doctrine*, II.6.7–8, tr. D. W. Robertson, Bobbs-Merrill, New York, 1958, pp. 37–8, and D. Aers, *Piers Plowman and Christian Allegory*, Arnold, London, 1975, pp. 54–5, and chapters 2–4 *passim* on exegesis.

26 Noonan, *Contraception*, pp. 256–7; see similar aspirations in *Cleanness*, ll. 697–708 in *The Poems of the Pearl Manuscript*, ed.

M. Andrew and R. Waldron, Arnold, London, 1978.

27 The Pluto-Proserpine episode is another critical and comic meditation by Chaucer on marriage and the male ego sanctioned by cultural norms his texts bring into question. This marriage is *explicitly* based on rape and seen as a winter-prison, mirroring the state in which Januarie confines May. Far from reinforcing the anti-feminist tradition, Chaucer exposes the double-think and dishonesty of male attitudes in this tradition, as he had done in *W of B Pr*. The picture of a male who 'ravysshed' a female accusing her of 'tresons' and praising Januarie as a 'worthy man' sums up the tradition at issue. The male's use of the Bible is also critically placed by Chaucer: compare ll. 2242–8 (Ecclesiastes 7: 29, Vulgate) with Proserpine's answers (ll. 2276–85, 2289–90, 2298–9) and Chaucer's support in *The Tale of Melibee*, ll. 1056, 1075–9. The Host's response is also used by Chaucer to illustrate commonplace male attitudes against which his art works (ll. 2419–40).

28 Kittredge's articles, 'Chaucer's discussion of marriage', *MPhil*, 9, 1911–12, pp. 435–67, reprinted in *Chaucer: Modern Essays in Criticism*, ed. E. Wagenknecht, Oxford University Press, 1959, see pp. 209–15 here: modern support of this position can be well represented by the following: R. E. Kaske, 'Chaucer's marriage group', pp. 45–65 in *Chaucer the Love Poet*, ed. Mitchell and Provost, see p. 65; G. White, '*The Franklin's Tale:* Chaucer or the critics', *PMLA*, 89, 1974, pp. 454–62; C. V. Kaske, 'Getting Round the *Parson's Tale*', in *Chaucer at Albany*, ed. R. H. Robbins Franklin, New York, 1975, pp. 160–3. For Robertson, *Preface to Chaucer*, Princeton University Press, 1963, pp. 470–2, 276, and his article in *Costerus*, 1, 1974, pp. 1–26. He has been extremely influential, even on many who could not be counted as his admirers.

29 I have not space to pursue the controversy over the Franklin in the *General Prologue* and the exchange with the Squire, but on the crucial ambivalence in Chaucer's portrayal, quite overlooked by Robertson, see J. Mann, *Chaucer and Medieval Estates Satire*, Cambridge University Press, 1973, pp. 152–9. The Franklin does indeed confuse social class and the quality of life at ll. 685–94, common enough in our civilization, but this does not mean he always does so nor that he is wrong in every area, nor that his dismissal of possessions (ll. 686–7) is simply hypocritical. Chaucer knew well enough that men habitually hold views which do not hold together coherently.

30 See n. 2, and on the rareness of the image of marriage here, Power, *Medieval Women*, pp. 19, 41, 38 ff.

31 For examples of the absence of Christianity, ll. 709–15, 1031–40, 1129–34, 1271–2, 1292–3; for a different perspective on the absence of Christianity see Kaske (op. cit. in note 28), though I see no grounds for claims about theories of *double truth* in Chaucer or his period, unlike the later thirteenth century: compare, G. Leff, *The*

Dissolution of the Medieval Outlook, Harper & Row, New York, 1976, chapters 1–3.

32 Much as the image of Gaunt in the *Book of the Duchess* has done (ll. 1285–91). In an exceptionally interesting article D. M. Murtaugh noted that many Christian traditions denied the existence of free will in women: 'Women and Geoffrey Chaucer', *ELH*, 38, 1971, pp. 473–92, here p. 485.

33 *Romance of the Rose*, tr. C. Dahlberg, Princeton University Press, 1971, pp. 154–71 (ll. 8355–9492). On the role of utopian thought in art Ernst Bloch is extremely interesting, *A Philosophy of the Future* (Herder, 1970), especially pp. 92–8. On orthodox Christian visions of a communist pre-lapsarian world, A. O. Lovejoy, 'The communism of St Ambrose', *Essays in the History of Ideas,* Johns Hopkins University Press, Baltimore Md, 1948, chapter 15.

34 Examples from I. Robinson, *Chaucer and the English Tradition*, Cambridge University Press, 1972; (the irresponsible assertions that 'The Franklin's theme is the same as Lawrence's in *Women in Love*' have nothing to do with Kittredge, of course: pp. 185, 187, 197); and B. F. Huppé, *A Reading of the Canterbury Tales*, University of New York, 1967, p. 171, and see Robertson, *Preface*, p. 471.

35 The Kittredge tradition represented here by Kaske, *Parson's Tale*, p. 63, C. A. Owen, *Pilgrimage and Storytelling*, University of Oklahoma, 1977, p. 208; G. White, *Franklin's Tale*; for the opposing reading of the episode, Robertson, *Preface*, p. 472, and David, *Strumpet Muse*, p. 189.

36 A. T. Gaylord, 'The promises in *The Franklin's Tale*', *ELH*, 31, 1964, pp. 331–65, here especially pp. 343, 345–57; and David, *Strumpet Muse*, pp. 187–8.

37 I believe that scholars who have applauded Arveragus' version of truth have been thoroughly refuted by David and Gaylord (n. 36 above). I would only add that his version of truth would actually sanctify *any* way of life or action, however evil; he fails to see that 'truth' needs grounding in a wider moral and metaphysical framework if it is to be more than a vacuous abstraction open to any content.

38 See ll. 937–42, 964–78, 1309–18, 1324–33; J. Huizinga, *The Waning of the Middle Ages*, Penguin, Harmondsworth, p. 123. For some acute comments on the romantic gardens in Chaucer, see Murtaugh, 'Women and Chaucer'.

39 David, *Strumpet Muse*, pp. 189–92; also Gaylord, pp. 332–41, 365.

40 Howard, *Idea*, p. 271.

41 For more recent examples of this tradition, R. B. Burlin, *Chaucerian Fiction*, Princeton University Press, 1977, pp. 140, 143–4; S. K. Heninger, 'The concept of order in Chaucer's Clerk's Tale', *JEGP*, 66, 1957, pp. 393–5; R. M. Jordan, *Chaucer and the Shape of Creation*, Harvard University Press, 1967, p. 204; D. W. Frese, *Ch Rev*, 8, 1973, pp. 133–4, 139.

42 D. Reiman, 'The real *Clerk's Tale*: or patient Griselda exposed', *Texas Studies in Literature and Language*, 5, 1963, pp. 356–73. See too the outstanding study by Elizabeth Salter, *Chaucer*, Arnold, London, 1962, pp. 37–70; also David, *Strumpet Muse*, chapter 10; there is also the line of Kittredge, in which the *ClT* is taken as an extreme response to the Wife of Bath's ideal of female sovereignty, before Chaucer resolves the debate in favour of views put by the Franklin. Most helpful aids in studying *ClT* are Petrarch's text and the French translation Chaucer also used, in Bryan and Dempster, *Sources and Analogues* chapter 11, and J. B. Severs, *The Literary Relationships of Chaucer's Clerk's Tale*, Yale University Press, 1942.

43 See ll. 311–12, 351–7, 449–62, 580–1, 619–23, 694–707; for explicit denunciation of his cruelty, ll. 734, 740, 785.

44 For other examples of Walter's psycho-spiritual sickness: ll. 617–23; 696–707; 732–5; 785–7. Contrast ll. 696–707 with Chaucer's sources, Bryan and Dempster, *Sources and Analogues*, pp. 316–19.

45 *Confessions* X.40.65 and see VIII.5.10, also analysing the maimed will. I have quoted the translation from P. Brown, *Augustine of Hippo*, Faber, London, 1967, see texts and discussions 149–50, 173–4.

46 *City of God*, XV. 7, XIV. 28, XIX. 15; also III. 14, IV. 3. See P. Brown, op. cit., pp. 326–7, 309 and H. A. Deane, *The Political and Social Ideas of St Augustine*, Columbia University Press, 1963, pp. 48–53.

47 See Severs, *Literary Relationships*, pp. 229–31 and Bryan and Dempster, *Sources and Analogues*, pp. 312–17, and *Clerk's Tale*, ll. 519–78, 673–86.

48 For studies of the historical and theoretical development of these implications, see M. Walzer, *The Revolution of the Saints*, Weidenfeld & Nicolson, London, 1966, and A. W. Gouldner, *The Dialectic of Ideology and Technology*, Macmillan, London, 1976.

49 Major works I have drawn on here include the following: M. J. Wilks, *The Problem of Sovereignty in the Later Middle Ages,* Cambridge University Press, 1964; A. S. McGrade, *The Political Thought of William of Ockham*, Cambridge University Press, 1974; G. De Legarde, *La naissance de l'esprit laïque au déclin du moyen âge*, new edition of vols. 4 and 5, Paris, 1962–3; *Trends in Medieval Political Thought*, ed. B. Smalley, Oxford, 1965, chapters 4 and 5; B. Tierney, *Ockham, the Conciliar Theory and the Canonists*, intr. H. A. Oberman, University of Pennsylvania, Philadelphia, 1971; W. Ullmann, *A History of Political Thought in the Middle Ages*, Penguin, Harmondsworth, 1965.

50 F. R. Scott, 'Chaucer and the parliament of 1386', *Speculum*, 18, 1943, pp. 80–6 and *Chaucer Life-Records* ed. M. M. Crow and C. C. Olson, Oxford University Press, 1966, pp. 364–9.

51 M. Schlauch, 'Chaucer's doctrine of kings and tyrants', *Speculum*, 20, 1945, pp. 133–56.

52 Wilks, *Problem of Sovereignty*, part 3, chapter 3; parts 5 and 6; and pp. 521, 526. McGrade, *Ockham*, here especially pp. 85–96, 103, 109–33, 169, 172, 185–9, 221–3.

53 M. J. Wilks, 'Chaucer and the mystical marriage in medieval political thought', *BJR*, 44, 1961–2, pp. 489–530, quoting p. 529; also E. H. Kantorowicz, *The King's Two Bodies*, Princeton University Press, 1957, pp. 212–23.

Chapter 7 Imagination, Order and Ideology: *The Knight's Tale*

1 See respectively Charles Muscatine, *Chaucer and the French Tradition*, University of California Press, 1964, chapter 6.2.1, especially pp. 181, 184; R. M. Jordan, *Chaucer and the Shape of Creation*, Harvard University Press, 1967, pp. 153, 157 (chapter 7); R. B. Burlin, *Chaucerian Fiction*, Princeton University Press, 1977, pp. 104–5 (chapter 5); similarly Howard, *Idea*, p. 245; P. M. Kean, *Chaucer and the Making of English Poetry*, Routledge & Kegan Paul, London, 1972, vol. 2, pp. 1–52; A. David, *The Strumpet Muse: Art and Morals in Chaucer's Poetry*, Indiana University Press, 1976, pp. 84–5.

2 Elizabeth Salter, *Chaucer: The Knight's Tale and the Clerk's Tale*, Arnold, London, 1962, pp. 9–36; R. Neuse, 'The Knight: the first mover in Chaucer's human comedy', *UTQ*, 31, 1962, reprinted from J. A. Burrow (ed.), *Chaucer*, Penguin, Harmondsworth, 1969, pp. 242–63; also involving relevant alternative readings to the prevalent orthodoxy are the following: H. J. Webb, 'A reinterpretation of Chaucer's Theseus', *RES*, 23, 1947, pp. 289–96; D. Underwood, *ELH*, 29, 1959, pp. 455–69; C. Mitchell, *MLQ*, 25, 1964, pp. 66–75. P. T. Thurston, *Artistic Ambivalence in Chaucer's Knight's Tale*, University of Florida, 1968, should be pertinent, but unfortunately sees Chaucer's chief and continual target as the knight-narrator, Palamon, Arcite and the women, finding Arcite's pain and death 'humorous' (l. 215) and revealing a 'Christian significance' which he fails to explain (l. 226), while he has nothing to say about the vital final speech of Theseus, 'so thoroughly explored by others' (l. 222). On the narrator see the sensible warnings in David, *Strumpet Muse*, pp. 76–8.

3 Henry of Lancaster offers a good example of conflict within an aristocrat contemporary with Chaucer, as J. Barnie has shown in *War in the Medieval Society*, Weidenfeld & Nicolson, London, 1974, pp. 62–5.

4 Webb, 'Chaucer's Theseus', p. 295.

5 Salter, *Chaucer*, p. 19.

6 For Chaucer's changes compare *Teseida*, II. st. 72–91 (*Opere Minori in Volgare*, vol. 2, Rizzoli, Milan, 1970); see Webb, 'Chaucer's Theseus' pp. 290–1. On medieval war, besides Barnie's study (n. 3 above), H. J. Hewitt's book should be of considerable

interest to students of medieval literature: *The Organization of War under Edward III*, Manchester University Press, 1966. For Chaucer's own critique of militarism and war, see *Tale of Melibee*, especially Robinson, pp. 169, 183–4.

7 See Webb, 'Chaucer's Theseus', pp. 293–4, 296; Honoré Bonet's statement is quoted by Barnie, *Medieval War*, p. 68.

8 On contemporary criticism of absolutism in relation to Chaucer, see discussion of *Clerk's Tale* at close of previous chapter and n. 48.

9 Lines 1967–2050: on the temples see Salter, *Chaucer*, pp. 17, 25–8. I have also read her as yet unpublished essay on 'Chaucer and Boccaccio: *The Knight's Tale*': I am extremely grateful to her for this, her published work and her conversations with me on Chaucer.

10 The phrase in quotation marks is from Elizabeth Salter's 'Chaucer and Boccaccio'; see too Salter, *Chaucer*, pp. 26–7. The continuities I describe would not surprise St Augustine as much as they would the modern admirers of Theseus: a famous passage in the *City of God* likens the order of kingdoms and of robber bands, asserting that the only difference is the *impunity* of legal rulers (IV. 4 and IV. 6: see the discussion by H. A. Deane, *The Political and Social Ideas of Augustine*, Columbia University Press, pp. 126–9).

11 Contrast *Teseida*, VII. st. 67 and IX. st. 2–4.

12 'Chaucer and Boccaccio', unpublished manuscript.

13 The class basis of Theseus' decision is made clear (ll. 2538–9). For contemporary criticism of tournaments Underwood, p. 462; to his examples it is worth adding Chaucer's admirer and friend, the Lollard knight Sir John Clanvowe, *The Two Ways*, ed. J. Scattergood, Brewer Press, 1976, pp. 69–70, condemning the glorification of militarism.

14 Webb, 'Chaucer's Theseus', p. 289, notes the 'tarnished' reputation of Theseus.

15 See ll. 1746–1869; for example of a recent admirer here, P. Elbow, *Oppositions in Chaucer*, Cambridge University Press, 1975, pp. 80–3, 90–3.

16 *Consolation of Philosophy*, III.m.12, Robinson, *Chaucer*, p. 358: see *Troilus and Criseyde*, IV, ll. 589–90, 617–18. For the neoplatonic framework to the *Consolation*, see the masterly study by P. Courcelle, *La consolation de philosophie dans la tradition littéraire*, Paris, 1967.

17 *LGW*, 1886–2227 and *HF*, 405–26.

18 Lines 1829–75: Theseus sees women as objects to be disposed of in political alliances for his own benefit, (contrast Nature in *PF*, 407–10, 624–30, and the discussion of Chaucer's treatment of these issues in chapter 6).

19 The quoted phrase is Elizabeth Salter's unpublished manuscript, 'Chaucer and Boccaccio'.

20 On secular theodicies, L. Kolakowski, *Marxism and Beyond*, Pall Mall Press, London, 1969, pp. 131–62.

21 For some interesting details of Chaucer's art here see W. C. Curry,

Chaucer and the Medieval Sciences, New York, 1926, pp. 139 ff. Saturn controlled the 'retentive virtue' which prevents the 'vertu expulsif' ejecting the 'venym', ensuring Arcite's slow death.

22 *Teseida*, X. st. 13–113.

23 Chaucer draws on the *Consolation of Philosophy* III. pr. 2 (and IV. pr. 6) for Arcite's meditation, but this is certainly no reason for scholars to assume that all Boethius' eclectic ideas were unquestioningly accepted as adequate solutions in the fourteenth century – quite the contrary, as most cursory acquaintance with the period's philosophy and theology reveals. To confirm this one could focus on just one major topic, such as the problem of future contingents and see thinker after thinker struggling with it in terms which show how Boethius's solution was not found adequate: eg., Ockham, *Predestination, God's Foreknowledge, and Future Contingents*, tr. M. McCord Adams and N. Kretzmann, Appleton-Century-Crofts, Englewood Cliffs, NJ, 1969, pp. 48–50 (and the editors' note p. 50 n. 54). See G. Leff, *Dissolution*, for an introductory account of major developments in late medieval thought, together with his *Medieval Thought,* Penguin, Harmondsworth, 1958, *Bradwardine and the Pelagians*, Cambridge University Press, 1957, *William of Ockham*, Manchester University Press, 1975.

24 For Chaucer's use of Boethius, *Consolation,* I.m5, and Salter, *Chaucer*, pp. 21–2; the comments in the previous note on attitudes to Boethius's metaphysics in the fourteenth century are relevant here too.

25 Line 2781; line 2782 includes reference to God which is an oath with no theological focus; similarly the references to Jupiter, ll. 2786–7, 2792. On Arcite's honesty, Salter, *Chaucer*, p. 29.

26 On developing distinctions between theological and philosophical argument see Leff, *Dissolution*, chapters 1 and 2, and *William of Ockham*, Manchester University Press, 1975, parts 1 and 2. I take the narrative voice here as the poet's, the voice I hear in *LGW*, Prologue F, 1–9, for instance; see David, *Strumpet Muse*, pp. 77–8. The poem does not have just one narrative voice; for example of the range compare the following: ll. 1201 (*write*, not speak), 1340–52 (court-quiz), 1459–60, 1465–6, 1668–78 (metaphysics of extreme determinism), 1995–2088 (Boccaccio's prayers take over as narrative 'I'), 2088, 2283–9 (prurience?), 2681–2 and 2807–26 (antifeminist cliché – or is there a double-take, a parody of such cliché by Chaucer, shared with the audience?)

27 For the positives, lines 1673–95, 2190–2205, 2483–7; the militaristic pursuits have been discussed, and these merge with the designs on Thebes (ll. 2970–4). For the miseries, also discussed above, 1995–2050, 2453–69 and Arcite's death 2743–814.

28 See scholars cited in note 1; on the area of Boethius here the caveat in note 23 applies.

29 Neuse, 'The Knight', p. 250: I do not, of course, agree with his view

of the tale as one carefully given to the particular Knight of the *General Prologue* ironizing against chivalry – see references to narrative voices (plural) in note 26, and on ambivalences in the *General Prologue*'s knight, C. Mitchell, *MLQ*, 25, 1964, pp. 66–75.

30 II. m.8; III. pr 10; IV. pr. 6; IV. m. 6.

31 'Chaucer and Boccaccio', unpublished manuscript; also Salter, *Chaucer*, p. 35. Obviously I disagree with her treatment of Theseus's speech as *Chaucer*'s attempt to impose a comforting Boethian resolution on intractable materials, seeing no more need to identify Theseus with Chaucer's views than those of Coriolanus with Shakespeare's.

32 For example of such criticism however, G. Leff, *William of Ockham*, Manchester University Press, 1975, chapters 5 and 6 (especially pp. 359–454); J. R. Weinberg, *Nicolaus of Autrecourt* (1948); Greenwood, 1969, chapters 2, 3, 5 (especially pp. 74–6, 95–113, 219); F. Coppleston, *A History of Philosophy*, vol. 3, Burns & Oates, 1960, pp. 67–8, 81–8, 123–7, 131–2.

33 Neuse, 'The Knight', p. 250.

34 II. m 8: see *Troilus and Criseyde*, III, ll. 1744–71, which re-creates the human dimension.

35 Neuse, 'The Knight', p. 250; Salter, p. 35. (Note the other contexts in which Chaucer uses this phrase, *Squire's Tale*, ll. 584–600 and *T & C*, IV, ll. 1275–589: in both cases the phrase advocates accommodation to wrong-doing, not metaphysical reflection.)

36 The duke calls the first mover 'Juppiter' (l. 3035) but this reference reminds us of lines 2438 ff., where Jupiter failed to create harmony and assented to Saturn's grisly exercise of power: Chaucer is hardly inviting us to dissolve his carefully constructed text and substitute a text such as the *Consolation*.

37 For the neoplatonism of the *Consolation*, see Courcelle, *La consolation*.

38 One could agree that this is one of the points where the narrative voice explicitly becomes that of the pilgrim-knight who will patch up an agreement relevant to the pilgrimage's *bonhomie* after the conflict between Host and Pardoner. On the plurality of narrative voices, note 26.

Index

Aers, D., 199–205 *passim*, 207–9 *passim*, 211, 214, 221, 224
Alexander, P. J., 211
Allen, J. B., 108, 216–17
Andrew, M. R., 224–5
Angelo Clareno, 62
Antichrist, 35, 57, 60, 208, 213
Arnold, T., 197, 213
Articles of Deposition (1399), 172
Atkins, J., 222
Augustine, St, 29, 73–4, 78, 146, 159, 171, 202, 208, 211, 218, 227, 229

Bald, R. C., 215
Barnie, J., 199, 228
Bayley, J., 221
Bennett, J. A. W., 65, 197, 206, 210, 211
Bernard Gui, 97–8, 214, 216
Bettenson, H., 204
Bird, R., 198
Bloch, E., 226
Bloomfield, M. W., 55–6, 62–3, 64, 67–70 *passim*, 74, 77, 199, 205, 207–9 *passim*, 211, 212
Boccaccio, G., 118, 123, 127, 129, 131, 176, 179–81 *passim*, 183, 185–6, 188, 219, 220, 228–31 *passim*
Bonet, Honoré, 177
Boethius, 80, 134, 139, 182, 184, 188–95 *passim*, 229–31 *passim*
Book of the Duchess, 83
Book of the Knight of the Tower, see Knight of the Tower
Book of Vices and Virtues, 18–19
Bradwardine, 218
Brenner, R., 200
Brock, P., 211
Brown, P., 208, 227
Bryan, W. F., 214, 227
Burlin, R. B., 224, 226, 228

Canticle of Canticles, 158–60, 224
Charland, Th.-M., 215
Chaucer, Geoffrey, ix, x, 43, 47, 80–173 *passim*, 214–31 *passim*; *see also under specific works*
Chrétien de Troyes, 146–7
Christ, 3, 6, 12–13, 19, 20, 30–1, 33, 35, 38–61 *passim*, 85, 86–8, 90, 95, 100, 101, 111–13, 139, 140, 154, 159, 202, 203, 204, 208, 215
Christine de Pisan, 220
Chrysostom, St John, 40
Church, 2–8 *passim*, 20, 24, 25, 31, 34, 35, 37, 38–79, *passim*, 94–116 *passim*, 143–73 *passim*, 204–14 *passim*
Clanvowe, Sir John, 229
Cleanness, 224–5
Cohn, N., 211
Commons' Petition (1376), 9–10
Complaint of Chaucer to his purse, 172
Confession, 38–61 *passim*, 76–7, 99–101, 114
Conlow, W. M., 215
Constantine, 51, 69, 74, 212
Coppleston, F., 231
Coulton, G. G., 218
Courcelle, P., 229, 231
Crow, M. M., 227
Curry, W. C., 229–30

Dahlberg, C., 226
Daiches, D., 198
David, A., 114, 141, 150, 168, 218, 219, 226–8 *passim*, 230
David, King, 64–5, 147–8, 215, 221, 223
Deane, H. A., 227, 229
De Beauvoir, S., 224
De Lagarde, G., 227

Delany, S., 81, 214, 217
Dempster, G., 214, 227
D'Entreves, A. P., 216
Dobson, R. B., 199, 200, 201, 210
Donaldson, E. T., xii, 63, 196, 197, 200, 202, 204, 205, 209, 210
Donne, John, 91, 101–2
Du Boulay, F. R. H., 199, 200, 205, 220, 222, 224
Duby, G., 199, 200, 222
Dunning, T. P., 205

Elbow, P., 215, 220, 229
English Works of Wyclif, 201, 212–13
Evans, A.P., 208, 214–15

Faulkner, D. R., 216
Ferrante, J., 223
Fines, J., 216
Finlayson, J., 109, 110, 217, 218
Fischer, J. H., 201
Fisher, J. H., 196, 218, 223, 224
Francis, W. W., 201
Frank, R. W., 201
Franklin's Tale, 160–9, 194, 225–6
Frappier, J., 146, 219, 223
Frese, D. W., 226
Friars, 35–6, 38–61 *passim*, 69–70, 201, 204
Froissart, 200, 201

Gaylord, A. T., 165, 166, 216, 226
General Prologue (to the *Canterbury Tales*), 95, 99, 103, 110, 139, 150, 175, 218, 231
Geremek, B., 198
Gist, M. A., 219
Goodman of Paris, 144, 146, 152, 160, 222
Gordon, R. K., 219
Gouldner, A. W., 82, 196, 214
Gower, John, x, 3, 135, 196, 197
Gradon, P., 197, 207, 219
Great Schism, 60
Gregory, St, 40, 47, 69

Handlynge Synne, 224
Hazelmayer, L. A., 94, 215
Helmholz, R. H., 222
Heninger, S. K., 226
Henry IV, 172
Henry of Lancaster, 228
Herbert, George, 93, 115
Hewitt, H. J., 199, 228–9
Hill, C., 212
Hilton, R., xi, 14, 15, 18, 197–201 *passim*, 210, 222
Hobsbawn, E., 211
Hodge, R., xi, 210
Holmes, G. A., 200
House of Fame, 84, 108, 182, 217, 223, 224
Howard, D. R., 81, 91, 93, 98, 102, 103, 105, 107, 169, 214–18 *passim*, 226, 228
Howell, C., 200
Hudson, A., 210, 216
Huizinga, J., 167, 226
Humbert of Romans, 90, 93
Huppé, B. F., 207, 211, 226
Hus, John, 213

Inquisition, 82, 87, 96–7,214–15, 216
Isaiah, 10, 66, 205

Jean de Meun, 62–3, 215
Jeremiah, 108
Jerome, St, 86, 89, 214
Jesus,*see* Christ
Joachim of Fiore, 62
John XXII, 97
John Ball, 17
John Wyclif, *see under* Wyclif
Jordan, R. M., 218, 224, 226, 228

Kaminsky, H., 210, 212
Kane, G., xii, 63, 197, 200, 202, 204, 205, 210
Kantorowicz, E. H., 228
Kaske, C. V., 109, 217
Kaske, R. E., 224, 225
Kean, P. M., 209, 224, 228
Kellogg, A. L., 94, 206, 215
Kelly, H. A., 145, 155, 217, 220,222–3
Kirk, E., 201, 207
Kittredge, G.L., 160, 162, 165, 225, 226, 227
Knight of the Tower, 144–5, 146, 151, 156, 160, 166, 167, 169, 170, 173, 222
Knight's Tale, 174–95, 228–31 *passim*
Kolakowski, L., 142, 222, 229
Kuhn, T. S., 196
Kretzmann, N., 230

Lakatos, I., 212
Lambert, M. D., 71, 97, 204, 209–13 *passim*, 215, 216
Langland, William, *see Piers Plowman*
Lanterne of Liȝt, 196–7, 213
Lawlor, J., 201, 218

Lazar, M., 146, 223
Le Bras, G., 198
Leff, G., xi, 9, 60–1, 70–1, 75, 87, 97, 198, 204, 205, 208–16 *passim*, 225–6, 230, 231
Legend of Good Women, 182, 229
Lerner, R. E., 9, 97, 198, 205, 211, 213, 215
Lollards, 3, 42, 59, 66, 70–8 *passim*, 96, 97, 104, 196–7, 208, 210, 212–13, 216
Loserth, I., 212
Lovejoy, A. O., 226
Luther, Martin, 101
Lydgate, x, 135
Lynch, J. H., 206

McAlpine, M., 140, 219–22 *passim*
McCall, J. P., 219, 220
McCord Adams, M., 230
MacDonald, F., xi
Macfarlane, A., 213
McGrade, A. S., 209, 227, 228
McGregor, Y., xi, 218, 219, 220
MacIntyre, A., 211
Mann, J., 47, 48, 81, 175, 196, 206–7, 214, 225
Manning, B. L., 204
Markus, R. L., 78
Martines, L., 222
Mathew, G., 223
Matthew, F. D., 201, 212–13
Merchant's Tale, 111–13, 139, 151–60, 224–5
Miller, E., 200
Miller, R. P., 96
Milton, John, 143, 174, 183, 222
Miskimin, H. A., 198, 199, 200
Mitchell, C., 222, 231
Mitler, E., 200
Mizener, A., 218
Mogan, J., 148, 222, 223
Mohl, R., 196
Mollat, M., 66, 198, 199, 201, 210
Muscatine, C., 81, 174, 179, 196, 207, 208, 214, 228
Musgrave, A., 196
Murtaugh, D. M., 226

Neuse, R., 174, 188, 190, 191, 228, 230, 231
Noonan, J. T., 145, 146, 155, 159, 217, 222–4 *passim*
Nichols, D., 199

Oberman, H. A., 204, 207, 216, 218
O'Faolain, J., 222
Oldcastle, Sir John, 70
Olson, C. C., 227
Owen, C. A., 226
Owen, N. H., 196
Owst, G. N., 41, 197, 205

Pantin, W. A., 204
Pardoner's Prologue, Tale and Epilogue, 89-106, 108, 115, 155, 215-16, 231
Parliament of Fowls, 229
Parson's Prologue and Tale, 106–14, 216–18
Paul, St, 31, 34, 85, 87, 88–9, 90, 91, 96, 98, 106, 108, 109, 145, 152, 159, 217
Payne, R.O., 117, 218
Pearsall, D.A., v, xi, 199, 200, 201, 202, 218
Peasants' Uprising (1381), 3, 13, 17, 19–20, 42, 66–7, 68, 200, 201, 210
Peter Chelcicky, 211
Peter John Olivi, 62
Petrarch, 227
Physician's Tale, 216, 220
Piers Plowman, 1–79 *passim*, 80–1, 83, 89, 94, 97–8, 104, 106–7, 108, 111, 115, 118, 139, 140, 155, 184, 187, 196–214 *passim*, 217, 222; and Anima, 39–40; and Charity, 30–1, 69, 74, 209; and Church, 2–8, 20, 24–5, 31, 34–5, 37, 38–79 *passim*, 204–14 *passim*; and Conscience, 8–11, 20, 25–6, 32, 34–7, 39, 50, 52, 55, 57, 60, 61, 64–8, 76, 78, 202, 203–4, 207, 210, 211; and Guile, 12, 35; and Haukyn, 25, 27–9, 197–8; and Holy Spirit, 4, 31–8, 41; and Hunger, 17–18, 36, 52; and Incarnation of God, 12–13, 30, 40–1; and Knights, 4–5, 7, 9–22, 33–5, 52, 66, 69, 71–8, 200; and Labourers, 9–20, 31–2, 73; and Meed, 7–11, 45–7, 50, 57, 63–8, 203; and Merchants, 3, 10, 20–3, 27–8, 32, 35, 50, 199; and Need, 50–1; and the Pardon, 20–3, 53, 201, 207; and Pardoners, 42–3, 205–6; and Patience, 25–8, 30, 55, 202, 208, 212; and Penance, 11–13, 28, 38–61 *passim*; and Piers, 13–22, 25–6, 35–7, 41, 52–3, 57, 60, 76, 78, 200, 202–3, 207, 208; and the Poor, 7–8, 19–23, 29–31, 202; and the Pope, 46, 57, 59, 71, 74; and

Piers Plowman (contd)
Reason, 6, 8, 11, 31–2, 52, 68; and Scripture, 55, 73; and Study, 55; and Theology, 7; and Tradesmen, 3, 7–8, 12, 27–8, 31–3, 197–8; and Trajan, 24, 202; and Will, 1–79 *passim*; and Wit, 55; and Ymaginatif, 40, 80–1; *see also under* Christ
Postan, M. M., 198
Power, E., 119, 142, 198, 219, 220, 222, 224, 225

Randall, L. M. C., 223–4
Rapp, F., 44–5, 205, 212, 213
Reeves, M., 209
Reiman, D., 169–70, 227
Retractions (of Chaucer), 106, 114–16
Richard II, 172
Richardson, H. G., 206
Roberts, R. P. ap, 219
Robertson, D. W., 117, 160, 165, 207, 214, 218–19, 223, 225
Robinson, F. N., xii, 214, 217, 218, 229
Robinson, I., 226
Romance of the Rose, 162–3, 226
Roover, R. de, 198
Rorig, F., 198
Ross, W. O., 196, 204, 205

Salter, E., v, xi, 138, 141, 174, 176, 180, 184, 189, 200, 206, 219, 221, 227, 228–31 *passim*
Satan, 35, 71
Scattergood, J., 229
Schlauch, M., 172, 227
Schmidt, A. V. C., 200, 202, 205–6
Scott, F. R., 227
Searle, E., 205
Sedgewick, G. G., 224
Select English Works of John Wyclif, 197, 213
Selections from English Wycliffite Writings, 210, 216
Severs, J. B., 224
Silverman, A. H., 223
Skeat, W. W., 199, 202, 205, 212
Smalley, B., 227
Songs of Songs, *see* Canticle
Southern, R. W., 46, 48–9, 50, 205–7 *passim*, 213, 215–16
Spearing, A. C., 41–2, 205
Squire's Tale, 231
Stockton, E. W., 197
Summoner's Tale, 88–9
Swinburn, L. M., 196, 213

Tale of Melibee, 225, 229
Tawney, R.H., 205
Tentler, T.N., 204
Thomas Aquinas, St, 101–2, 146, 203, 216, 223
Thomas, K., 216
Thomas of Wimbledon, 2–3, 10–11, 196
Thompson, A. H., 206
Thomson, S. H., 213
Thrupp, S., 21–2, 198, 201, 203, 211
Thurston, P. T., 228
Tierney, B., 227
Trinkaus, C., 204, 216
Troilus and Criseyde, 117–42 *passim*, 150, 157, 167, 218–22 *passim*, 231

Ullmann, W., 227
Underwood, D., 228

Veale, E. M., 198
Virgin Mary, 159
Virgoe, R., xi

Wakefield, W. L., 208, 214
Waldensians, 77, 96
Waldron, R., 224–5
Walzer, M., 227
Webb, H., 175–7 *passim*, 228, 229
Weinberg, J.R., 231
Wenzel, S., 107, 217
White, B., 200
White, G., 225, 226
Wife of Bath's Prologue, and the Wife, 83–9, 97, 146–52, 156–7, 159, 164, 224, 225, 227
Wilks, M. J., 172, 209, 212, 227, 228
Willard, C. C., 220
William of Ockham, 214, 227, 230–1
Williams, A., 215
Williams, G. A., 198
Wittig, J. S., 202
Wolff, P., 66, 198, 199, 210
Wright, T., 208
Wyclif, John, 3, 65, 66, 70–2, 74, 75, 77–8, 98, 197, 208, 210, 212–13

Young, K., 219